TEAC

JUMP RIGHT IN
THE MUSIC CURRICULUM

| CYNTHIA C. TAGGART | ALISON M. REYNOLDS | WENDY H. VALERIO | JENNIFER M. BAILEY | DIANE LANGE | EDWIN E. GORDON |

DAVID G. WOODS
FIRST EDITION CO-AUTHOR

GIA PUBLICATIONS, INC.
CHICAGO

Jump Right In Editions

Jump Right In: The General Music Series

Kindergarten
- J237   Teacher's Edition
- J237CD   3-CD set
- J237P   Piano Accompaniment

Grade 2
- J239   Student Book
- J239T   Teacher's Edition
- J239CD   Compact disc set
- J239P   Piano Accompaniment

Grade 4
- J241   Student Book
- J241T   Teacher's Edition
- J241CD   Compact disc set
- J241P   Piano Accompaniment

Grade 1
- J238   Student Book
- J238T   Teacher's Edition
- J238CD   Compact disc set
- J238P   Piano Accompaniment

Grade 3
- J240   Student Book
- J240T   Teacher's Edition
- J240CD   Compact disc set
- J240P   Piano Accompaniment

Jump Right In: The Original Edition
- J13   Jump Right In Song Collection (two spiral-bound volumes)

Jump Right In: The Instrumental Series
- J177   Revised Parents' Guide
- J315   Revised Teacher's Guide for Band Books 1 and 2
- J317   Revised Teacher's Guide for Strings Books 1 and 2
- J249   Composition Book 1 (all instruments)
- J167   Solo Book 1–Writing (all instruments)
- J168   Solo Book 2–Writing (all instruments)

Band Instrumentation
- Flute
- Clarinet
- Oboe
- Bassoon
- Alto Sax
- Tenor Sax
- Trumpet
- Horn in F
- Trombone
- Baritone BC
- Baritone TC
- Tuba
- Percussion
- Recorder

Strings
- Violin
- Viola
- Cello
- Bass

Jump Right In: The Music Curriculum (Kindergarten)
Teacher's Guide Book
Cynthia C. Taggart, Alison M. Reynolds, Wendy H. Valerio, Jennifer M. Bailey, Diane Lange, and Edwin E. Gordon.

Dancing Bear by Doug Nichol © 1974 by Doug Nichol. Used by permission.

Fireman, Fireman by Doug Nichol © 1975 by Doug Nichol. Used by permission.

Full Moonlight Dance by Karen Beth © 1977 Karen Beth. Published by Catkin Music, B.M.I.

Hot Dog by Doug Nichol © 1974 by Doug Nichol. Used by permission.

I Wonder as I Wander by John Jacob Niles © 1934 (renewed) by G. Schirmer, Inc. (ASCAP). International copyright secured. All rights reserved. Used by permission.

Oh, I'll Build a Snowman by Doug Nichol © 1978 by Doug Nichol. Used by permission.

Popcorn by Doug Nichol © 1974 by Doug Nichol. Used by permission.

One Summer Day by Jacob Gade, from *Botsford Collection of Folk Songs* by Florence Botsford. Copyright © 1929 (renewed) by G. Schirmer, Inc. (ASCAP). International copyright secured. All rights reserved. Used by permission.

Peas by Doug Nichol © 1974 by Doug Nichol. Used by permission.

Cover design, layout and illustration: Martha Chlipala

J237T
ISBN: 978-1-57999-776-2

Copyright © 2010 GIA Publications, Inc.
7404 S Mason Ave
Chicago IL 60638

www.giamusic.com
All rights reserved
Printed in the United States of America

Table of Contents

Jump Right In: The Comprehensive Music Curriculum vii
Three-stage Approach to Learning vii
Classroom Activities viii
Learning Sequence Activities viii
Coordination of Classroom Activities and Learning Sequence Activities viii
Developing Vocabulary: Language and Music ix
    Language Vocabulary Development ix
    Music Vocabulary Development x
Understanding Music through Audiation of Tonalities and Meters xi
    Tonality and Meter xi
        Tonality xi
        Meter xii
Modes of Performance xiii
    Singing xiii
    Chanting xiii
    Moving xiii
    Playing Instruments xiv
    Listening xiv
    Music Reading xiv
Using the Teacher's Edition xv
    Lesson Planning xvi
    Lesson Plan for Early in the Year xvii
    Lesson Plan for the Middle of the Year xviii
    Lesson Plan for Late in the Year xviii
Scope and Sequence xx
Music Aptitude xxiv
Measurement Evaluation, and Testing xxiv
Coordination with Instrumental Music xxv
Philosophy of *Jump Right In* xxvi

Hello, Everybody 2
The Braes O'Yarrow 4
This Lady She Wears a Dark Green Dress 6
Jeremiah, Blow the Fire 8
All Pretty Little Horses 10
Arirang 12
Peas 14
The Elephant 16
Down in Village of Valtou 18
Sleep, My Darling (*Sofda Unga Astin Min*) 20
Blow the Balloon 22
Five Little Pumpkins 24
Floppy Scarecrow 28
The Ghost of John 30
America the Beautiful 32
Open-Close 34
Graceful Simo (*Simo Ligeri*) 36

Table of Contents

Full Moonlight Dance 38

The Sure Hope 40

Go to Sleep 42

Sometimes I Feel Like a Motherless Child 44

One Summer Day 46

Do You See That Bird There? 48

Hato Popo (Little Pigeons) 50

The Squirrel 52

The Ardelean Woman 54

Shake, Shake, Shake 56

The Volga Boat Song 58

Bim Bam 60

Early to Bed 62

Over the River and through the Wood 64

Turkey Song 66

Five Little Muffins 68

Mos Mos (Cat Song) 70

Two Little Sausages 72

Sleep, My Babe (*Dors, Dors, 'Tit Bébé*) 74

The Elephant Song 76

My Little Ducklings 78

Zion's Children 80

In the Window 82

Popcorn 84

Personent Hodie (Celebrate Joyously) 86

America 88

Baloo, Lammy 90

Coventry Carol 92

As Joseph Was A-Walking 94

I Wonder as I Wander 96

O Little Town of Bethlehem 98

Away in a Manger 100

Softly 102

Children's Lullaby 104

Oh, I'll Build a Snowman 106

I'm a Little Snowflake 108

Walking with My Mom 110

Darling, Goodnight 112

You'll Sound as Weird as Me 114

Bí, Bí, Og Blaka (Flip, Flap, and Flutt'ring) 116

Dance from Zalongou 118

The Star-Spangled Banner 120

London Bridge 122

Toss and Catch 124

Five Little Speckled Frogs 126

Horses 128

Everybody Do This! 130

iv

Table of Contents

Swing a Lady	132
Dancing Bear	134
Yangtze Boatmen's Chantey	136
Blow the Man Down	138
Blow the Winds Southerly	140
Tsamico Dance	142
Will Winter End?	144
Roll That Big Ball Down to Town	146
Hani Kouni	150
Scandinavian Folk Song	152
City Line Avenue	154
Elephants and Kitty Cats	156
High Bird	158
Barnacle Bill	160
See How I'm Jumping	162
Shalom Chaverim	166
The Greenland Whale Fishery	168
Fire House	170
Wild Dog on Our Farm	172
Funny Puppy	174
Sidewalk Talk	176
Jim Along Josie	178
Bre'r Rabbit, Shake It	180
Tisket, A-Tasket	182
Baa, Baa, Black Sheep	184
Sakura	186
My Name Is Little Yellow Bird	188
Little Train	190
Engine, Engine	192
Old MacDonald Had a Farm	196
The Old Gray Cat	198
Little Wind	200
Who Has Seen Wind?	202
Ophelia' Letter Blow 'Way	204
Fireman, Fireman	206
Lullaby from Cyprus	208
The Nothing Song	210
The Bell Peter	212
Gipsy Ipsy	214
The Sky Has Clouded	218
Clapping Land	220
Only My Opinion	224
Rain on the Green Grass	226
This Old Man	228
Johnny Works with One Hammer	230
The Chickens They Are Crowin'	232
Lazy Bones	234
Nanny Goat	236

Table of Contents

Jumbo Elephant 238

Scarborough Fair 240

Punchinella 242

To Market, To Market 244

Hot Dog 246

Toodala 248

Thessaly *Syrtos* Dance 250

Humpty Dumpty 252

Little Rondo 254

Draw a Bucket of Water 258

Fair Rosie 260

Mary Wore a Red Dress 264

Row, Row, Row Your Boat 268

Index A	Alphabetical Listing of Songs and CD Tracks	271
Index B	Songs by Arranger, Composer, or Transcriber	273
Index C	Songs by Chanting	274
Index D	Songs by Connections: Art, Literature, Social Studies, and Science	274
Index E	Songs by Coordination with Instrumental Music	274
Index F	Songs by Form	275
Index G	Songs by Games and Dances	275
Index H	Songs by Listening	276
Index I	Songs by Listening Lesson	276
Index J	Songs by Manipulatives	276
Index K	Songs by Meter	276
Index L	Songs by Movement	278
Index M	Songs by Music Concept	281
Index N	Songs by National, State, or Ethnic Origin	285
Index O	Songs by Performance Instrument	286
Index P	Songs by Singing	286
Index Q	Songs by Subject Matter	288
Index R	Songs by Tonality	289

JUMP RIGHT IN:
The Comprehensive Music Curriculum

THREE-STAGE APPROACH TO LEARNING

The authors of *Jump Right In: The Music Curriculum* believe that the most effective method for teaching music to children uses a three-stage approach called Whole/Part/Whole. The approach is described briefly and presented in chart form below.

Stage 1 Experience music in all tonalities, meters, and timbres in Classroom Activities. Techniques may include singing, chanting, moving, dancing, listening, playing instruments, creating and improvising, reading, writing, and performing. At Stage 1, students experience music in a holistic way. Music content, such as different tonalities and meters, is introduced in Stage 1. In kindergarten, children are immersed in this stage.

Stage 2 Study music through Learning Sequence Activities. During Learning Sequence Activities, children respond by themselves and in a group to patterns performed by the teacher. Students are studying the parts of music by learning a specific vocabulary of tonal and rhythm patterns. Music skills, such as the association of tonal and rhythm solfege and music reading, are introduced in Stage 2. For more information on the specific skills that are introduced during Learning Sequence Activities, see the 2006 edition of Edwin E. Gordon's *Learning Sequences in Music: Skill, Content, and Patterns* published by GIA.

Stage 3 Understand music in all tonalities and meters in Classroom Activities. Content experienced in Stage 1 is woven together with skills learned in Stage 2 to provide understanding and comprehension of music. This understanding results in students engaging in musical activities in a more sophisticated way than at Stage 1. As in Stage 1, students experience music in a holistic way.

STAGE 1	STAGE 2		STAGE 3
WHOLE	**PART**		**WHOLE**
Experience the Whole	Study the Parts		Understand and Comprehend the Whole
CLASSROOM ACTIVITIES	**LEARNING SEQUENCE ACTIVITIES**		**CLASSROOM ACTIVITIES**
Singing	Discrimination:	Inference:	Singing
Chanting	Aural/Oral	Generalization Aural/Oral	Chanting
Moving and Dancing	Verbal Association	Generalization Verbal	Moving and Dancing
Playing Instruments			Playing Instruments
Playing Games	Partial Synthesis	Creativity/Symbolic	Playting Games
Creating and Improvising	Symbolic Association	Generalization Symbolic	Creating and Improvising
Reading and Writing Music			Reading and Writing Music
Performing	Composite Symthesis	Theoretical Understanding	Performing

JUMP RIGHT IN: THE MUSIC CURRICULUM

CLASSROOM ACTIVITIES

During Classroom Activities, students are actively engaged in music making through singing, chanting, moving, and playing instruments. They also apply to listening what they have learned while making music. When involved in Classroom Activities, students are learning music holistically; they are learning musical repertoire and are learning musical concepts by experiencing them in context.

Jump Right In: The Music Curriculum Teaching Plans are classroom activities that are designed for use by all teachers, regardless of their knowledge of or commitment to Music Learning Theory and Learning Sequence Activities. The activities described in the Teaching Plans are similar to the activities used in many general music classrooms, except that they are sequential and can be linked in a meaningful way to Learning Sequence Activities.

LEARNING SEQUENCE ACTIVITIES

The audiation of tonal and rhythm patterns is the cornerstone of Music Learning Theory. Just as we derive musical meaning in language through the organization of words, in music we derive musical meaning through the organization of tonal patterns within a tonality and rhythm patterns within a meter.

In kindergarten, pattern instruction is informal and presented in the context of Classroom Activities. However, in the later grades, during Learning Sequence Activities, students are engaged in more formal tonal pattern and rhythm pattern instruction. Through this instruction, students are learning specific patterns in a tonal or metric context, which will serve as a musical vocabulary for performance, to compare to music that they hear or perform, and with which to create. Students also learn specific skills, such as association of tonal and rhythm solfege and reading music during Learning Sequence Activities. The patterns and skills are sequenced according to the results of extensive research into how children learn music.

When teaching Learning Sequence Activities, the teacher is able to adapt instruction to the individual needs of the students. Although all students learn the same skill, such as music reading, those students with high aptitude sing, chant, read, and write more patterns and patterns that are more difficult in addition to the patterns that are read by other students. This prevents students with higher aptitudes from getting bored and students with lower aptitudes from getting frustrated.

Teachers who would like to teach Learning Sequence Activities to their students should purchase *Tonal Register Books One* and *Two*, *Rhythm Register Books One* and *Two*, and the *Reference Handbook for Using Learning Sequence Activities*, 2001 Edition. All are published by GIA Publications, 7404 S. Mason Ave., Chicago, IL 60638 (www.giamusic.com). Before beginning to teach Learning Sequence Activities, an appropriate test of music aptitude should be given to all students. Read the section on "Measurement, Evaluation, and Testing" for more information about music aptitude testing.

COORDINATION OF CLASSROOM ACTIVITIES AND LEARNING SEQUENCE ACTIVITIES

In kindergarten, children engage almost entirely in Classroom Activities as they build their music listening vocabularies and are immersed in the tonal and rhythm systems of music. In the later grades, to provide a complete and well-balanced music education for children, teachers should use both Classroom Activities and Learning Sequence Activities during every class period and coordinate one with the other. Although many teachers may choose to coordinate Classroom Activities and Learning

Sequence Activities according to their curricular goals, this is done for the teacher in *Jump Right In: The Music Curriculum*.

Each "Coordination with Learning Sequence Activities" plan in books 1-6 is related to the Classroom Activity "Teaching Plan" on the facing page of the Teacher's Edition and includes related teaching suggestions for two tonal skill levels and two rhythm skill levels. If your students are studying at the Aural/Oral skill level in Learning Sequence Activities, teach the Classroom Activity Lesson Plan and use the Coordination with Learning Sequence Activities plan for the Aural/Oral units. If your students are studying at the Verbal Association skill level in Learning Sequence Activities, then use the Coordination with Learning Sequence Activities plans for Verbal Association units..

For those teachers who wish to coordinate Classroom Activities and Learning Sequence Activities according to their own curricular goals, here are a few simple guidelines. Students should learn new tonal and rhythm content in Classroom Activities, and they should learn new skill levels in Learning Sequence Activities. New content includes a rich variety of tonalities, meters, and timbres, many of which will be unfamiliar to students. New skills include the initial study of familiar content at a deeper skill level. Once a new skill is experienced in Learning Sequence Activities, it may be applied to Classroom Activities.

DEVELOPING VOCABULARY:

LANGUAGE AND MUSIC

Children learn music and language in a similar manner. Both are aural arts, learned initially through listening. Early listening experience in music and language forms the foundation for further learning. It is what we have heard that creates in each of us the listening vocabulary to eventually speak, sing, and chant, and to hear and understand complex forms.

LANGUAGE VOCABULARY DEVELOPMENT

In order to develop an adequate speaking vocabulary in language, the child must first develop a listening vocabulary by hearing the whole language spoken for and to him or her by language-competent parents. Parents are usually patient and understanding language teachers. They speak to and for their child from the moment of birth throughout infancy, toddlerhood, and beyond.

Parents seem to have an innate understanding that they should speak to and for their infant, even though the child does not speak back in language for several months, or perhaps for a year or more. They do not expect the child to imitate parent speech immediately. They nurture the child's language development through continuous speech modeling and language interaction and through language play between parent and child.

It is parent-modeled speech and language interaction that creates the child's listening vocabulary and gives the child the readiness to speak language. The words eventually spoken by the child are the ones that have been heard. The listening vocabulary is reflected in the speaking vocabulary. The child's listening and speaking vocabularies are developed in the home during the preschool years.

By providing a spoken language model and by encouraging their children to learn to speak, parents provide informal guidance in language, helping their children to develop the readiness to participate in formal instruction in reading and writing when they reach school age. By the time a child enters public school, five or six years of immersion in informal language guidance in the home should have taken place. Children who have experienced a rich and varied listening, interacting, and speaking environment in the home enter school with the foundation to learn to read and write.

In order to develop adequate speaking, reading, and writing vocabularies in language, the child must first develop a listening vocabulary by hearing adults speak and by interacting with adults in language. The listening vocabulary forms the foundation for all language learning. It is from the words and phrases that the child hears and the meanings acquired simultaneously that the child develops his speaking vocabulary. It is from the speaking vocabulary that the reading vocabulary and, ultimately, the writing vocabulary develops.

MUSIC VOCABULARY DEVELOPMENT

In order to develop an adequate speaking vocabulary in music, the child must first develop a listening vocabulary by hearing the whole language of music with a variety of tonalities, meters, timbres, tempos, and styles. That whole language of music should be performed for and to the child by musically competent parents.

With music, although parents may also be patient and loving, they may not understand how to teach their child. Because music and language are both learned aurally, parents should perform music to their child at least as often and as fluently as they perform language. Ideally, parents should sing and chant to and for their children musically just as they speak to and for them in language. The listening and interacting experience builds the listening vocabulary in music that leads to music performance, understanding, and comprehension.

The listening vocabulary forms the foundation for all other vocabularies in music. It is parent-modeled music performance and interaction that create the child's listening vocabulary and give the child the readiness to sing, chant, and move. The listening vocabulary is reflected in the speaking vocabulary. The tonal and rhythm patterns and songs eventually sung and chanted by the child are derived from what the child has heard. It is during the early preschool years that the child's listening and speaking vocabularies in music should be developed through informal guidance in the home.

By providing a music model that includes singing, chanting, and movement to music, and by helping their children learn to sing, chant, and move, parents make it possible for their children to develop the readiness to participate in formal music instruction when they reach school age. By the time a child enters public school, five or six years of immersion in informal music guidance in the home should have taken place.

Children who have experienced a rich and varied listening, interacting, and performing musical environment in the home enter school with the foundation to learn to sing songs, chant, create and improvise, and to read and write music. Unfortunately, many parents are not as comfortable providing music models for their children as they are providing language models for their children. Many children enter school without the necessary readiness to participate in formal music instruction. That readiness must then be provided by the music teacher in the first few years of music instruction in school.

In order to develop adequate singing, speaking, and moving vocabularies in music, the child must first develop a listening vocabulary by hearing the whole language of music sung, spoken, and played for and to him or her by musically competent parents, or, if necessary, by a music teacher in school. The child is drawn into language learning and music learning through modeling and social interaction. Children learn to speak the language they hear; they learn to chant, sing, and move to the music they hear. In order for children to learn music, parents and teachers must model music for them, and parents, teachers, and children must interact in music as they do in language. The four vocabularies of music are presented below.

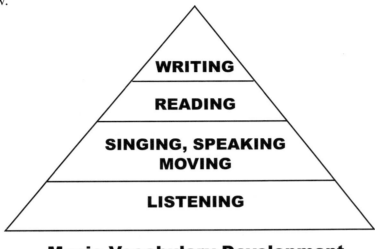

Music Vocabulary Development

UNDERSTANDING MUSIC THROUGH AUDIATION OF TONALITIES AND METERS

TONALITY AND METER

Throughout the entire series, teachers will find songs in a rich variety of tonalities and meters and songs and chants in many meters. The names of the tonality and of the meter are provided in the leftmost column of each lesson plan in the teacher's editions of *Jump Right In: The Music Curriculum.*

You may use the songs, chants, and lesson plans in *Jump Right In: The Music Curriculum* whether or not you are teaching Learning Sequence Activities to your students. It is beneficial for all children to hear, perform, and understand music in a variety of tonalities and meters, regardless of the text used for teaching or of the framework for classroom activities. Many of the songs and chants in this curriculum may be adapted beautifully for use in music classrooms guided by Orff or Kodály teachers. Classroom teachers as well may feature the variety of tonalities and meters in classroom lessons that include a music component.

TONALITY

Tonality is taught in *Jump Right In: The Music Curriculum* using a tonal system with a movable DO and a LA-based minor. A simple chart of tonality names and their corresponding resting tone names is provided below.

JUMP RIGHT IN: THE MUSIC CURRICULUM

Tonality	Resting Tone
Major	DO
Dorian	RE
Phrygian	MI
Lydian	FA
Mixolydian	SO
Aeolian	LA
Harmonic Minor	LA
Melodic Minor	LA
Locrian	TI

If you teach your students Learning Sequence Activities in the later grade levels, you will use the above-written syllables to name resting tones when your students complete the Verbal Association, Generalization-Verbal, and Creativity/Improvisation Units. If you are not using Learning Sequence Activities or the Coordination with Learning Sequence Activities, you may create your own techniques to help your students understand tonality through use of resting tone audiation and tonal solfege.

METER

Meter is taught in *Jump Right In: The Music Curriculum* using a rhythm solfege system based on beat function. The rhythm solfege is not based on rhythm duration or on notation as are some other systems. A simple chart of meter names and their corresponding macrobeat and microbeat names is provided below.

Meter	Macrobeat	Microbeats
Usual Duple	DU	DU DE
Usual Triple	DU	DU DA DI
Usual Combined	DU	DU DA DI DU DE
Unusual Paired	DU	DU BE DU BA BI
Unusual Unpaired	DU	DU BE DU BE DU BA BI

Notice that in this rhythm solfege system the macrobeat is named DU in all meters. The consistent use of one syllable, DU, to represent the strong beat in all meters will help students organize their rhythmic movement to macrobeats and develop their rhythm solfege as well. To further aid teachers and their students in understanding and comprehending meter, rhythm syllables beginning only with the letter D are used for microbeats in the usual meters, and rhythm syllables beginning with the letter B are used for microbeats in the unusual meters.

If you are teaching your students Learning Sequence Activities in the later grade levels, you will use the rhythm syllables written on page [x] to chant rhythm patterns and the meter names to label meters when your students are learning in the Verbal Association and Generalization-Verbal Units featured in the first-grade book. If you are not using Learning Sequence Activities or the Coordination

xii

with Learning Sequence Activities, you may create your own way to help your students understand meter through use of macrobeat and microbeat movement and audiation and rhythm solfege.

MODES OF PERFORMANCE

SINGING
Singing is the most fundamental means of musical performance. Singing is musically rich because it involves both the rhythmic and the tonal elements of music. When singing, students have an opportunity to apply what they have learned aurally to their own musical performance without needing to develop other sophisticated technical skills such as those needed to play an instrument. Through *Jump Right In: The Music Curriculum,* students will develop readiness for singing and will regularly engage in singing, both in groups and in solo. For example, in kindergarten, students learn to sing songs, the resting tone, and tonal patterns.

MOVING
Movement is essential to musical development, for whenever one performs or listens to music with comprehension, one is also covertly or even overtly moving to that music. Movement provides fundamental readiness for the understanding of rhythm and style. Through *Jump Right In: The Music Curriculum*, students will develop beat competency. In addition, students will develop the ability to move stylistically and learn beginning folk dance skills.

CHANTING
Chanting is a means of vocal rhythmic performance. Opportunities for students to chant in groups and in solo are provided throughout the *Jump Right In: The Music Curriculum* Teaching Plans. Students eventually learn to chant ostinati and chant in parts. As with singing, students have an opportunity to apply what they have learned aurally to their musical performance without needing to develop the sophisticated technical skills needed for performance on an instrument.

PLAYING INSTRUMENTS

Students who have been actively engaged in music making through singing, chanting, and moving will learn to apply what they have learned to playing instruments. First, students will develop readiness by observing models and by having an opportunity to explore the instruments with no expectation toward correctness. Second, they will transfer what they have learned to audiate to their instrumental performances. Third, they will develop instrumental technique. In kindergarten, students will have opportunities to see appropriate instrumental technique modeled and to develop instrumental readiness.

MUSIC READING

Children learn to understand language aurally and to speak before they learn to read and write. Likewise, students learning music must first learn to comprehend aurally and perform music before they learn to read music. From the beginning of instruction using *Jump Right In: The Music Curriculum*, students begin to develop the necessary readiness for learning to read music. They develop a rich aural and oral music vocabulary. Eventually, through guided instruction, they will learn to recognize this vocabulary in notation. In kindergarten, students develop readiness for music reading and writing.

LISTENING

Listening is essential for learning music. In order to develop appropriate musical concepts, students must listen to and observe excellent musical models. Eventually, students who were actively engaged in music making through singing, chanting, moving, and playing instruments will be able to apply to listening what they have learned while making music.

USING THE TEACHER'S EDITION

Lesson plans in *Jump Right In: The Music Curriculum* are presented in a consistent format. Each plan includes (1) a key to the plan, which lists activity type, tonality, meter, resting tone, macrobeats, microbeats, materials and the purposes for that Teaching Plan, (2) an age-appropriate Teaching Plan for use in your classroom.

In addition, you will find the music notation for the melody of the song and Enrichment Bubbles, which can include one or more related activities, such as Coordination with Instrumental Music, Teaching Tips, lesson extension ideas, listening lessons, and special connections to language arts, social studies, science, math, and art. Below is a plan with the parts labeled.

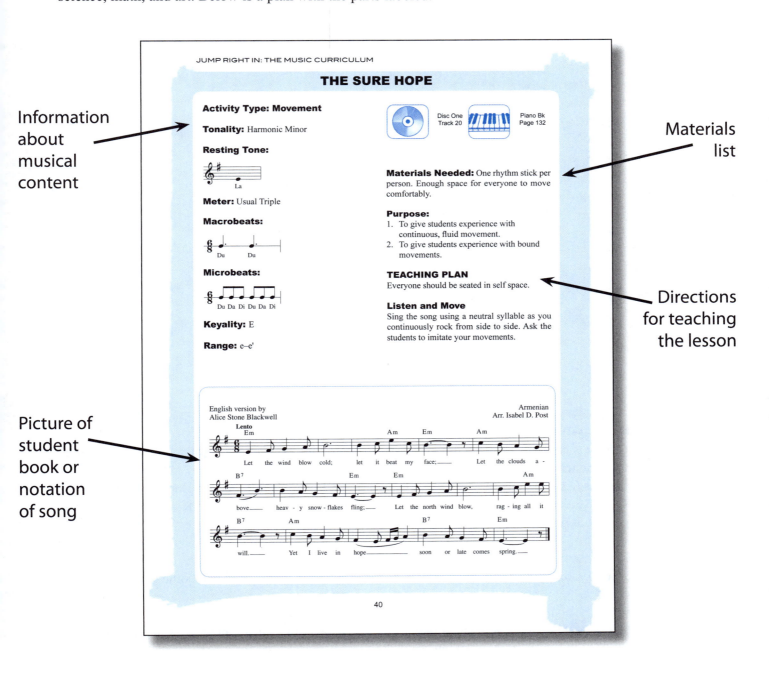

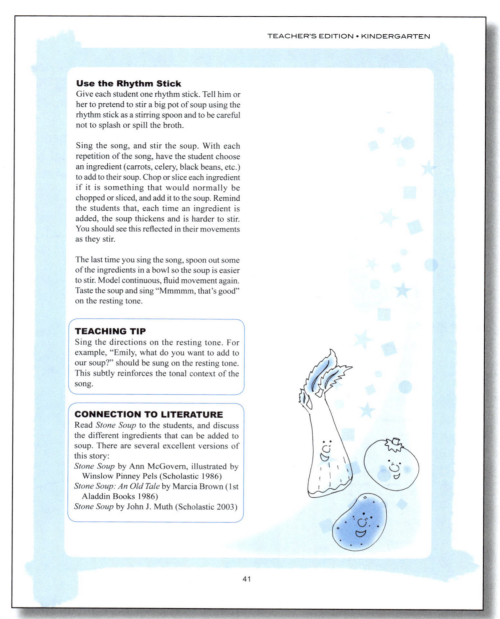

LESSON PLANNING

The Teaching Plans in the Teacher's Editions are not the same as lesson plans. For a successful lesson plan, teachers will want to draw from several of the Teaching Plans. In fact, a teacher may include portions of as many as seven or eight Teaching Plans in a single lesson plan, depending upon the age of the students and the pace of instruction. When planning a lesson, teachers should keep several of the following general principles in mind.

1. Every lesson plan should include a balance of tonalities and meters.
2. Every lesson plan should include some activities with a tonal focus and some with a rhythmic focus.
3. Every lesson plan should include a mixture of musical material that the students experience for the first time as well as musical material that has been introduced in past lessons and is being explored in more depth or reviewed.

4. Every lesson plan should include opportunities for individual musical responses from students, for it is through these individual responses that a teacher can most accurately determine the musical achievement levels of the students and subsequently adapt instruction to meet the individual needs of those students.

5. Every lesson plan should provide a balance of activity types, including movement, singing, chanting, listening, and instrumental performance.

6. Lesson plans need to be fluid. Sometimes what a teacher has planned may not be the best course to follow as an actual music class unfolds. A teacher should always be sensitive to the needs and responses of the students and adapt lesson plans in action as needed.

The Teaching Plans in the Teacher's Edition are generally in order of student readiness; therefore, the plans later in the book are more difficult for students than those in the beginning of the book. However, many fundamental concepts, such as the audiation of resting time and movement with continuous flow, along with others, appear throughout the entire Teacher's Edition.

The following lesson plans can serve as examples for how a teacher might plan a lesson for use with kindergarten students.

Lesson Plan for Early in the Year

1. **Hello, Everybody:** Sing "Hello, Everybody" when you meet the students at the door of your classroom. Continue singing as they follow you in to the room and take their seats in a circle. (Students will become used to being met at the door with music and walked into the room in a musical way each class period. In this way, music class begins the moment the students set foot in the music room.) Students have already completed the first part of the "Hello, Everybody" Teaching Plan, so at this point, choose a student to serve as a movement leader as suggested in the second portion of the Teaching Plan. (Curricular goals: understanding of pathways in movement, body awareness)

2. **All the Pretty Little Horses:** Because this is a short Teaching Plan, follow all the instructions. When asking students to sing the resting tone, ask both the entire class and individual students to respond. (Curricular goals: audiation of resting tone and exposure to Aeolian tonality; continuous, fluid movement; individual tonal response to provide an opportunity for the assessment of individual achievement)

3. **The Elephant:** As this Teaching Plan is also short, you can complete it in its entirety in one class period. However, you will probably want to review it in the next class period to allow the information and learning to solidify. (Curricular goals: audiation of rhythm patterns in Usual Triple meter; discrimination of rhythm patterns as being the same or different.)

4. **Do You See That Bird There?:** Complete the "Move Alone" part of the Teaching Plan. Save "Move with a Partner" for the next class period. (Curricular goals: continuous, fluid movement; exposure to multiple tonalities and meters in a single song)

5. **Shake, Shake, Shake:** Complete entire Teaching Plan. (Curricular goals: experiencing fast and slow through movement)

6. **Volga Boat Song:** The students have already completed "Move Alone" and "Move with Partners" in previous lessons and are familiar with the song. Complete the "Move as a Class" portion of the

JUMP RIGHT IN: THE MUSIC CURRICULUM

Teaching Plan. (Curricular goals: experience with bound movement; exposure to Aeolian tonality; audiation of and movement to macrobeats in Usual Duple meter)

Lesson Plan for the Middle of the Year

1. **Little Train:** Meet students at the door and sing "Little Train" as you walk them into the classroom. At the end of the song, they should all be sitting in their places in the circle. They have already been introduced to the song in the previous class period and have completed the "Sing and Move" and "Create Movements" part of the Teaching Plan. Invite the students to sing with song with you. Then pass out rhythm sticks and review the "Create Movements" portion of the Teaching Plan with the students singing, if they are able, and moving. (Curricular goals: audiation of and movement to macrobeats in Usual Duple meter; creative movement; instrumental readiness through the use of rhythm sticks)

2. **My Name Is Little Yellow Bird:** Start singing the song a you walk around the room, gently tapping students on their shoulders as a signal for them to silently put their rhythm sticks in the collection basket in the center of the circle. The students have already completed the "Identify Macrobeats" portion of the Teaching Plan in a previous lesson. Introduce the activities in the "Creating Responses" portion of the Teaching Plan. This should be repeated in the next class period as well to give more students an opportunity to respond individually. (Curricular goals: creative melodic response in Major Tonality and Usual Duple meter)

3. **Little Wind:** The students completed the "Flow with Pulsations" portion of the Teaching Plan in a previous lesson. Get out the Hoberman Sphere, and finish the Teaching Plan. (Curricular goals: audiation of Dorian tonality; individual tonal response to provide an opportunity for the assessment of individual student achievement)

4. **The Bell Peter:** The students have already completed the "Listen and Move" portion of the Teaching Plan in a previous class period. Quickly review that portion of the Teaching Plan, and complete the "Move with a Partner" portion. (Curricular goals: exposure to Dorian tonality; Audiation of and movement to macrobeats in Usual Triple meter)

5. **Johnny Works with One Hammer:** Introduce the song by teaching the "Sing and Move" portion of the Teaching Plan. (Curricular goals: continuous, fluid movement to a traditional song; development of body awareness and coordination)

6. **The Firehouse:** The students have already completed the "Move to Microbeats and "Vocal Exploration" portion of the Teaching Plan. Give the students streamers, and complete the "Move with Streamers" portion of the Teaching Plan. (Curricular goals: audiation of movement to macrobeats in Usual Duple meter; experience with preparatory breath as a bridge to audiation.)

Lesson Plan for Late in the Year

1. **Everybody Do This!:** Sing "Everybody Do This!" when you meet the students at the door. Move into the classroom as if flying, with your arms extended, bending your knees and flowing as much as possible. Continue singing as the students follow you in to the room, imitating your movement and taking their seats in a circle. Students have already completed the first part of the "Everybody Do This!"

xviii

Teaching Plan, so once the students are seated, add pulsations to your flow using your elbows, sing the song once more, and move on to the next activity. (Curricular goals: continuous fluid movement with pulsations)

2. **Tsamico Dance:** This is the first time that students have experienced this song. Complete the "Move and Listen" and "Imitate" portions of the Teaching Plan. Next class period, review those portions of the Teaching Plan, and go on to "Create Patterns." (Curricular goals: preparation for rhythm creativity; individual rhythm response to provide an opportunity for the assessment of individual student achievement; extension of rhythm pattern vocabulary; exposure to the music of another culture)

3. **City Line Avenue:** The students have already completed "Identify Macrobeats and Microbeats" and "Walk to Microbeats," although this was less successful than you had hoped in the last class period. Ask the students to stand up and flow with pulsations in their hands while chanting TUH to microbeats as you sing the song to reinforce the audiation of microbeats. Then complete the "Reinforce Resting Tone" portion of the lesson plan. (Curricular goals: reinforcement of the audiation of microbeats through continuous flow with pulsations; audiation of resting tone in Mixolydian tonality; exposure to Mixolydian tonality)

4. **Dancing Bear:** Complete the Listening Lesson for "Dance of the Jesters" found in the "Dancing Bear" lesson plan. (Curricular goals: exposure to instrumental music through listening and discussion; continuous, fluid movement with pulsations)

5. **Mary Wore a Red Dress:** The students have already completed the "Greet the Children and Introduce the Song" and the "Invite Students to Sing Song" portions of the Teaching Plan. Review the song. Then complete the "Introduce the Chord Root Melody" portion of the Teaching Plan, and, if the students display readiness, move on to the "Teach the Chord Root Melody" portion of the Teaching Plan. (Curricular goals: audiation of harmony in Major tonality)

6. **Lazy Bones:** The students completed the Teaching Plan last class period. However, they needed more experience to solidify their learning. Choose different students to "wake up" the class than you did in the previous class period. (Curricular goal: audiation of microbeats in Usual Duple meter; individual movement to beat to provide an opportunity for the assessment of individual student achievement; engagement in a traditional song and game; exposure to two tempos and meters in the context of a single song)

7. **London Bridge:** The students have already completed the entire Teaching Plan. However, you are playing the game again to give more individual students an opportunity to perform tonal patterns in solo. (Curricular goals: individual tonal response to provide an opportunity for the assessment of student achievement; engagement in a traditional song and game.)

SCOPE AND SEQUENCE

		Singing					Chanting				Stylistic Movement								Beat Movement					
	Page Number	Readiness	Unison	Solo	Ostinato	Creativity	Unison	Solo	Ostinato	Creativity	Readiness	Body Awareness	Self Space	Shared Space	Flow	Weight	Space	Time	Readiness	Pulsations	Bilateral	Alternating	Locomotor	Creativity
Hello Everybody	2											•	•		•		•							
The Braes O'Yarrow	4	•									•	•				•	•						•	
This Lady Wears a Dark Green Dress	6	•	•								•	•				•							•	
Jeremiah Blow the Fire	8	•	•									•				•								
All the Pretty Horses	10	•	•									•				•								
Arirang	12	•	•								•	•				•								
Peas	14	•	•				•				•	•	•		•		•		•	•			•	
The Elephant	16						•	•		•		•												
Down in the Village of Valtou	18										•				•		•							
Sleep, My Darling	20	•	•	•							•	•												
Blow the Balloon	22	•										•				•		•						
Five Little Pumpkins	24	•	•							•		•												
Floppy Scarecrow	28											•				•			•	•			•	
The Ghost of John	30	•	•									•				•								
America the Beautiful	32											•	•											
Open-Close	34		•				•					•												
Graceful Simo	36											•		•		•	•		•	•				
Full Moonlight Dance	38											•				•	•							
The Sure Hope	40	•										•				•								
Go to Sleep	42	•	•									•				•								
Sometimes I Feel Like a Motherless Child	44	•										•	•			•								
One Summer Day	46											•				•			•	•				
Do You See That There Bird	48											•				•	•							
Hato Popo	50	•	•				•					•							•	•	•			
The Squirrel	52											•				•	•	•					•	
The Ardelean Woman	54							•			•	•				•	•							
Shake, Shake, Shake	56											•						•						
The Volga Boat Song	58											•	•			•			•	•				
Bim Bam	60	•	•								•	•												
Early to Bed	62							•		•		•											•	
Over the River and through the Woods	64						•	•	•			•										•	•	
Turkey Song	66	•	•				•	•		•		•							•					
Five Little Muffins	68						•					•							•					
Mos Mos	70						•	•				•				•		•						
Two Little Sausages	72						•	•		•		•							•	•				
Sleep, My Babe	74	•	•		•							•												
The Elephant Song	76									•		•	•											
My Little Ducklings	78											•						•					•	•
Zion's Children	80											•				•		•	•	•				
In the Window	82	•	•									•							•	•				
Popcorn	84						•					•							•	•	•		•	
Personet Hodie	86	•	•								•	•				•			•	•				
America	88	•	•				•					•				•			•	•	•			
Baloo, Lammy	90										•	•				•								
Coventry Carol	92						•		•			•							•	•		•		
As Joseph was a Walking	94						•	•			•	•	•		•		•							
I Wonder as I Wander	96	•	•									•				•								
O Little Town of Bethleham	98										•	•				•							•	
Away in a Manger	100		•				•						•			•						•	•	
Softly	102						•				•	•	•			•	•		•	•	•			
Children's Lullaby	104	•	•								•	•				•								
Oh, I'll Build a Snowman	106						•				•	•	•			•			•	•				
I'm a Little Snowflake	108							•		•		•				•								
Walking With My Mom	110									•	•	•	•		•	•	•	•					•	
Darling Goodnight	112	•	•	•								•				•								
You'll Sound as Weird as Me	114	•	•								•	•				•			•	•				
Bi, Bi, Og Blaka	116	•	•	•							•	•												
Dance from Zalongou	118										•	•			•	•			•	•				
The Star Spangled Banner	120	•	•				•					•				•			•	•	•			
London Bridge	122			•		•	•		•	•	•	•							•		•	•	•	
Toss and Catch	124	•	•								•	•				•			•	•				
Five Little Speckled Frogs	126	•			•							•								•				
Horses	128	•					•					•							•	•			•	
Everybody Do This	130	•	•									•							•	•				
Swing A Lady	132																								
Dancing Bear	134															•			•	•				
Yangtze Boatman's Chantey	136	•	•	•								•	•										•	

SCOPE AND SEQUENCE

	Dance					Concepts									Harmony	
	Readiness	Circle Games	Action Songs	Instrumental	Listening	Resting Tone	S/D Rhythm	S/D Tonal	Macrobeats	Microbeats	Timbre Recog.	Dyn/Expression	Phrase	Form	Readiness	Page Number
Hello Everybody					•											2
The Braes O'Yarrow					•											4
This Lady Wears a Dark Green Dress					•	•			•							6
Jeremiah Blow the Fire					•	•			•	•						8
All the Pretty Horses				•	•	•					•					10
Arirang				•	•	•					•					12
Peas		•			•				•							14
The Elephant					•	•	•		•	•						16
Down in the Village of Valtou				•	•						•					18
Sleep, My Darling					•	•							•			20
Blow the Balloon					•											22
Five Little Pumpkins			•		•	•			•							24
Floppy Scarecrow					•											28
The Ghost of John					•	•			•					•		30
America the Beautiful				•	•	•					•	•				32
Open-Close			•		•				•	•						34
Graceful Simo					•						•					36
Full Moonlight Dance					•											38
The Sure Hope					•	•			•	•						40
Go to Sleep					•	•		•					•			42
Sometimes I Feel Like a Motherless Child				•	•	•					•					44
One Summer Day					•				•							46
Do You See That There Bird					•											48
Hato Popo					•	•			•	•						50
The Squirrel				•	•											52
The Ardelean Woman				•	•						•					54
Shake, Shake, Shake					•							•				56
The Volga Boat Song				•	•				•		•					58
Bim Bam					•	•										60
Early to Bed					•			•								62
Over the River and through the Woods				•	•				•		•					64
Turkey Song			•		•			•	•							66
Five Little Muffins			•		•				•							68
Mos Mos					•											70
Two Little Sausages					•			•	•							72
Sleep, My Babe					•					•						74
The Elephant Song			•		•		•	•								76
My Little Ducklings				•	•				•		•					78
Zion's Children					•			•	•	•						80
In the Window				•	•	•			•	•					•	82
Popcorn					•				•	•						84
Personet Hodie					•	•										86
America				•	•				•	•	•					88
Baloo, Lammy					•							•	•			90
Coventry Carol					•			•	•	•	•					92
As Joseph was a Walking					•	•					•					94
I Wonder as I Wander					•	•					•		•		•	96
O Little Town of Bethleham		•			•				•				•			98
Away in a Manger					•	•			•		•		•			100
Softly									•	•						102
Children's Lullaby					•	•					•				•	104
Oh, I'll Build a Snowman					•							•				106
I'm a Little Snowflake					•			•								108
Walking With My Mom					•			•								110
Darling Goodnight						•										112
You'll Sound as Weird as Me					•				•	•						114
Bí, Bí, Og Blaka					•											116
Dance from Zalongou					•											118
The Star Spangled Banner				•	•	•			•	•	•					120
London Bridge		•	•		•	•			•		•					122
Toss and Catch					•					•						124
Five Little Speckled Frogs						•			•	•						126
Horses					•				•	•						128
Everybody Do This			•		•				•	•						130
Swing A Lady		•			•				•							132
Dancing Bear				•	•				•	•	•			•		134
Yangtze Boatman's Chantey					•	•			•			•				136

xxi

SCOPE AND SEQUENCE

	Page Number	Singing					Chanting				Stylistic Movement								Beat Movement					
		Readiness	Unison	Solo	Ostinato	Creativity	Unison	Solo	Ostinato	Creativity	Readiness	Body Awareness	Self Space	Shared Space	Flow	Weight	Space	Time	Readiness	Pulsations	Bilateral	Alternating	Locomotor	Creativity
Blow the Man Down	138												•	•										
Blow the Winds Southerly	140	•	•	•									•	•										
Tsamico Dance	142						•	•		•			•	•									•	
Will Winter End?	144	•	•	•									•		•	•	•	•					•	
Roll That Big Ball Down to Town	146		•									•	•			•	•	•		•				
Hani Kouni	150	•	•										•	•			•						•	
Scandinavian Folk Song	152												•										•	
City Line Avenue	154	•	•										•				•						•	
Elephants and Kitty Cats	156												•				•							
High Bird	158											•	•											
Barnacle Bill	160	•																						
See How I'm Jumping	162	•	•				•			•			•						•	•				
Shalom Chaverim	166	•	•	•							•	•	•		•								•	
The Greenland Whale Fishery	168	•	•			•							•	•									•	
Fire House	170	•										•	•			•					•		•	
Wild Dog on Our Farm	172				•							•	•								•	•		
Funny Puppy	174			•		•							•								•			
Sidewalk Talk	176						•							•	•	•			•	•	•			
Jim Along Josie	178	•	•	•									•										•	
Bre'r Rabbit Shake It	180	•	•										•		•		•							
Tisket, A Tasket	182	•	•									•	•	•									•	
Baa, Baa, Black Sheep	184	•	•								•		•		•	•								
Sakura	186	•	•	•								•	•		•		•	•						
My Name is Little Yellow Bird	188			•		•							•										•	•
Little Train	190		•										•										•	
Engine, Engine	192	•					•			•						•	•	•		•	•			•
Old MacDonald Had a Farm	196											•	•			•								
The Old Grey Cat	198												•				•		•	•	•		•	
Little Wind	200	•	•	•									•		•		•		•	•	•			
Who Has Seen the Wind?	202	•	•	•		•							•											
Ophelia' Letter Blow 'Way	204	•	•	•									•											
Fireman, Fireman	206	•	•	•		•							•	•										
Lullaby from Cyprus	208						•						•						•	•	•		•	
The Nothing Song	210												•			•	•						•	
The Bell Peter	212										•	•	•	•										•
Gipsy Ipsy	214		•	•		•					•	•												
The Sky Has Clouded	218	•	•				•					•	•						•	•				
Clapping Land	220	•	•				•						•			•	•							
Only My Opinion	224	•	•	•								•	•										•	
Rain on the Green Grass	226										•	•	•	•										
This Old Man	228	•	•	•		•					•	•	•	•										
Johnny Works With One Hammer	230						•	•		•			•		•		•							
The Chickens They Are Crowin'	232												•				•							
Lazy Bones	234																	•			•			
Nanny Goat	236	•	•	•									•		•	•								
Jumbo Elephant	238												•			•	•					•	•	
Scarborough Fair	240											•	•	•	•	•	•	•	•	•			•	
Punchilla	242												•				•							
To Market, To Market	244							•			•		•				•							
Hot Dog	246												•											
Toodala	248	•	•							•	•		•		•	•	•	•	•	•			•	
Thessaly *Syrtos* Dance	250												•		•	•	•						•	
Humpty Dumpty	252						•						•				•	•	•	•				
Little Rondo	254	•	•	•		•	•	•		•	•	•	•											
Draw a Bucket of Water	258												•	•								•	•	
Fair Rosie	260	•	•	•									•				•		•	•				
Mary Wore a Red Dress	264	•	•	•			•			•			•						•	•				
Row, Row, Row Your Boat	268		•										•		•	•	•	•	•				•	

SCOPE AND SEQUENCE

	Dance				Listening	Concepts									Harmony	Page Number
	Readiness	Circle Games	Action Songs	Instrumental	Listening	Resting Tone	S/D Rhythm	S/D Tonal	Macrobeats	Microbeats	Timbre Recog.	Dyn/Expression	Phrase	Form	Readiness	Page Number
Blow the Man Down				•	•				•	•	•					138
Blow the Winds Southerly					•	•			•							140
Tsamico Dance				•	•		•		•							142
Will Winter End?				•		•										144
Roll That Big Ball Down to Town									•	•						146
Hani Kouni										•			•	•		150
Scandinavian Folk Song				•	•				•	•	•		•			152
City Line Avenue					•	•			•							154
Elephants and Kitty Cats					•											156
High Bird					•											158
Barnacle Bill				•	•	•			•		•			•		160
See How I'm Jumping							•		•							162
Shalom Chaverim				•	•				•		•		•			166
The Greenland Whale Fishery					•				•	•		•				168
Fire House		•			•											170
Wild Dog on Our Farm					•											172
Funny Puppy							•		•							174
Sidewalk Talk					•				•	•						176
Jim Along Josie					•	•			•							178
Bre'r Rabbit Shake It					•	•										180
Tisket, A Tasket		•			•				•							182
Baa, Baa, Black Sheep					•	•										184
Sakura				•	•				•		•		•			186
My Name is Little Yellow Bird					•				•							188
Little Train				•					•	•						190
Engine, Engine			•		•				•	•						192
Old MacDonald Had a Farm				•	•						•					196
The Old Grey Cat		•		•	•				•		•					198
Little Wind		•			•	•										200
Who Has Seen the Wind?					•									•		202
Ophelia' Letter Blow 'Way						•							•			204
Fireman, Fireman					•			•								206
Lullaby from Cyprus					•				•	•						208
The Nothing Song					•								•			210
The Bell Peter				•	•	•			•	•						212
Gipsy Ipsy					•			•								214
The Sky Has Clouded					•	•	•		•							218
Clapping Land									•	•						220
Only My Opinion					•	•										224
Rain on the Green Grass					•											226
This Old Man				•	•	•			•	•						228
Johnny Works With One Hammer					•		•			•				•		230
The Chickens They Are Crowin'													•			232
Lazy Bones		•			•					•						234
Nanny Goat					•	•		•								236
Jumbo Elephant					•				•							238
Scarborough Fair				•	•				•	•	•	•				240
Punchilla		•			•				•							242
To Market, To Market				•	•				•	•						244
Hot Dog				•	•				•							246
Toodala				•	•	•			•							248
Thessaly Syrtos Dance				•	•				•		•		•			250
Humpty Dumpty									•	•						252
Little Rondo					•		•	•								254
Draw a Bucket of Water		•			•											258
Fair Rosie					•					•						260
Mary Wore a Red Dress					•	•	•		•						•	264
Row, Row, Row Your Boat			•	•	•				•				•		•	268

xxiii

MUSIC APTITUDE

Every child has potential to achieve in music. This potential, called music aptitude, is normally distributed among the population at birth and is developmental. Simply put, the quality of a child's music environment affects the level of a child's music aptitude until that child is approximately nine years old. After that time, a child will be able to achieve in music to the level that his or her stabilized music aptitude and musical environment will allow. In light of this, the importance of general music instruction for young children becomes clear. Elementary general music teachers are not only responsible for teaching children music; they are also responsible for maintaining and improving children's lifelong potential to learn music.

Really, children have several aptitudes that relate to music. Some children are stronger tonally and others are stronger rhythmically. We, as teachers, must know the levels of our students' music aptitudes in order to teach to individual differences. We need to challenge those with high aptitudes by presenting them with tasks that will challenge them to achieve to their full potential, and we need to give students with low aptitude extra help. This will prevent boredom for some and frustration for others.

MEASUREMENT, EVALUATION, AND TESTING

The authors of *Jump Right In: The Music Curriculum* recommend that teachers use a variety of measurement tools to evaluate students' music aptitude and music learning. Standardized tests are measurement tools that provide evidence of reliability and validity and, therefore, make it possible for individual teachers to measure objectively their own students' musical performances and learning. Recommended measures fall naturally into two categories: standardized tests of music aptitude and tests of music achievement. The test types are presented below in chart form.

STANDARDIZED TEST OF MUSIC APPITUDE	TESTS OF MUSIC ACHIEVEMENT
Primary Measures of Music Audiation a test of developmental music aptitude for children in kindergarten through third grades	**Iowa Tests of Music Literacy** a standardized, multilevel test of tonal and rhythm listening, reading, and writing skills for students in fourth through twelfth grades
Intermediate Measures of Music Audiation a test of developmental music apitude for children in first through fourth grades	**Performance Based Music Achievement Tests** with standardized, administration procedures, recorded performances, and rating scales that include at least three dimensions (tonal, rhythm, and expression) to provide objective information about each student's music performance.
Musical Apitude Profile a test of stablized music apitude for children in fourth through twelfth grades	**Paper and Pencil Music Acievement Tests** with standardized answer sheets and administration procedures to provide objective information about each student's understanding of what they have learned

In first grade and beyond, a standardized music aptitude test should be administered to all students prior to instruction so teaching may be directed toward each student's individual strengths and weaknesses. The purpose of administering a standardized music test is to improve instruction. With objective information about each student's music aptitudes, teachers can plan effective teaching to meet each student's needs. With objective information about each student's music achievement, or music learning, teachers can better evaluate student progress and each student's relative standing within a group of peers.

COORDINATION WITH INSTRUMENTAL MUSIC

Jump Right In: The Music Curriculum is the only educational music series for children in grades K–6 that features full integration and coordination with a published instrumental music series. *Jump Right In: The Instrumental Series* features recordings of excellent instrumental soloists on woodwind, brass, strings, and percussion instruments throughout. The authors of *Jump Right In: The Music Curriculum* believe that children should hear excellent instrumental performances of familiar and unfamiliar songs to build their listening vocabularies of instrumental tone colors, performance styles, and timbres. By listening to the instrumental recordings, children will hear excellent performances by professional performers on each of the band and orchestra instruments.

Throughout *Jump Right In: The Music Curriculum* students may hear solo performances on the following instruments:

Violin	Bass Clarinet
Viola	Soprano Saxophone
Cello	Alto Saxophone
Bass	Tenor Saxophone
Guitar	Baritone Saxophone
Soprano Recorder	Trumpet
Piccolo	Flügelhorn
Flute	French Horn
Alto Flute	Euphonium
Oboe	Trombone
English Horn	Tuba
Clarinet	Xylophone
Bassoon	Marimba

Instrumental solo recordings are performed by students and artist-faculty from the Eastman School of Music in Rochester, New York. Choral recordings are performed by the Westminster Choir of Rider University. Orchestral and band recordings were drawn from the performance recording libraries of the University of Michigan School of Music and the University of Arizona School of Music.

To make the most of their music potential, teachers should include in children's musical experiences a rich variety of tonalities and meters, timbres, tempos, and styles. When teachers provide many opportunities for children to hear performers on band and orchestra instruments playing music in many tonalities and meters, children's musical environments are enriched and their potential for understanding and comprehending music is increased

PHILOSOPHY OF *JUMP RIGHT IN*

In writing *Jump Right In: The Music Curriculum,* we have tried to achieve several goals.

First, we believe that music is learned in the same way that a language is learned. Children interact with language first by listening and experimenting with it; we have no expectation for correctness. Eventually, children develop solid listening and, eventually, speaking vocabularies. Only after they can already understand spoken language and speak themselves do they learn to read and write. We have sequenced the instruction of *Jump Right In: The Music Curriculum* to parallel this learning process. Students first develop extensive aural and oral music vocabularies. Only then do we introduce music reading and writing. Because music is learned aurally and orally, teachers must serve as models of excellent musicianship. As a result, we have written our Teaching Plans so that teachers must sing, chant, move, play, and create in order to teach successfully. Teachers should provide the musical models to which their students aspire, for unless students have excellent aural models, they will be unable to learn music efficiently.

Second, we have tried to achieve a balance of tonalities and meters when choosing repertoire to include in the series. Most of the music heard in the United States is in Major tonality and Duple meter. However, our understandings of Major tonality and Duple meter are limited because we have nothing with which to compare them. By involving our students in making music in less frequently heard tonalities and meters, they will not only develop an understanding of the unusual tonalities and meters, but they will also have a better and richer understanding of Major and Duple. In other words, they will learn what Major and Duple are by learning what they are not.

Third, we have tried to involve students in music of other cultures. When choosing repertoire, we included many songs from other countries and cultures and presented those songs in as authentic a form as possible. We have also encouraged teachers to go beyond what is written in the main Teaching Plans and explore the cultural context of the songs with students.

Fourth, we believe that students should be given opportunities to perform alone as well as in a group. Only by performing alone can students gain a full understanding of their own performances. By hearing students perform alone, teachers will be able to assess the progress of individuals rather than the overall progress of a group. In this way, the teacher will be better able to address the needs of individual students.

Finally, we have written all books so that they conform to the National Standards of MENC: The National Association for Music Education. By teaching the plans as they are presented within *Jump Right In: The Music Curriculum,* students will have the opportunity to achieve all of the goals as defined for each of the levels within the National Standards document.

Jump Right In
Kindergarten
Teacher's Guide
Lesson Plans

JUMP RIGHT IN: THE MUSIC CURRICULUM

HELLO, EVERYBODY

Activity Type: Movement

Tonality: Major

Resting Tone:

Meter: Usual Duple

Macrobeats:

Microbeats:

Keyality: D

Range: d–d'

 Disc One Track 1

 Piano Bk Page 64

Materials Needed: Recording. Enough space for everyone to move comfortably.

Purpose:
1. To increase body awareness.
2. To help students learn to move shoulders, elbows, ankles, hips, and wrists in isolation.

TEACHING PLAN
Everyone should be seated in self space.

Matching Body Part Isolations and Time
Have the students sit in a circle with their legs crossed. Ask them to copy your movements as you play the recording or sing the song. (If your students are adept at using self space, you may have them stand for this activity.)

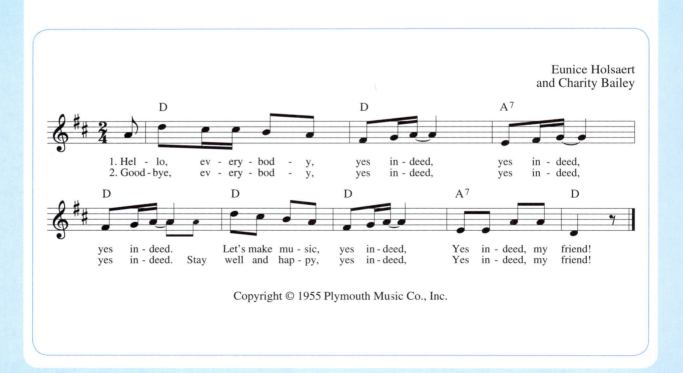

Eunice Holsaert and Charity Bailey

Copyright © 1955 Plymouth Music Co., Inc.

TEACHER'S EDITION • KINDERGARTEN

Begin by moving only one shoulder in curvy pathways during the first half of the song. Switch, and move the other shoulder in curvy pathways during the second half of the song.

Repeat the activity using the following parts of the body:
- one elbow and then the other
- one ankle and then the other
- one hip and then the other
- one wrist and then the other.

Discuss how it feels to move parts of the body in isolation. The students will discover that it is easier to move some than others. That is the beginning of body awareness. You might say something such as, "Though we each have one body, each body has many parts that work together."

Using Movement Leaders
Finish the lesson by allowing individual students to be movement leaders. Ask one student to select a body part. All other students will imitate the leader's movement and tempo. Play the recording or sing the song, and allow the student to lead the movement. After the first two phrases of the recording, instruct the student to switch to the other shoulder, elbow, etc. Repeat the activity with several different leaders. Be sure to have the students select several parts of the body.

FOR THE MUSIC TEACHER
On another day, you can extend this activity. Repeat the activity using matching pairs of body parts. For example, move both shoulders, ankles, or wrists at the same time. The students will experience body part duets. They will need to adjust their standing and sitting to accommodate.

JUMP RIGHT IN: THE MUSIC CURRICULUM

THE BRAES O' YARROW

Activity Type: Movement

Tonality: Aeolian

Resting Tone:

La

Meter: Usual Triple

Macrobeats:

Du Du

Microbeats:

Du Da Di

Keyality: G

Range: d–f'

Materials Needed:
Enough space so that everyone can move comfortably.

 Disc One Track 2

 Piano Bk Page 26

Purpose:
1. To help students audiate resting tone in Aeolian tonality.
2. To give students experience with continuous, fluid movement.

TEACHING PLAN
Everyone should be seated in self space.

Making Soup
Tell the students that you are going to make a huge pot of soup and that they will be responsible for choosing the ingredients. Ask them to hold their imaginary stirring spoons with both hands, as they will be stirring a large pot. Sing the song. As you sing, hold your imaginary spoon and stir an imaginary pot of soup. Involve your entire upper body in the stirring.

4

TEACHER'S EDITION • KINDERGARTEN

When you have finished singing and stirring, sing the following on the resting tone: "What should we put in our soup?" Do not talk during the activity. Always sing questions and directions on the resting tone. Call on a student and mime putting that ingredient in the soup. If the ingredient would normally need to be chopped, pretend to chop it before adding it to the soup. Then sing the song again and stir. Repeat this several times, adding a new ingredient to the soup for each repetition of the song.

You can include the concept of bound flow in this activity as well. Tell the students that the soup is getting thicker and more difficult to stir as you add each ingredient.

TEACHING TIP
Sometimes students will suggest things that are not normal soup ingredients. Feel free to accept their ideas and make nontraditional soups, allowing the students to be somewhat silly.

FOR THE MUSIC TEACHER
Singing verbal instructions on the resting tone or on the resting tone and dominant serves several purposes. First, it reinforces the fundamental pitches of the tonality for the students and helps them audiate that tonality. Second, it helps the students audiate for the entire activity. When a teacher talks, audiation tends to be inhibited. Finally, singing facilitates vocal health on the part of the teacher. Switching back and forth between talking and singing is vocally taxing. Staying in a light, healthy singing voice that is a good model for children is less stressful on the vocal mechanisms.

EXTENDING THE ACTIVITY
You can extend this activity by having children stir with different parts of their bodies to promote body awareness. Have the students stir with their heads, their elbows, their hips, and their feet. Have them jump into their pots of soup and stir with their entire bodies.

JUMP RIGHT IN: THE MUSIC CURRICULUM

THIS LADY SHE WEARS A DARK GREEN DRESS

Activity Type: Listening, Movement, Singing

Tonality: Major

Resting Tone:

Do

Meter: Usual Duple

Macrobeats:

Du Du

Microbeats:

Du De Du De

Keyality: D

Range: d–b

Materials Needed: Enough space for everyone to move comfortably.

 Disc One Track 3

 Piano Bk Page 137

Purpose:
1. To help students learn to listen.
2. To give students experience following a conductor.
3. To help students learn to breathe before they sing.

TEACHING PLAN
Everyone should be seated in self space.

Listen and Move
Tell the students that they will be listeners and movers. Remind them that listening is the most important job of each musician.

Tell the students to copy your movements as you sing a song for them. Perform the song and rock from side to side on macrobeats. Check to make sure the students copy your movements.

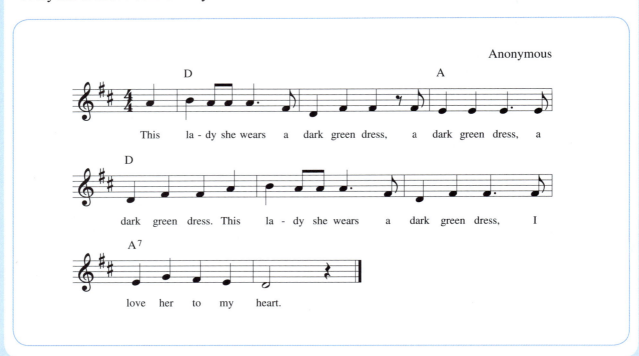

6

Sing the Resting Tone

Say, "Listen to this pitch." Sing the resting tone using BUM. Sing on the resting tone, "Watch my hands; they will tell you when to breathe. When I gesture to you, take a breath and sing the pitch I just sang to you." Perform a breath gesture for the students to sing the resting tone.

Sing, "Now, think that pitch." Give the students a moment to think the pitch. Sing, "Watch my hands. Take a breath and sing the pitch you were thinking." Again, give a clear breath gesture as you breathe and sing the pitch with the students. Sing, "Your job is to remember that pitch."

Sing, "I am going to sing the song again. Sometimes I will pause. Then I will show you when to breathe and sing the pitch you were thinking." Perform the song, and pause every two or four measures to give the breath gesture and sing the resting tone with the students.

Finish by singing the song again and having the students copy your continuous shoulder and spine movements. After you sing the last pitch, ask the students to watch your hands, breathe, and sing the last pitch of the song with you.

JUMP RIGHT IN: THE MUSIC CURRICULUM

JEREMIAH, BLOW THE FIRE

Activity Type: Movement

Tonality: Pentatonic

Resting Tone:

Do

Meter: Usual Duple

Macrobeats:

Du   Du

Microbeats:

Du De Du De

Keyality: D

Range: d–d'

 Disc One Track 4

 Piano Bk Page 72

Materials Needed: One or two chiffon scarves per person. Enough space for everyone to move comfortably.

Purpose
1. To reinforce coordinated breathing.
2. To allow observation of a correct visual model of continuous, fluid movement.

TEACHING PLAN
Everyone should be seated in self space at the beginning of the lesson. Later, all will move into standing self space.

Teach the Song
Teach the song using the Rote Song Teaching Procedure found in the Reference Manual.

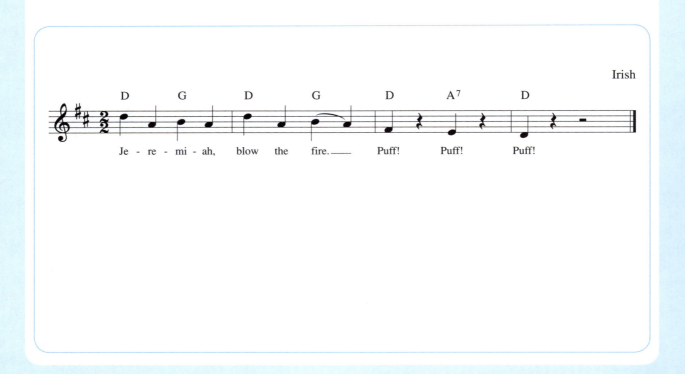

TEACHER'S EDITION • KINDERGARTEN

Model Movement and Breath

Ask the students to watch you move in a continuous, fluid way to the music using one or two chiffon scarves. At the end of the chant, open one scarf, take a large breath, and blow the scarf as high in the air as possible toward the ceiling. Allow the scarf to float to the ground, and sing the resting tone when the scarf (scarves) land.

Sing and Move

Give each student one or two chiffon scarves. Tell students that they are going to sing and copy the movements you just demonstrated. Sing the song as the students move with flow and blow their scarves into the air.

FOR THE MUSIC TEACHER

The purpose of this activity is to reinforce coordinated breathing. Musicians audiate what they are about to perform during the breath before performing. One way to encourage coordinated audiation and breathing in your students is to be a good musical model. Always cue them to sing by giving both a breath and a preparatory gesture. Also, always take a preparatory breath before you sing. Eventually this will become a habit for you and your students.

JUMP RIGHT IN: THE MUSIC CURRICULUM

ALL THE PRETTY LITTLE HORSES

Activity Type: Listening, Movement, Singing

Tonality: Aeolian

Resting Tone:

Meter: Usual Duple

Macrobeats:

Microbeats:

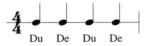

Keyality: E

Range: B–d′

 Disc One Track 5

 Piano Bk Page 2

Materials Needed: Enough space for everyone to move comfortably.

Purpose:
1. To help students learn to listen and move in response to music.
2. To give students experience moving carefully with bound flow.
3. To help students learn to sing resting tone in Aeolian tonality.

TEACHING PLAN
Everyone should be seated in self space.

Listen and Move with Bound Flow
Tell the students to copy your movements as you sing a song for them. Ask them to be listeners and movers. Remind them that listening is the most important job for each musician.

10

Place your arms as if cradling a baby. Check to see that the students have copied your movement. Begin to rock carefully, as though you have a baby in your arms, as you being to sing the song. If any students begin to sing with you, stop and ask the students to remind you of their jobs (listening and moving). Begin again. Repeat the process until all students are listening and moving. When all students demonstrate listening and moving competency, continue to move as you sing the entire song.

Ask the students to describe your movements. Were you rocking carefully or carelessly? When you are rocking carefully, you are using bound flow. When you are being careful with a baby, you are using bound flow.

Sing the Resting Tone
Say, "Listen to this pitch." Sing the resting tone using the neutral syllable BUM.

On the resting tone, sing, "Watch my hands, they will tell you when to breathe and sing. Now, think the pitch that I just sang. When you think music, you are audiating." Give the students a moment to think the pitch. Say, "Watch my hands. Take a breath and sing the pitch you were thinking." Again, give a clear breath gesture as you breathe and sing the pitch with the students. Sing, "Your job is to remember that pitch."

Sing, "I am going to sing the song again. Sometimes I will pause. Then, I will show you when to breathe and sing the pitch that you are audiating." Perform the song, and pause every two or four measures to give the breath gesture and sing the resting tone with the students.

COORDINATION WITH INSTRUMENTAL MUSIC
Play the solo flute recording of "All the Pretty Little Horses" from *Jump Right In: The Instrumental Series* (J229CD, track 80). Ask the students if they can identify the instrument without looking at a picture of it. If a student is able, ask that student how he or she knew. If no one is able to identify the instrument, show the students a picture of the flute using Instrument Card 8. Tell the students that the flute is called a wind instrument because it makes a sound when you blow into it.

Ask the students to name a part of the body. Once it has been identified, tell them that, as they listen to the recording, they should move that part of the body with continuous flow. Play the recording and move. Choose a new part of the body to move in a continuous, fluid style with each repetition of the recording.

JUMP RIGHT IN: THE MUSIC CURRICULUM

ARIRANG

Activity Type: Movement, Singing

Tonality: Multitonal (Pentatonic, Aeolian)

Resting Tone:

Meter: Usual Triple

Macrobeats:

Microbeats:

Keyality: G

Range: d–d'

 Disc One Track 6

 Piano Bk Page 10

Materials Needed: Scarves. Recording. Enough space for everyone to move comfortably.

Purpose:
1. To give students an opportunity to move with continuous, fluid movement.
2. To reinforce the audiation of resting tone.
3. To give students an opportunity to experience high, medium, and low levels of space.

TEACHING PLAN
Everyone should be standing in self space.

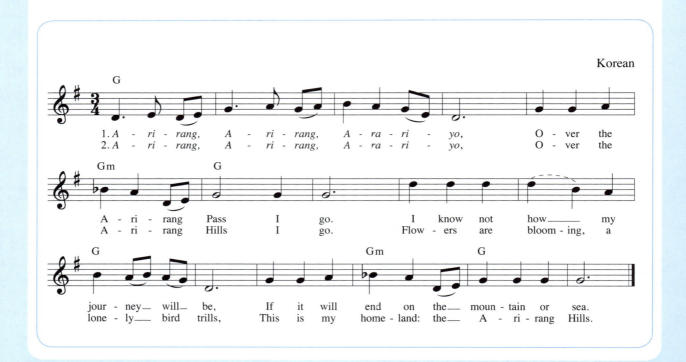

12

TEACHER'S EDITION • KINDERGARTEN

Move

Play the recording of "Arirang." As students listen, model continuous, fluid movement using different parts of the body (e.g., arms, shoulders, hips, knees) as a means of developing a movement vocabulary. Play the recording again, and invite students to move their bodies, exploring the space around them through continuous, fluid movement.

Use Scarves

You may extend the activity by using scarves. Give each a student a scarf and invite him or her to "dip the scarf in paint." Modeling continuous, fluid movement, paint the room with the scarf. Remind them to paint all the areas in the room, not just what is in front of them. Stretch high to the ceiling and low to the floor. Once students demonstrate continuous, fluid movement with scarves, add a resting tone drone to the song. As students paint with scarves, invite them to sing the resting tone as you sing the melody.

LISTENING LESSON

Play a recording that uses a gentle, flowing style, such as "Père Lachaise" from *Paris Sketches* by Martin Ellerby (Disc One, Track 7). This band recording is in a gentle style, much like that of Erik Satie. Ask the students to describe the style of the music. Guide them to use words such as "flowing," "gentle," and "soft." Ask the students how those musical qualities might be shown if they were to move. Continue the discussion, and give individual students an opportunity to demonstrate what such movement might look like. Play the recording, and ask the students to move throughout the room as if floating on clouds. Remind them that they should move with their entire bodies and not just their feet. Play the recording, and move with them, exaggerating the qualities of your movements so that they serve as a model for the students.

JUMP RIGHT IN: THE MUSIC CURRICULUM

PEAS

Activity Type: Movement, Singing

Tonality: Lydian

Resting Tone:

Fa

 Disc One Track 8

 Piano Bk Page 106

Meter: Usual Triple

Macrobeats:

Du Du

Microbeats:

Du Da Di Du Da Di

Keyality: G

Range: d–d′

Materials Needed: Enough space for everyone to move comfortably.

Purpose:
1. To help students learn to audiate the resting tone and a melody in Lydian tonality.
2. To help students increase their body awareness in self and shared space.
3. To give students an opportunity to chant rhythm patterns in Usual Triple meter.

TEACHING PLAN

Everyone should be standing in stationary self space.

Introduce the Song

Tell students that you will sing and move using continuous flow with pulsations. Invite them to imitate your movement and to audiate the song silently. Model continuous, fluid movement with pulsations to macrobeats as you sing the song, and observe students who are coordinating themselves with your movement.

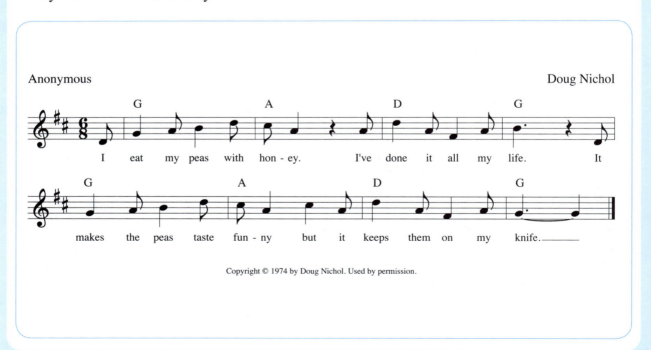

Anonymous — Doug Nichol

I eat my peas with hon-ey. I've done it all my life. It makes the peas taste fun-ny but it keeps them on my knife.

Copyright © 1974 by Doug Nichol. Used by permission.

Establish Tonality and Sing the Resting Tone

Singing the sequence of tones notated below, establish tonality using neutral syllables. Gesture for students to audiate. Then sing the resting tone using BUM. Gesture for the students to breathe and sing the resting tone with you.

Invite the students to audiate the resting tone as they move again, this time freezing if you stop singing the melody. Remind them to look at you when they freeze and that you will gesture for them to breathe and sing the resting tone while they are frozen.

Review Self and Shared Space

Review the definitions of self space and shared space. Ask the students, "Which is the label for space in which you are touching someone or something?" (Answer: shared.) Ask students which lyrics in the song suggest shared space. (Answer: honey sticking to the knife and peas.)

Invite the students to play a game. Assign students partners. Tell the students that, as before, when they hear you sing, they are to audiate silently and move using continuous flow with pulsations. When you stop singing, they are to freeze in shared space. Each time, before you sing the beginning of the song, announce a part of the body for partners to share when you stop singing. As students become coordinated with their movement and the game, invite several students to share space together when they freeze. Eventually, invite the students to use locomotor movements through space during singing; have them use stationary, shared space with the suggested parts of the body with those around them each time they freeze. When the students accomplish this, they can breathe just before sharing space and sing the resting tone when they touch. This does not need to occur in unison, as long as students sing BUM briefly and then freeze in silence.

Usual Triple Patterns

Play the game again, but when the song finishes, the students should freeze in self space and echo four-macrobeat Usual Triple meter patterns. Then they should resume their locomotor movements whenever you sing the song again.

JUMP RIGHT IN: THE MUSIC CURRICULUM

THE ELEPHANT

Activity Type: Chanting

Meter: Usual Triple

Macrobeats:

Microbeats:

Materials Needed: Two puppets with mouths that open.

Purpose:
1. To identify same and different rhythm patterns.
2. To chant patterns in Usual Triple meter.

TEACHING PLAN
Everyone should be seated in self space.

 Disc One Track 9   Piano Bk Page 41

Chanting
Teach the poem using the Rote Song Teaching Procedure found in the Reference Manual.

Focus on Patterns
Between repetitions of the poem, chant several four-macrobeat rhythm patterns in Usual Triple meter using the neutral syllable BAH and gesture for students to imitate your patterns.

Focus on "Same" and "Not the Same"
Tell students that you are going to chant two patterns and you want them to show you using their hands if the patterns are the same or not the same. Explain and demonstrate how they should do this using two closed hands for "the same" and one open and one closed hand for "not the same."

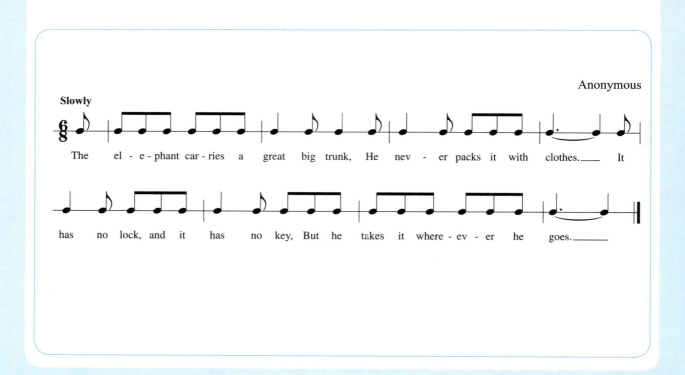

16

Use the Puppets

Use one puppet to chant a four-macrobeat rhythm pattern and the other to chant the same pattern. Ask students if those patterns were the same or not the same. Have them show you with their hands. Repeat with two patterns that are different.

Then, perform the chant. Give the students "same" and "not same" four-macrobeat rhythm patterns between repetitions of the chant.

FOR THE MUSIC TEACHER

Tell one student that the puppet is going to chant a pattern and that he or she can choose to chant the same pattern or not the same pattern. Use one of the puppets to chant a pattern. Have the student chant in response. Ask the class to show you with their hands whether those patterns were the same or not the same.

CONNECTION TO LITERATURE

Read *The Biggest Nose* by Kathy Caple (Houghton Mifflin 1988). Discuss how the elephant has the biggest nose and tries to hide her flaw by tying it in a knot. Talk with students about how we all have attributes that make us uncomfortable about ourselves but that these are part of what makes each of us unique.

FOR THE MUSIC TEACHER

When introducing the concepts of same and different, some children respond with more accuracy to the term "not same" rather than "different." As you teach same/different lessons throughout this book, use both terms ("not same" and "different") to facilitate student learning.

JUMP RIGHT IN: THE MUSIC CURRICULUM

DOWN IN THE VILLAGE OF VALTOU

Activity Type: Movement

Tonality: Harmonic Minor

Resting Tone:

La

Meter: Usual Triple

Macrobeats:

Microbeats:

Keyality: A

 Disc One Track 10

 Piano Bk Page 38

Range: e–e'

Materials Needed: Recording. Enough space for everyone to move comfortably.

Purpose:
1. To give students experience with continuous, fluid movement.
2. To give students an opportunity to explore high, middle, and low levels of space.
3. To give students an opportunity to explore open and closed shapes.
4. To help students develop body awareness.

TEACHING PLAN
Everyone should be seated in self space.

TEACHER'S EDITION • KINDERGARTEN

Move with Flow

Play the recording of "Down in the Village of Valtou." As the students listen, model continuous, fluid movement with your arms. Play the recording again, and invite the students to move with continuous, fluid movement. Ask the students what other parts of the body they could move with continuous flow. Model continuous, fluid movement using head, shoulders, arms, torso, hips, legs, and feet.

Extend the Activity

To extend the activity, invite the students to freeze like a statue. Model different shapes the students can make with their bodies (open or closed, using different levels of space). Tell them that, when the song is sung, they are to move their bodies using continuous, fluid movement, but if the song stops they are to freeze like statues. Sing the song, and allow the students to move and freeze. Choose students who are using open and closed shapes in different levels of space, and discuss their shapes with the rest of the class. Sing the song again, and allow the students to explore how they move in space.

COORDINATION WITH INSTRUMENTAL MUSIC

Play the solo euphonium recording of "Down in the Village of Valtou" from *Jump Right In: The Instrumental Series* (J199CD, track 13). Show the students a picture of the euphonium using Instrument Card 22, and ask if anyone can identify the instrument in the picture and recording. If one of the students is successful, ask the student how he or she knew the answer. Point out that the euphonium looks similar to a tuba, but that it is smaller.

Give each student a scarf. Play the recording, and tell students that it is their job to keep their scarves slowly moving through space for the entire time that the song is playing. Allow them to move throughout the room as long as they stay in self space. This means they cannot touch anything or anyone else. Play the recording, and watch the students move to see who is able to demonstrate continuous flow with the scarf.

JUMP RIGHT IN: THE MUSIC CURRICULUM

SLEEP, MY DARLING (*SOFDA UNGA ASTIN MIN*)

Activity Type: Singing, Solo Singing, Movement

Tonality: Harmonic Minor

Resting Tone:

Meter: Usual Duple

Macrobeats:

Microbeats:

Keyality: G

Range: d–c'

Disc One
Track 11

Piano Bk
Page 124

Materials Needed: Recording. Bean bags. Enough space for everyone to move comfortably.

Purpose:
1. To help students audiate and sing the resting tone in Harmonic Minor tonality.
2. To give students an opportunity to move with continuous, fluid movement.
3. To help students develop body awareness.

TEACHING PLAN

Everyone should be seated in self space.

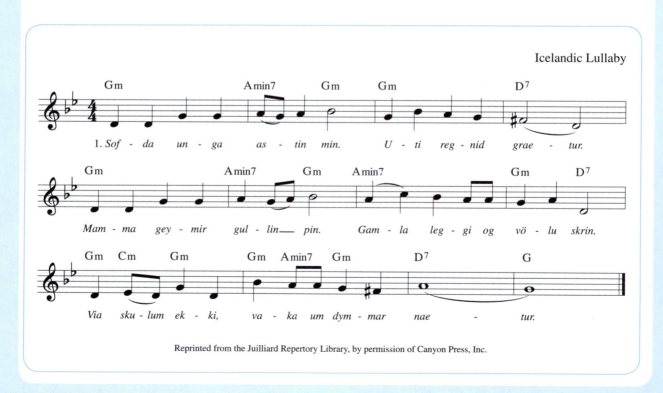

Reprinted from the Juilliard Repertory Library, by permission of Canyon Press, Inc.

Identify Resting Tone

Ask the students listen to the song and try to audiate the resting tone. Sing the song using a neutral syllable, or play the recording. When the song is complete, take an audiation breath and sing the resting tone for the students. Breathe and gesture for the students to echo you. Tell them that you are going to pause during the song and gesture for them to sing the resting tone, so they should continue to audiate it as you sing. Also tell them that sometimes you will gesture for the whole class to sing, using both hands, and sometimes you will gesture for one person to sing, using one hand. Sing the song, pausing at phrase points. During the pause, breathe and gesture for individuals or the class to sing the resting tone.

Use the Bean Bags

Give each student a bean bag. Balance your bean bag on the back of your hand, and gesture for the students to do the same. Sing the song, moving the bean bag in a continuous, fluid way while you sing. At the end of the song, sing the dominant, and then drop the bean bag on the floor. Sing the resting tone when the bean bag lands on the ground. Ask the students for another part of the body upon which they can balance their bean bags. Sing the song again as the students balance their bean bags and move the new body part with flow. At the end, sing the dominant pitch, and then drop the bean bag and sing the resting tone. Repeat this several more times, each time using a different part of the body as suggested by the students.

TEACHING TIP

You can individualize instruction when asking students to sing the resting tone at phrase points. Some places in the song make audiating and singing the resting tone difficult. For example, if you pause after two measures, the melody is still within the tonic function, making the resting tone easier to audiate. If you pause after four measures, the melody is underpinned with dominant harmonies, which makes the resting tone more difficult to audiate and sing. Ask the students who are strongest tonally to sing the resting tone in the most difficult places, and ask those who are less advanced tonally to sing the resting tone when it is easier to audiate.

JUMP RIGHT IN: THE MUSIC CURRICULUM

BLOW THE BALLOON

Activity Type: Movement

Tonality: Major

Resting Tone:

Meter: Usual Duple

Macrobeats:

Microbeats:

Keyality: E-flat

Range: e-flat–g

Disc One
Track 12

Piano Bk
Page 22

Materials Needed: Recording. Enough space for everyone to move comfortably.

Purpose:
1. To give students an opportunity to move in a continuous, fluid style.
2. To give students an opportunity to move in open and closed shapes.
3. To model an audiation breath for students.
4. To help students develop an awareness of time.

TEACHING PLAN
Everyone should be seated in self space.

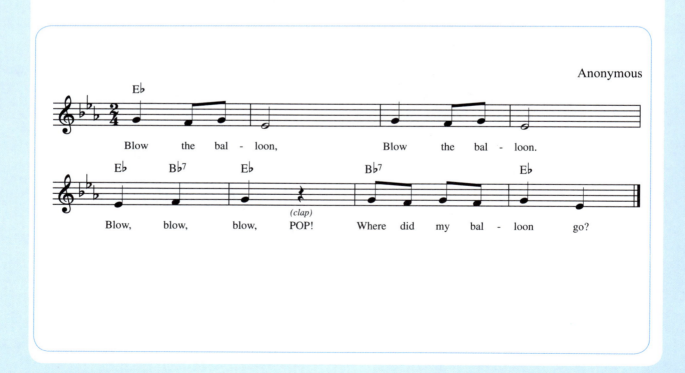

22

Move

Play the recording of "Blow the Balloon." As the students listen, pretend your hands are a balloon, and blow up the balloon. This demonstrates moving from a closed to an open shape using continuous, fluid movement. (An open shape will take up a lot of space, without parts of the body touching. A closed space will take up only a little space, with parts of the body touching.) At the end of the song, let your balloon pop by demonstrating free flow and indirect space. Play the recording again, and invite the students to blow up their own balloons. Model taking a breath before each phrase.

Label Movement Qualities

Extend the activity by transferring the movement to the entire body. Ask the students to describe what a closed shape looks like versus an open shape. Ask the students the difference between the shape of a deflated balloon and an inflated balloon. Invite the students to show you closed and open shapes. Ask them to use self space and make a closed shape. Sing the song, and watch students "inflate" into their open shapes. Watch their movement as they pop, and ask them to describe that movement. Is it quick or slow? Did they fall directly to the ground or indirectly through the space? Sing the song again so that students may adjust their movements.

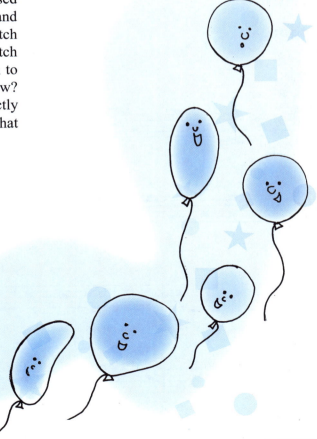

FIVE LITTLE PUMPKINS

Activity Type: Movement, Singing

Tonality: Major

Resting Tone:

Meter: Usual Duple

Macrobeats:

Microbeats:

Keyality: G

Range: d–e'

Disc One
Track 13

Piano Bk
Page 52

Materials Needed: Enough space for everyone to move comfortably.

Purpose:
1. To help students learn to listen and move.
2. To give students experience following a conductor.
3. To reinforce the skills needed to breathe and sing.

TEACHING PLAN ONE

Everyone should be seated in self space.

Teacher's Edition • KINDERGARTEN

Listen and Move

Tell the students to copy your movements as you sing a song for them. Tell the students that they will be listeners and movers. Remind them that listening is the most important job for musicians. Sing the song, and perform actions for the words as follows.

"Five little pumpkins sitting on a gate" = five fingers of one hand sit on opposite forearm

"Oh my it's getting late" = worried face with hands on cheeks

"There are witches in the air" = point to imaginary witches on broomsticks

"But we don't care" = defiantly cross arms on chest

"Let's run and run and run" = move arms as if running

"I'm ready for some fun" = proudly tap thumb on chest

"Oooo" = make sweeping motion with spine, shoulders, and arms

"Out" = tap both hands on floor

"Five little pumpkins rolled out of sight" = roll arms quickly and tuck body into a ball

Sing the Resting Tone

Say, "Listen to this pitch." Sing the resting tone using the neutral syllable BUM. Sing on the resting tone, "Watch my hands, they will tell you when to breathe. Take a breath and sing that pitch." Breathe and gesture for the students to sing the resting tone. Sing, "Now, think that pitch." Give the students a moment to think the pitch. Say, "Watch my hands. Take a breath and sing the pitch you were thinking." Again, give a clear breath gesture as you breathe and the students sing the resting tone. Say, "Your job is to remember that pitch."

Sing on the resting tone, "I am going to sing the song again. Sometimes I will pause. Then I will show you when to breathe and sing the pitch you were thinking." Perform the song, and pause every two or four measures to give the breath gesture so the students sing the resting tone. Finish by singing the song with the movements.

25

FIVE LITTLE PUMPKINS (continued)

TEACHING PLAN TWO

Activity Type: Movement, Singing
Everyone should be seated in self space.

Materials Needed: Enough space for everyone to move comfortably.

Purpose: To give students an opportunity to discriminate if tonal patterns are same or different.

Move and Sing
Students should be familiar with the song and the resting tone activities from Teaching Plan One. Have the students copy your movements from that plan as you sing the song.

Imitate and Identify Same and Different Tonal Patterns
Sing the following tonal pattern on BUM. Give the students a breath gesture, and have them repeat the pattern.

Tell the students that the pattern is the first tonal pattern of the song. Have them listen for that pattern as you sing the first measure of the song again using BUM.

Sing the following tonal pattern using BUM. Give the students a breath gesture, and have them repeat the pattern.

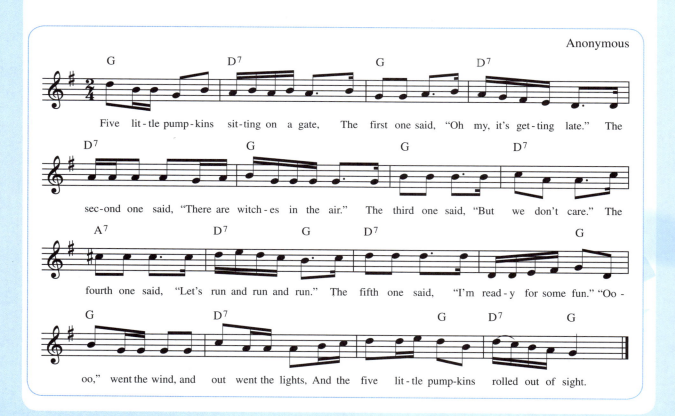

Tell the students that the pattern above is also from the song. Have them listen for that pattern as you sing measures 12 and 13 of the song on BUM.

Tell the students to listen as you sing each pattern again. Tell the students the two patterns are different. Have the students hold up two hands that are different (one open and one closed) and repeat the word "different."

Sing the first pattern, and then sing it again. Tell the students that those patterns are the same. Have the students hold up two hands that are the same (both open or both closed), and repeat the word "same."

Play the Game
Play a same and different game using the two patterns. Have the students show you with their hands whether the two patterns you perform are the same or different.

JUMP RIGHT IN: THE MUSIC CURRICULUM

FLOPPY SCARECROW

Activity Type: Movement

Meter: Usual Duple

Macrobeats:

Microbeats:

Materials Needed: Recording. Enough space for everyone to move freely.

Purpose:
1. To give students experience with pulsating flow in Usual Duple meter.
2. To allow students to explore open and closed shapes.

 Disc One Track 14

 Piano Bk Page 55

TEACHING PLAN

Everyone should be standing in self space. Play the recording of "Floppy Scarecrow." Ask the students what scarecrows do and what they look like. Invite them to make their own scarecrow statues in self-space. Perform the chant again, and model pulsating flow throughout. Invite the students to move with pulsating flow as well. At the end of the chant, have them freeze into a new scarecrow statue. Repeat this process several times.

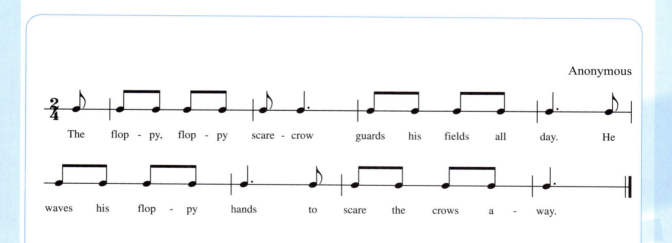

FOR THE MUSIC TEACHER
Pulsated flow is one of the foundations of rhythm learning. With pulsated flow, students learn not only to feel the beats but also to experience the spaces between the beats. This is essential for developing a sense of consistent tempo.

JUMP RIGHT IN: THE MUSIC CURRICULUM

THE GHOST OF JOHN

Activity Type: Singing, Movement

Tonality: Aeolian

Resting Tone:

Meter: Usual Duple

Macrobeats:

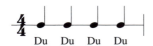

Microbeats:

Keyality: E

Range: B–e'

 Disc One Track 15

 Piano Bk Page 58

Materials Needed: Recording. Enough space for everyone to move comfortably.

Purpose:
1. To help students learn to coordinate movement and singing.
2. To give students experience with same and different without labels.

TEACHING PLAN

Everyone should be seated in self space.

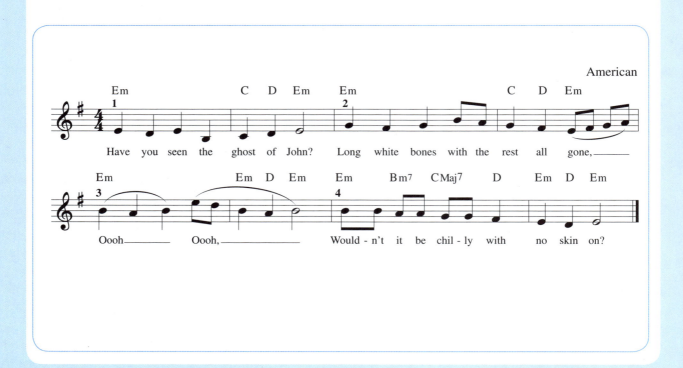

30

Introduce the Song

Invite the students to listen and audiate as you sing the song. Sing the melody as you move through the room, using continuous flow to pantomime the words of the song. Invite the students to imitate your movements in seated self space. Tell them that it will be their turn to sing later and that they should be sure to audiate so they will be ready to sing. Sing the song, and perform the movement several times.

Invite Students to Sing and Move

On a different day, after students have heard the melody several times by reviewing the introduction to the song above, invite them to sing and move. Do not sing with them. They may need to listen to you sing again and move to the song several more times before they are able to sing it without you.

Establish Tonality: Sing Resting Tone and Patterns

Establish tonality by singing the sequence of tones notated below.

Then sing the resting tone using BUM, and invite the students to sing the resting tone with you by giving them a breath gesture as a cue for when to sing. Then invite them to be your echo. Sing the patterns notated below on this page. After you sing each pattern, give the students a breath gesture as a cue to sing.

Compare Melodies

Tell students that you are going to sing "The Ghost of John" as they know it. Establish tonality, and then sing it for them as notated. Then ask them to audiate. Tell them you will sing it again. They are to decide whether it sounds the same or different. Tell them that, at the end, you will invite them to describe what they heard.

Sing the song in Major tonality. After you finish singing, the students might answer that it sounds the same as before because they were listening to the same words. Also, they might have answered "the same" because they were audiating macrobeats, microbeats, and rhythm patterns. Finally, they might answer that it is different because they audiate the difference in the tonal patterns and tonality. The activity is designed for comparison purposes. It is acceptable if students cannot describe why they answered in a particular way or if they guess. Make a note of their responses. Close this activity by singing the song in Aeolian tonality.

JUMP RIGHT IN: THE MUSIC CURRICULUM

AMERICA THE BEAUTIFUL

Activity Type: Movement, Singing

Tonality: Major

Resting Tone:

Do

Meter: Usual Duple

Macrobeats:

Du Du

Microbeats:

Du De Du De

Keyality: C

Range: d–e'

Disc One Track 16   Piano Bk Page 6

Materials Needed:
Parachute. Recording. Enough space for everyone to move comfortably.

Purpose:
1. To give students an opportunity to move with continuous, fluid movement.
2. To guide students to audiate phrases.
3. To familiarize students with an American patriotic song.

TEACHING PLAN
Everyone should be seated in self space.

Move
Play the recording of "America the Beautiful." As students listen, model continuous, fluid movement in the arms, arching through each phrase. Play the song again, and invite the students to move as you moved.

Katharine Lee Bates / Samuel A. Ward

O beau-ti-ful, for spa-cious skies, For am-ber waves of grain, For pur-ple moun-tain maj-es-ties A-bove the fruit-ed plain! A-mer-i-ca! A-mer-i-ca! God shed His grace on thee, And crown thy good with broth-er-hood, From sea to shin-ing sea!

TEACHER'S EDITION • KINDERGARTEN

Use the Parachute

You may extend the activity using a parachute. Invite students to gather around the edge of the parachute. Play the recording again. Move the parachute up and down to each phrase of the song. At the end of the song, lift the parachute high into the air, and sing the dominant pitch of the song. Bring the parachute down to the ground. When the parachute reaches the ground, sing the resting tone. Repeat the movement, and invite students to sing the dominant and resting tone pitches. Repeat the entire activity.

COORDINATION WITH INSTRUMENTAL MUSIC

Play the cello recording of "America the Beautiful" from *Jump Right In: The Instrumental Series* (J201CD, track 1). Ask the students if they can identify the instrument on the recording. Show them a picture of the cello using Instrument Card 3. Ask them if any of them play cello or know someone who does. Listen to their answers. If one of the students plays the cello, ask him or her to bring the instrument in to demonstrate it during the next class period. Repeat the Teaching Plan, this time with the cello performing rather than the vocal recording of the song.

JUMP RIGHT IN: THE MUSIC CURRICULUM

OPEN–CLOSE

Activity Type: Movement, Singing, Chanting

 Disc One Track 17

 Piano Bk Page 102

Tonality: Major

Resting Tone:

Meter: Usual Duple

Macrobeats:

Microbeats:

Keyality: G

Range: d–d'

Materials Needed: Enough space for everyone to move comfortably.

Purpose:
1. To give students an opportunity to perform traditional actions to the melody.
2. To give students experience chanting rhythm patterns in Usual Duple meter.

TEACHING PLAN

Everyone should be seated in self space.

Perform the Movements

Ask the students to audiate the song silently and imitate your movements as you sing. Sing the melody using text, and perform the actions as described in the song.

Hold up both hands in front of you with palms facing your students before you begin. The following actions should be performed to macrobeats:

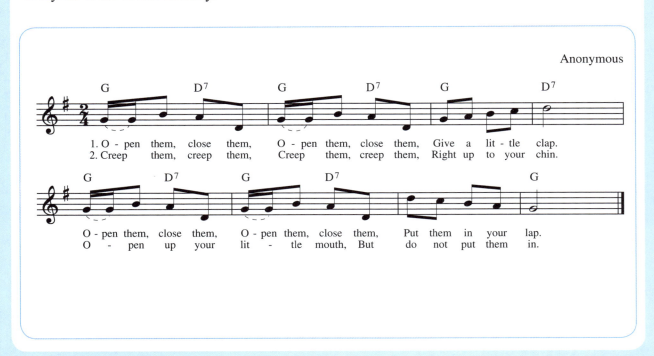

34

- "Open them"–spread fingers out
- "Close them"–close fingers
- "Give a"–spread fingers out
- "Little"–close fingers
- "Clap"–spread fingers out

(On the second beat of the held note, clap your hands.)

Repeat the actions above for "Open them, close them. Open them, close them, put them in your lap." On the second beat of the held note "lap," place your hands in your lap.

For "Creep them, creep them. Creep them, creep them, right up to your chin," slowly walk your fingers up from your lap to your chin to microbeats.

Perform "Open up your little mouth, but do not put them in" by swaying from side to side to microbeats as you leave your hands on your chin.

On the second macrobeat of the word "chin," put your hands quickly behind your back, and open your mouth as though you have been surprised.

Return to this song and activity on different days, and invite children to sing with you after they have had an opportunity to hear the song several times and perform the movements.

Audiate and Move to the Song
After the students are able to sing and move to this song, ask them to silently audiate the melody and words in tempo while performing the actions.

Establish Meter
On a different day, after the students have had a chance to sing and move to this song, introduce rhythm patterns in Usual Duple meter. Gesture for the students to audiate as you establish meter by chanting the following pattern using BAH.

Bah Bah Bah   Bah Bah Bah

Chant four-macrobeat patterns in Usual Duple meter. Invite the students to echo you by giving them a breath gesture. To do this, indicate a breath on the fourth macrobeat of each pattern you chant for them. Indicate for them to chant on the first macrobeat following your pattern.

GRACEFUL SIMO (SIMO LIGERI)

Activity Type: Movement

Tonality: Harmonic Minor

Resting Tone:

La

Meter: Usual Duple

Macrobeats:

Du   Du

Microbeats:

Du De Du De

Disc One
Track 18

Piano Bk
Page 60

Keyality: A

Range: c–e'

Materials Needed: Two pom-poms for each student. Enough space for everyone to move comfortably.

Purpose:
1. To give students experience with continuous, fluid movement.
2. To give students experience with Harmonic Minor tonality.

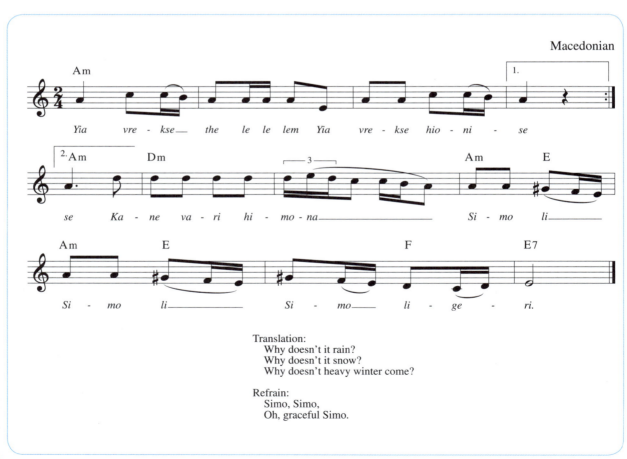

Macedonian

Yia vre - kse— the le le lem Yia vre - kse hio - ni - se
se Ka - ne va - ri hi - mo - na— Si - mo li—
Si - mo li— Si - mo— li - ge - ri.

Translation:
  Why doesn't it rain?
  Why doesn't it snow?
  Why doesn't heavy winter come?

Refrain:
  Simo, Simo,
  Oh, graceful Simo.

36

TEACHER'S EDITION • KINDERGARTEN

TEACHING PLAN
Everyone should be seated in self space.

Model and Describe Movement
Ask the students to watch you move and to be prepared to describe your movement. With a pom-pom in each hand, sing the song or play the recording and move with flow, pulsating each macrobeat. At the end of the song, sustain the last note and shake your pom-poms as vigorously as you can.

In your movement, be certain to use all of the space that you can reach, including the space behind you, above your head, and low to the ground. Ask the students to describe your movement, guiding the discussion so that they notice how you flowed and that you pulsated on macrobeats, using as much space as possible without moving your feet. They should also notice that you did something different at the end of the song. You may need to model the movements several times before the students notice and identify all of the movement characteristics.

Move
Give each student two pom-poms. Ask everyone to stand in self space. Remind them that this means that they will not be touching anyone else. Tell them that they should move exactly as you did, pretending that their pom-poms are paint brushes and that they are painting polka dots around their self space. Ask a student what color the polka dots should be this time. Sing the song while they move as you did in your modeling. As they are shaking their pom-poms at the end of the song on the sustained pitch, sing the following on that pitch: "You are shaking the blue (or other color) paint off your paint brushes. What color should be put on now?"

Take student suggestions for a new paint color. Ask the students to sing rather than speak the name of the paint color. Everyone should continue shaking the paint brushes until a new color has been decided upon and you begin singing the song again. Once you begin singing the song with the students moving, you should, if possible, only sing, not speak, throughout the entire activity. Repeat the activity several times, imagining a new paint color for each repetition of the song.

TEACHING TIP
Singing instructions rather than speaking them has several benefits. First, singing keeps an activity more in the musical domain. As soon as you begin talking, the students attend to language rather than music. When you are singing the instructions, at least at some level, they attend to both music and language. Second, singing instructions on the tonic or dominant helps reinforce the most important pitches in most tonalities. Therefore, it supports the development of students' tonal audiation skills.

Finally, singing the instructions is better for your vocal health. Switching back and forth between singing and speaking makes you more vocally tired than consistently singing in a light, correctly produced singing voice. In this context, sing instructions on tonic or sometimes dominant as much as possible, rather than speaking them.

FULL MOONLIGHT DANCE

Activity Type: Movement

Tonality: Aeolian

Resting Tone:

La

Meter: Unusual Paired

Macrobeats:

Microbeats:

Keyality: G

Range: d–d'

Disc One
Track 19

Piano Bk
Page 56

Materials Needed: Recording. Enough space for everyone to move comfortably.

Purpose:
1. To help students increase body awareness.
2. To help students learn to move parts of the body in duet.
3. To give students an opportunity to move parts of the body in curvy pathways and straight pathways.

TEACHING PLAN

Everyone should be seated in self space with crossed legs.

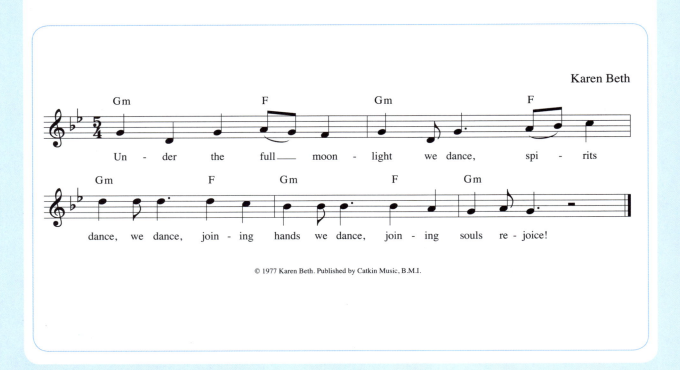

© 1977 Karen Beth. Published by Catkin Music, B.M.I.

Body Part Isolations and Pathways

Tell the students to pretend to write with a marker on both of their elbows. Ask them to move their elbows (the markers) in curvy pathways when they hear the recording. They should be drawing as many pretend curvy lines as possible. Begin singing the song or playing the recording, and check to make sure that the students are moving their elbows in curvy pathways.

Repeat the activity, but ask the students to draw very straight lines with their elbows. Check to make sure the students are drawing straight pretend lines, and offer reminders if necessary.

Repeat the activity using the following body parts: shoulders, hips, ankles, toes, knees, eyebrows, fingers, and wrists.

Discuss how it feels to move body parts by themselves in curvy pathways and straight pathways. Your students will discover that it is easier to move some body parts in curvy pathways than it is to move others. That is the beginning of body awareness.

Using Movement Leaders

Next, allow individual students to be movement leaders. Ask a student to select a pair of matching parts of the body and the types of pathways he or she would like the class to demonstrate. All other students will follow the leader's body parts and pathways. Sing the song or play the recording, and allow the student to lead the movement.

Repeat the activity with several different leaders. Be sure to have the students select a variety of parts of the body.

Body Part Duets

On another day, repeat the activity using parts of the body that do not match. The students will experience combinations such as shoulder/hip, elbow/knee, and wrist/ankle. The body parts could follow the same type of pathway (both straight or both curvy), or each of the body parts could follow a different pathway type (one curvy and one straight).

JUMP RIGHT IN: THE MUSIC CURRICULUM

THE SURE HOPE

Activity Type: Movement

Tonality: Harmonic Minor

Resting Tone:

Meter: Usual Triple

Macrobeats:

Microbeats:

Keyality: E

Range: e–e'

 Disc One Track 20

 Piano Bk Page 132

Materials Needed: One rhythm stick per person. Enough space for everyone to move comfortably.

Purpose:
1. To give students experience with continuous, fluid movement.
2. To give students experience with bound movements.

TEACHING PLAN
Everyone should be seated in self space.

Listen and Move
Sing the song using a neutral syllable as you continuously rock from side to side. Ask the students to imitate your movements.

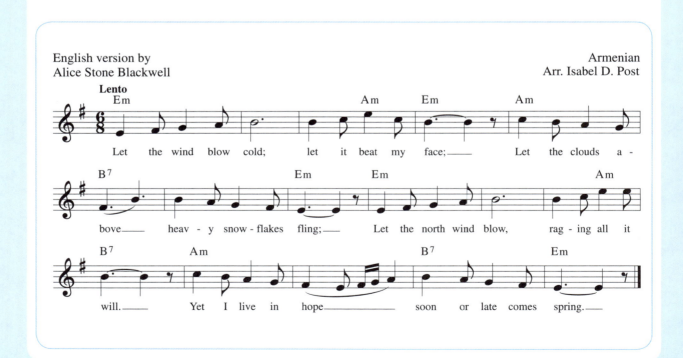

English version by Alice Stone Blackwell

Armenian
Arr. Isabel D. Post

Let the wind blow cold; let it beat my face;___ Let the clouds a-bove___ heav-y snow-flakes fling;___ Let the north wind blow, rag-ing all it will.___ Yet I live in hope___ soon or late comes spring.___

TEACHER'S EDITION • KINDERGARTEN

Use the Rhythm Stick
Give each student one rhythm stick. Tell him or her to pretend to stir a big pot of soup using the rhythm stick as a stirring spoon and to be careful not to splash or spill the broth.

Sing the song, and stir the soup. With each repetition of the song, have the student choose an ingredient (carrots, celery, black beans, etc.) to add to their soup. Chop or slice each ingredient if it is something that would normally be chopped or sliced, and add it to the soup. Remind the students that, each time an ingredient is added, the soup thickens and is harder to stir. You should see this reflected in their movements as they stir.

The last time you sing the song, spoon out some of the ingredients in a bowl so the soup is easier to stir. Model continuous, fluid movement again. Taste the soup and sing, "Mmmmm, that's good" on the resting tone.

TEACHING TIP
Sing the directions on the resting tone. For example, "Emily, what do you want to add to our soup?" should be sung on the resting tone. This subtly reinforces the tonal context of the song.

CONNECTION TO LITERATURE
Read *Stone Soup* to the students, and discuss the different ingredients that can be added to soup. There are several excellent versions of this story:
Stone Soup by Ann McGovern, illustrated by Winslow Pinney Pels (Scholastic 1986).
Stone Soup: An Old Tale by Marcia Brown (1st Aladdin Books 1986).
Stone Soup by John J. Muth (Scholastic 2003).

41

GO TO SLEEP

Activity Type: Singing, Audiation, Movement

Tonality: Harmonic Minor

Resting Tone:

La

Meter: Usual Duple

Macrobeats:

Microbeats:

Keyality: E

Range: e–b

 Disc One Track 21

 Piano Bk Page 59

Materials Needed: Bean bag. Enough space for everyone to move freely.

Purpose:
1. To help students audiate resting tone in Harmonic Minor tonality.
2. To give students an opportunity to perform the resting tone.
3. To give students the opportunity to move in a continuous, fluid style.
4. To help students audiate same and different tonal patterns.

TEACHING PLAN
Everyone should be seated in self space.

Identify Resting Tone
Ask the students to listen to the song as you sing it. Sing the song while balancing a bean bag on your hand and moving with flow. At the end of

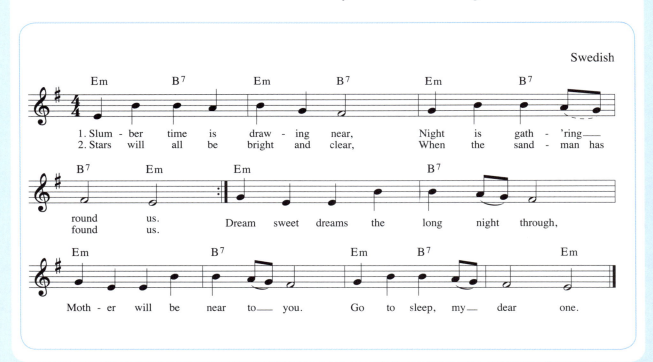

JUMP RIGHT IN: THE MUSIC CURRICULUM

the song, let the bean bag fall from your hand, and sing the resting tone when it hits the floor.

Tell the students that you just performed the resting tone, and ask them to sing it. Then tell them that you are going to sing the song again and that they should sing the resting tone whenever the bean bag falls from your hand and lands on the floor. Sing the song, occasionally allowing the bean bag to fall at phrase endings.

Same and Different
Ask the students to listen to two patterns in Minor tonality. Sing one tonic pattern and one dominant pattern in Harmonic Minor in the keyality of the song. Tell the students that the two patterns do not sound the same; they sound different. Put your hands in front of you with one hand in a fist and the other hand open. Tell the students that your two hands look different from one another. Ask the students to show you two hands that look different. Then ask them to make their two hands look the same. (Some students will choose to make both of their hands into fists, and others will choose to open both hands. Both responses are appropriate.)

Sing pairs of tonal patterns, and ask the students to show you with their hands whether the two patterns in the pair are the same or different. Then sing the song, and perform two tonal patterns after each song repetition. Ask the students to show you "same or different hands" to represent whether the two patterns are the same or different.

Assessment
Ask the students to tell you about the text of the song. They should say that it is about sleeping at night. Ask the students to find an empty spot on the floor and lie on their backs as if they were going to go to sleep in their beds. Tell them that you want them to move their arms in a continuous, fluid style as you sing the song. Demonstrate what this would look like, and then sing the song as they move. Tell the students that you are going to sing two tonal patterns at the end of the song. Then, while still lying down, they should show you with their hands whether the two patterns are the same or are different.

Perform the song while they move their arms with flow. Then sing two tonal patterns, and observe whether their hands match the patterns. After this, tell them whether the patterns were the same or different. Then ask them to close their eyes, and repeat this process several times with their eyes closed. This allows you to make notes concerning which students can successfully identify same and different tonal patterns in Harmonic Minor.

> **TEACHING TIP**
> This Teaching Plan should be taught over several class periods. Perhaps the first class period could include the bean bag activity with the singing of resting tone, the second class period could include the introduction of "same and different hands" to represent tonal patterns being the same and different, and the third class period could include the students lying on their backs and doing the activity with their eyes closed.

43

JUMP RIGHT IN: THE MUSIC CURRICULUM

SOMETIMES I FEEL LIKE A MOTHERLESS CHILD

Activity Type: Movement, Singing

Tonality: Harmonic Minor

Resting Tone:

La

Meter: Usual Duple

Macrobeats:

Microbeats:

Keyality: D

Range: A–a

 Disc One Track 22

 Piano Bk Page 126

Materials Needed: One bean bag per person. Enough space for everyone to move comfortably.

Purpose:
1. To give students experience with continuous, fluid movement to music.
2. To sing resting tone in Harmonic Minor tonality.

TEACHING PLAN

Everyone should be seated in self space in a circle.

Listen and Move

Give bean bags to the students, and ask them to copy your movements. Sing the song on a neutral syllable, and balance the bean bag on the back of your hand. At the conclusion of the song, drop the bean bag on the floor and sing the resting tone.

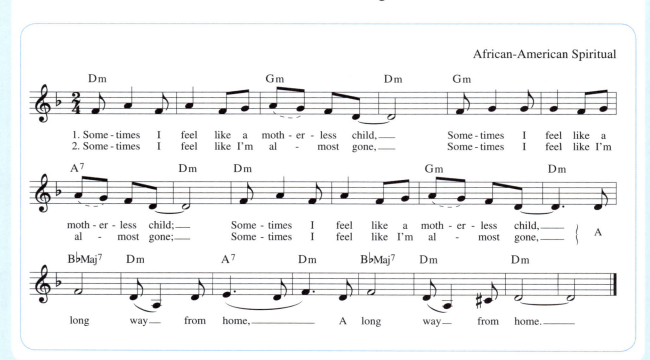

Place the bean bag on other body parts (foot, elbow, and knee), and take it for a continuous, fluid movement ride. At the conclusion of the song, drop the bean bag on the floor, and sing the resting tone.

CONNECTION TO SCIENCE

Give the students different objects (straws or books) and ask them to balance them on various parts of their bodies. For example, have students balance the straw on their index fingers. Lead them to discover that the straw must be equally distributed to balance properly. Discuss why some objects are difficult to balance and others are easy.

COORDINATION WITH INSTRUMENTAL MUSIC

Play the alto saxophone recording of "Sometimes I Feel Like a Motherless Child" from *Jump Right In: The Instrumental Series* (J299CD, track 4). Ask the students whether, without seeing the picture, they can identify the instrument on the recording. If a student can identify the instrument, ask how the student knew. If no one can identify the instrument, show the students a picture of the alto saxophone using Instrument Card 16. Tell the students that this instrument makes a sound when you blow into it, so it is called a wind instrument.

Tell the students that you are going play both the alto saxophone recording of the song and the vocal recording of the song. After they listen to both, ask them to tell you how the recordings are the same and how they are different. Play both recordings, and then lead the discussion. Although the discussion may not be very sophisticated at this point, it gives the students an opportunity to learn to talk about music. They may focus on the tempo, volume, instrumentation, and mood of the recordings. Some may even notice the tonal difference between the two recordings.

JUMP RIGHT IN: THE MUSIC CURRICULUM

ONE SUMMER DAY

Activity Type: Movement

Tonality: Harmonic Minor

Resting Tone:

La

Meter: Usual Triple

Macrobeats:

Du   Du

Microbeats:

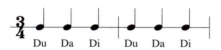
Du Da Di Du Da Di

 Disc One Track 23   Piano Bk Page 100

Keyality: G

Range: f-sharp–e'

Materials Needed: Recording. Enough space for everyone to move freely.

Purpose: To give students experience with continuous, fluid movement with pulsations.

TEACHING PLAN

Everyone should be seated in self space at the beginning of the lesson. Later, all will move into standing self space.

Jacob Gade, from *Botsford Collection of Folk Songs* by Florence Botsford

Copyright © 1929 (renewed) by G. Schirmer, Inc. (ASCAP). International copyright secured. All rights reserved. Used by permission.

46

Listen to the Recording

Play the recording, or sing the song using a neutral syllable. Move your arms and upper body with continuous, fluid movements as you listen. Ask the students to copy your continuous, fluid movements. Play the recording, or sing the song again using a neutral syllable, and move as you did before.

Watch and Describe

Tell the students to watch your movement because you are going to change it. Play the recording again. This time, add pulsations on the microbeats while moving with continuous, fluid movement. Ask students to describe your movements. They should have noticed that the flow continued but that you added pulsations. Guide them to notice that the pulsations were on the microbeats.

Listen and Move

Ask students to copy your continuous, fluid movements with pulsations. Play the recording again, and move as you did before.

Play the recording several times, and alternate between continuous, fluid movement and continuous, fluid movement with pulsations.

CONNECTION TO ART

This activity allows students to connect flow in movement to flow in art. Spray shaving cream on a table. Ask children to draw pictures and create flowing, abstract designs in the cream. Demonstrate what a flowing design looks like and describe its characteristics before the children create their own designs.

DO YOU SEE THAT BIRD THERE?

Activity Type: Movement

Tonality: Multitonal

Resting Tone:

Meter: Multimetric (Usual Duple, Usual Combined, Usual Triple)

Macrobeats:

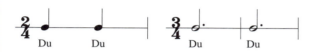

Microbeats:

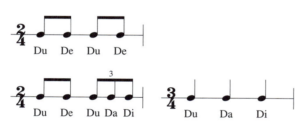

 Disc One Track 24

 Piano Bk Page 36

Keyality: C, D

Range: c–e-flat'

Materials Needed: Recording. Enough space for everyone to move comfortably.

Purpose:
1. To give students experience with continuous, fluid movement.
2. To give students an opportunity to coordinate movement with a partner.

TEACHING PLAN

Everyone should be seated in self space.

Teacher's Edition • Kindergarten

Move Alone

Play the recording of "Do You See That Bird There?" Ask the students to describe how a bird moves through the sky. Model continuous, fluid movement with your arms to mimic how a bird moves. Play the recording again, and invite the students to move with continuous flow. Play the recording again, and invite the students to move freely throughout the room, still modeling continuous, fluid movement with their arms.

Move with a Partner

To extend the activity, demonstrate mirror movement with a partner. Ask a student to be your partner, and mirror his or her continuous, fluid movement. Pair the students together, and ask them to decide who will go first. Sing the song for the students or play the recording and observe the pairs moving in mirror images. Choose a pair to demonstrate their flowing movements for the class. Repeat, allowing the second partner to lead the activity.

49

HATO POPO (LITTLE PIGEONS)

Activity Type: Listening, Movement

Tonality: Major

Resting Tone:

Meter: Usual Duple

Macrobeats:

Microbeats:

Keyality: G

Range: g–f-sharp'

Disc One
Track 25

Piano Bk
Page 63

Materials Needed: Enough space for everyone to move comfortably.

Purpose:
1. To help students learn to listen and move.
2. To give students experience moving continuously with pulsations.
3. To help students audiate and sing the resting tone.

TEACHING PLAN
Everyone should be seated in self space.

Listen and Move
Tell the students that they will be listeners and movers. Remind them that listening is the most important job of a musician.

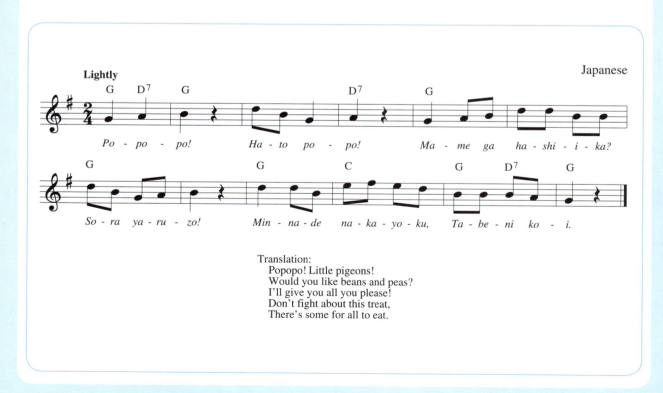

Translation:
Popopo! Little pigeons!
Would you like beans and peas?
I'll give you all you please!
Don't fight about this treat,
There's some for all to eat.

Have the students sit with crossed legs, copying your movements as you sing the song and perform bilateral microbeat pulsations with your hands. Never perform the microbeat pulsations in the same place twice in a row. Keep moving the microbeats all around on the floor, on your legs, and in the air. Use your spine to assist your use of continuous flow.

Sing the song again, this time performing macrobeat pulsations. Have the students copy your bilateral macrobeat pulsations as you sing.

Then sing the song a third time with microbeat pulsations again. Now have the students copy your bilateral microbeat pulsations while they chant TUH to microbeats to help coordinate their tongues with their body movements.

Sing the song, this time pulsing to macrobeats. Have the students copy your bilateral macrobeat pulsations while they chant BAH to macrobeats to aid in the awareness of the differences between microbeats and macrobeats and to facilitate audiation of meter.

Sing the Resting Tone
Sing on the resting tone, "Listen to this pitch." Sing the resting tone using the neutral syllable, BUM. Sing, "Watch my hands, they will tell you when to breathe. When my hands tell you to do so, take a breath and sing the pitch." Breathe and gesture for the students to sing the resting tone. Say, "Now, think that pitch." Give the students a moment to think the pitch. Say, "Watch my hands. Take a breath, and sing the pitch you were thinking." Again, give a clear breath gesture as you breathe, and then have the students sing the pitch. Sing, "Your job is to remember that pitch."

Remember and Audiate the Resting Tone
Sing, "I am going to sing the song again. Sometimes I will pause. Then, I will show you when to breathe and sing the pitch you were thinking." Perform the song, and pause every two or four measures to give the breath gesture for the students to sing the resting tone.

FOR THE MUSIC TEACHER
The use of TUH and BAH as neutral syllables for microbeats and macrobeats will serve as readiness for chanting using rhythm syllables at a later time. Both of these syllables are forward in the mouth, making them easy to perform. Chanting in this way helps the students coordinate their bodies with their audiation.

JUMP RIGHT IN: THE MUSIC CURRICULUM

THE SQUIRREL

Activity Type: Movement, Chanting

Meter: Unusual Paired

Macrobeats:

Microbeats:

Disc One
Track 26

Piano Bk
Page 128

Materials Needed: Enough space for everyone to move comfortably.

Purpose:
1. To give students experience with Unusual Paired meter.
2. To give students an opportunity to explore space by making open and closed shapes.

TEACHING PLAN
Everyone should be seated in self space.

Introduce the Chant
If there is space in the room, invite the students to lie down on their backs with their eyes closed and to audiate your chant. Ask them to imagine a forest full of amazing and interesting trees as they audiate.

Perform the chant several times through. When you perform several repetitions without pausing, be certain to begin the next repetition on the macrobeat directly following the last one.

After you have repeated the chant several times, ask the students to open their eyes but remain lying down. Invite a discussion about the words to the chant. Guide them to describe the forest they imagined.

Transcribed by Kyungsil Jung

52

Make Shapes

Tell the students that you will perform the chant again and they will rise slowly to the shape of trees in the forest. They should grow continuously during the chant, freezing at the end. As you chant, observe students' movements. Ask the students to remember the tree shapes they have created.

Model an open shape created by one student's tree. An open shape will take up a lot of space, with parts of the body touching. Ask the students to copy your shape. Say, "This is an open shape." Do not define it at this time. Then invite the students to return to their original tree shapes while you perform the chant.

Model a closed shape created by one of the students' trees. (A closed shape will take up only a little space, with parts of the body touching.) Ask the students to copy your shape. Say, "This is a closed shape." Do not define it at this time. Then invite the students to return to their original tree shapes while you perform the chant again.

Use Continuous Flow to Tell the Squirrel's Story

Invite the students to use continuous flow in standing, stationary self space to illustrate what the squirrel in the story is doing. Invite them to use the space all around them. Ask them to audiate the chant while they flow, pretending to be squirrels. Tell them that when you finish the chant they are to stop moving. Perform the chant, and observe students who are coordinating themselves to the music as they move.

Play a Game

Invite five students to be squirrels. The remaining students will be the forest. Ask the trees in the forest to make a shape that is open or closed. Tell them that the squirrels will use continuous flow in locomotor self space to illustrate the story as before. When the chant is finished, squirrels will stop their movements next to a tree. Then each will label whether his or her tree is making an open shape or a closed shape. (It is possible that the shape will be both open and closed.) After each squirrel labels his or her tree, the students should trade roles. Continue until all students have had a turn being a squirrel or until students lose interest in the activity.

JUMP RIGHT IN: THE MUSIC CURRICULUM

THE ARDELEAN WOMAN

Activity Type: Movement

Tonality: Harmonic Minor

Resting Tone:

Meter: Usual Duple

Macrobeats:

Microbeats:

Keyality: E

Range: d-sharp–e'

 Disc One Track 27

 Piano Bk Page 8

Materials Needed: Hand drum and mallet. Tambourine. Recording. Enough space for everyone to move comfortably.

Purpose: To combine strong and gentle motions with body awareness and continuous flow.

TEACHING PLAN

Everyone should be standing in self space in scattered formation. Model and discuss strong and gentle continuous flow.

54

How Would You Move If You Had Happy Hips?

Invite the students to move using continuous flow in silence. Ask them to tell you which body parts they can move to make sure that their whole bodies are moving with flow (hips, back, shoulders, flexible knees).

Ask them to rest for a moment by closing their eyes and standing still. Then ask them to imagine how they would move if their hips were happy. After a moment to imagine, invite them to open their eyes and show you their happy hips as they move with continuous flow. If necessary, model the desired movement (light and gentle) for them.

How Would You Move If You Had Sad Hips?

Repeat the happy hips sequence, this time asking students to imagine and then move with sad hips. If necessary, model the desired movement (strong and heavy) for them.

Repeat these two types of movements, emphasizing different parts of the body. After giving the students several opportunities to move, assist them in labeling their continuous flow as being strong or gentle.

Choose Your Movement

Ask students to choose one of the two types of movements emphasizing different body parts. Notice students' movements. Pay specific compliments to individuals by labeling the body parts that they are emphasizing while moving with strong or gentle movement.

Move with Music

Tell students you will play a melody for them. While they listen, they may move their whole bodies with continuous flow in stationary self space. Tell them that, if they hear a hand drum as they listen, they should move with strong, continuous flow. If they hear the tambourine, they should move with gentle, continuous flow.

Play the Percussion Instruments

Play the recording of "The Ardelean Woman." To signal that the students should move with strong, continuous flow, play the ostinato notated below during the melody.

To signal that the students should move with gentle, continuous flow, play the ostinato notated below during the melody.

JUMP RIGHT IN: THE MUSIC CURRICULUM

SHAKE, SHAKE, SHAKE

Activity Type: Movement, Chanting

Meter: Usual Duple

Macrobeats:

Microbeats:

 Disc One Track 28

 Piano Bk Page 119

Materials Needed: Enough space for everyone to move comfortably.

Purpose: To help students experience the concepts of fast and slow through movement.

TEACHING PLAN
Everyone should be seated in self space.

Move
Perform the chant, shaking your hands very slowly as you flow with your arms during the first part and suddenly quickly at the end. The text invites the students to join in with your movements. If they do not, ask them to move with you. Perform the chant again, substituting "feet" for "hands" in the chant and in the movement.

Ask students whether they have ideas for what parts of the body they could shake slowly and quickly. Perform the chant multiple times, incorporating each of their suggestions. If they cannot perform the motions without standing, ask the students to stand for the remainder of the activity.

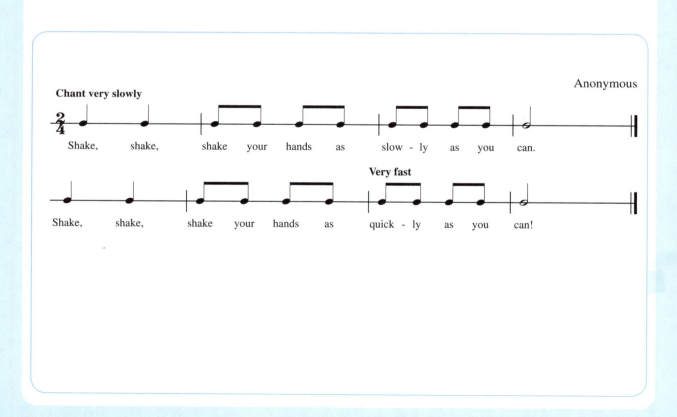

56

Teacher's Edition • KINDERGARTEN

FOR THE MUSIC TEACHER
Students need many experiences with creative movement to be able to perform music stylistically and to develop rhythmicity. For this reason, we have included many movement activities in *Jump Right In: The Music Curriculum* that are designed to help students experience the range of movement possible with their bodies. These movement activities are based on the work of Rudolf Laban. For more information about Laban's work, read his book *The Mastery of Movement*, revised by Lisa Ullmann in 1988 and published by Northcote House Publishing.

Another book with additional ideas for creative movement is *Dance for Young Children: Finding the Magic in Movement* by Sue Stinson (American Alliance for Health, Physical Education, Recreation 1988).

57

JUMP RIGHT IN: THE MUSIC CURRICULUM

THE VOLGA BOAT SONG

Activity Type: Singing, Movement

Tonality: Aeolian

Resting Tone:

Meter: Usual Duple

Macrobeats:

Microbeats:

Keyality: G

Range: g–e-flat'

 Disc One Track 29

 Piano Bk Page 147

Materials Needed: Hand drum. Long, thick rope. Enough space for everyone to move comfortably.

Purpose:
1. To help students experience bound movement.
2. To give students an opportunity to audiate and move to macrobeats in Usual Duple meter.
3. To help the students experience flowing movement with pulsations.

TEACHING PLAN

Everyone should be seated in self space.

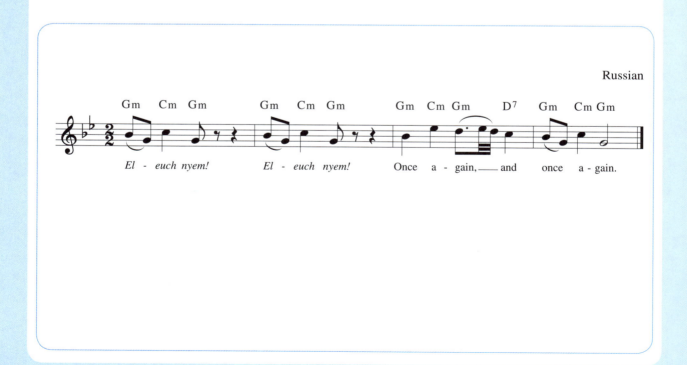

Move Alone

Ask the students to watch your movement and be ready to describe it when you have finished singing the song. Stand, sing the song, and move your entire body with flow, making large pulsations to the macrobeats of the song. Ask the students to describe your movement, and guide the discussion so that they notice both the flow and the pulsations.

Ask the students to stand in self space and to move as you did while you sing the song. Sing the song, playing macrobeats on a hand drum to help students audiate.

Move with Partners

Ask the students to find partners and sit facing them. Tell them that you are going to sing a song and that they are going to join hands with their partner and row to macrobeats. Next, tell them that you are playing macrobeats on the hand drum to help them know when to row. Sing the song, and play macrobeats on the hand drum while you watch the students move.

Move as a Class

Place a long, thick rope in a straight line on the floor. Divide the class in half. Have one half of the class walk to one end of the rope and grab on, facing the middle of the rope, and have the other half hold the other end of the rope. (They should be in tug-of-war formation, with every student holding the rope at some point and facing the middle of the rope.) You should stand at the middle of the rope and hold on with both hands to help guide their movement practice.

Practice the movement first without music. Chant "pull" as you gently pull the rope to the right. Then chant "pull" as you move the rope to the left. Practice the movements in the tempo of the macrobeats of the song. Once the students are comfortable moving back and forth in tempo, sing the song while their movement continues.

TEACHING TIP

The macrobeats of this song are difficult to audiate because they are slow. As a result, the students may have more difficulty than usual moving to the macrobeats. Providing a hand drum reinforcement for the macrobeats will facilitate imitation and later audiation of the macrobeats. However, if students are already audiating the macrobeats well at this tempo, you can remove the hand drum reinforcement. Your eventual goal should be to have them move to macrobeats without reinforcement.

TEACHING TIP

If some students are struggling to find the beat, make sure to pair them with others who are rhythmically strong during the partner movement portion of the Teaching Plan. Those students who are rhythmically unsure usually adjust their movements to match the movements of the stronger students, enabling them to imitate and, eventually, to audiate the macrobeats as modeled by their partners.

COORDINATION WITH INSTRUMENTAL MUSIC

Play the solo bass recording of "The Volga Boat Song" from *Jump Right In: The Instrumental Curriculum* (J201CD, track 24). Show the students a picture of the bass using Instrument Card 4. Show the students pictures of the rest of the string family using Instrument Cards 1 through 3. Ask the students to identify what is the same about all of the instruments and what is different. Tell them that they are all members of the string family because of the strings that get bowed or plucked to make a sound. Then repeat the final activity of the Teaching Plan using the bass rather than the vocal recording.

JUMP RIGHT IN: THE MUSIC CURRICULUM

BIM BAM

Activity Type: Listening, Movement, Singing

Tonality: Harmonic Minor

Resting Tone:

La

Meter: Usual Duple

Macrobeats:

Microbeats:

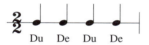

Keyality: D

Range: d–a

 Disc One Track 30

 Piano Bk Page 21

Materials Needed: Enough space for everyone to move comfortably.

Purpose:
1. To help students learn to listen.
2. To help students learn to follow a conductor.
3. To help students learn to breathe and sing.

TEACHING PLAN
Everyone should be seated in self space.

Listen and Move with Flow
Tell the students to copy your movements as you sing a song for them. Remind them that they will be listeners and movers and that listening is the most important job of a musician.

60

TEACHER'S EDITION • KINDERGARTEN

Perform the song while moving your shoulders and spine continuously. (Think of your shoulders making figure eights, and let your spine go with the flow). Check to make sure the students are copying your continuous, flowing movements.

Sing the Resting Tone

Sing on the resting tone, "Listen to this pitch." Sing the resting tone using the neutral syllable BUM. Again sing on the resting tone, "Watch my hands; they will tell you when to breathe. Take a breath and sing that pitch." Breathe and gesture for students to sing the resting tone. Say, "Now, think that pitch." Give the students a moment to think the pitch. Say, "Watch my hands. Take a breath and sing the pitch you were thinking." Again, give a clear breath gesture as you breathe, and sing the pitch with the students. Say, "Your job is to remember that pitch."

Say, "I am going to sing the song again. Sometimes I will pause. Then, I will show you when to breathe and sing the pitch you were thinking. Perform the song and pause every two to four measures to give the breath gesture, and sing the resting tone with the students.

Finish by singing the song again and having the students copy your continuous shoulder and spine movements. After you sing the last pitch, ask the students to watch your hands, breathe, and sing the resting tone of the song with you.

TEACHING TIP

When working with young musicians, find times to emphasize the skill of listening. Listening is the most important job of the musician because it comes in to play in the success of every musical activity.

EARLY TO BED

Activity Type: Singing, Chanting, Rhythm Creativity, Movement

Tonality: Major

Resting Tone:

Do

Meter: Usual Triple

Macrobeats:

Du   Du

Microbeats:

Du Da Di   Du Da Di

Keyality: F

Range: c–f'

 Disc One Track 31

 Piano Bk Page 40

Materials Needed: Two puppets of any variety. Enough space for everyone to move freely.

Purpose:
1. To give students experience creating rhythm patterns in Usual Triple meter.
2. To give students an opportunity to move to macrobeats in Usual Triple meter.

TEACHING PLAN
Everyone should be standing in self space.

Move to Macrobeats
Sing the song while swaying to macrobeats with your arms fully extended. Your feet should leave the ground in alternating motion to macrobeats, and your knees should bend to allow a full-body sway. Sing the song again, and ask the students to join you in your movements.

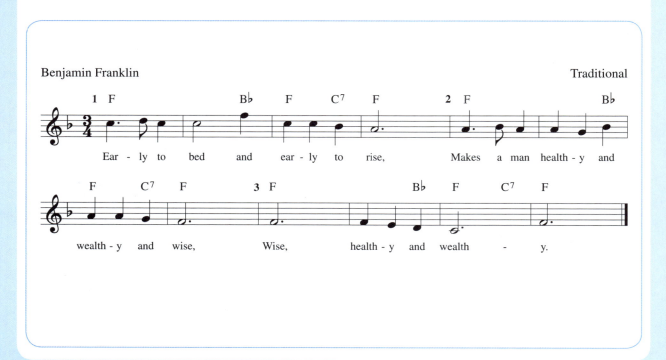

TEACHER'S EDITION • KINDERGARTEN

Rhythm Conversation

Ask the students to describe what happens in a conversation. Guide the discussion so that they realize that, in a conversation, the people talking generally say different things rather than the same thing. Tell the students that you are going to have a rhythm conversation with individual students between repetitions of the song.

Place a puppet on each of your hands. Ask the students to tell you whether the puppets echoed one another or whether they had a conversation. Sing the song and then chant a four-macrobeat pattern using BAH while moving the mouth of one of the puppets. Have the other puppet echo the pattern. Ask the students whether it was a conversation and why or why not. Guide them to realize that the patterns were the same, so it was not really a conversation. Repeat, this time having the two puppets chant different patterns.

Remove one of the puppets from your hands. Tell the students that one of them will have a conversation with the remaining puppet after you sing the song while they sway. As you sing, the students should sway to macrobeats. At the end of the song, chant a four-macrobeat pattern to one student. That student should create a different four-macrobeat pattern in response. Repeat this process several times, giving a variety of students an opportunity to create rhythm patterns.

TEACHING TIP

Sometimes students have difficulty thinking of their own patterns. Often students echo the patterns rather creating their own. If this happens, ask the students to start the conversations; in other words, the student chants first, and the puppets respond. This way, the students will not have a pattern to imitate. When doing this, some students will chant out of metric context or will create patterns that are longer or shorter than four macrobeats. These students are not audiating meter fully. This type of activity can be valuable to you as a teacher in providing insight into the audiational development of individual students in the classroom.

JUMP RIGHT IN: THE MUSIC CURRICULUM

OVER THE RIVER AND THROUGH THE WOOD

Activity Type: Movement, Chanting

Tonality: Major

Resting Tone:

Do

Meter: Usual Triple

Macrobeats:

Du   Du

Microbeats:

Du Da Di Du Da Di

Disc One
Track 32

Piano Bk
Page 104

Keyality: D

Range: d–d'

Materials Needed: Temple blocks and mallets. Enough space for everyone to move comfortably.

Purpose:
1. To help students audiate and move in Usual Triple meter.
2. To give students an opportunity to chant a pattern in solo.

Lydia Maria Child

2. Over the river and through the wood,
   And straight through the barnyard gate.
   We seem to go so very slow,
   And it's hard to wait.
   Over the river and through the wood,
   Now Grandmother's cap I spy.
   Hurrah for the fun! The pudding's done?
   Hurrah for the pumpkin pie!

3. Over the river and through the wood,
   Now soon we'll be on our way.
   There's feasting and fun for every one,
   For this is Thanksgiving day.
   Over the river and through the wood,
   Get on, my dapple grey.
   The woods will ring with songs we sing,
   For this is Thanksgiving day.

64

TEACHING PLAN
Everyone should be seated in self space.

Perform the Song
Sing the first verse of the song for the students while performing macrobeats on your lap in parallel motion. Ask the students to copy your movement as soon as they are able. Sing the song again, playing the following ostinato on temple blocks.

Ask the students to describe the sound of the temple block ostinato and tell you whether it sounds like anything described in the text of the song. (They may identify it as sounding like horses' hooves. If not, give them that suggestion.)

Movement
Ask the students to stand in self space. Tell them that, when you begin singing the song, you want them to gallop around the room. Remind them to stay in self space; they may not touch another person. Sing the song, and play the temple-block ostinato as an aural guide for their movements. At the end of the song, create and chant a four-macrobeat rhythm pattern using BAH. Gesture for the students to echo your pattern. Sing the song again, and perform another pattern for the students to echo.

Solo and Group Pattern Performance
Tell the students that after you sing the song you will either gesture for the entire class to echo your pattern or for one student to echo the pattern. If you want the entire class to echo, you will gesture with both hands, and if you want an individual to echo, you will look at that student and gesture with one hand. Perform the song several more times as the students gallop. Between each repetition of the song, gesture either to an individual or the entire class to echo your improvised patterns.

CONNECTION TO LITERATURE
Sing the entire song for the students, and, after each verse, discuss the text of the song. The following questions may be used to stimulate the discussion.

Verse One:
Where were they going?
What was the weather like for their trip?
Who do you think was travelling?

Verse Two:
In what type of house do the grandparents live?
What is the family having for dessert?
Have you ever had pumpkin pie? If so, when?

Verse Three:
What holiday is mentioned in this song?

Give several students an opportunity to describe their Thanksgiving traditions.

Read *The Thanksgiving Story* by Alice Dagliesh and Helen Sewell (Athenaeum reissue edition 1988). Discuss the origins of the Thanksgiving celebration with the students. Ask individual students to identify what makes them thankful.

COORDINATION WITH INSTRUMENTAL MUSIC
Play the solo oboe recording of "Over the River and Through the Woods" from *Jump Right In: The Instrumental Series* (J299CD, track 34). Show the students a picture of an oboe using Instrument Card 10. Ask a middle school or high school student who plays oboe to come to your classroom and demonstrate the instrument.

JUMP RIGHT IN: THE MUSIC CURRICULUM

TURKEY SONG

Activity Type: Movement, Chanting, Singing, Rhythm Creativity

 Disc One Track 33

 Piano Bk Page 144

Tonality: Aeolian

Resting Tone:

La

Meter: Usual Duple

Macrobeats:

Microbeats:

Keyality: F

Range: c–f'

Materials Needed: Recording. Enough space for everyone to move comfortably.

Purpose:
1. To give students an opportunity to move using continuous flow with microbeat pulsations.
2. To give students an opportunity to perform actions to macrobeats in Usual Duple meter.
3. To give students an opportunity to chant and create rhythm patterns in Usual Duple meter.

TEACHING PLAN

Everyone should be standing in stationary self space.

66

Move Using Continuous Flow with Pulsations

Ask the students to audiate silently and imitate your movement. Sing the song or play the recording, and move using continuous flow with pulsations to microbeats. Be certain to put each pulsation in a different place in space and to move with pulsations using several different parts of the body.

Notice which students coordinate their movements, and compliment them on their use of space. Invite students who are modeling coordinated, continuous flow with pulsations to demonstrate their movements for the class.

Create Actions to the Song Lyrics

Ask the students to describe what the song is about. Repeat the singing and moving if necessary. Then ask them to help you create actions to go with the words of the song. Take students' suggestions, and perform them showing a macrobeat pulse as you move.

After many opportunities to hear and move to this song, invite the students to sing the song without you. Use the following preparatory sequence as a cue for them to sing.

Imitate Usual Duple Rhythm Patterns

On a different day, complete the previous activity. Then establish Usual Duple meter using the preparatory sequence below. Chant four-macrobeat patterns in Usual Duple, and gesture for the students to breathe on the fourth macrobeat of your pattern.

Create Rhythm Patterns

After singing the song and/or chanting patterns, invite the students to create their own rhythm patterns. Tell them to audiate a rhythm pattern silently. Then tell them that you will sing the song, but at the end you will silently audiate four macrobeats instead of singing "feet looked awful dirty." Ask them to raise their hands when you reach that place.

After most of the students indicate they are aware of where "feet looked awful dirty" occurs in the song, tell them you will give them a breath gesture and they should audiate their four-macrobeat rhythm pattern silently. Then invite individuals to breathe and chant their patterns when you give them the breath gesture. When individuals are ready, they can chant in solo. For this activity, there is no "wrong" pattern. Accept any answer the students give.

JUMP RIGHT IN: THE MUSIC CURRICULUM

FIVE LITTLE MUFFINS

Activity Type: Movement, Chanting

 Disc One Track 34

 Piano Bk Page 51

Meter: Usual Duple

Macrobeats:

Microbeats:

Materials Needed: Enough space for everyone to move comfortably.

Purpose:
1. To learn a traditional chant.
2. To give students experience with macrobeat movement in Usual Duple meter.

TEACHING PLAN
Everyone should begin the lesson seated in self space. Later, all will move into standing self space.

Listen
Perform the chant, and pantomime the movements of the poem. Hold up five fingers on one hand to represent the muffins, with one finger on the other hand representing the child walking toward and into the shop. The child should buy the muffin (press one of the muffin fingers down) and then run away. Repeat for each verse, until no fingers remain held up.

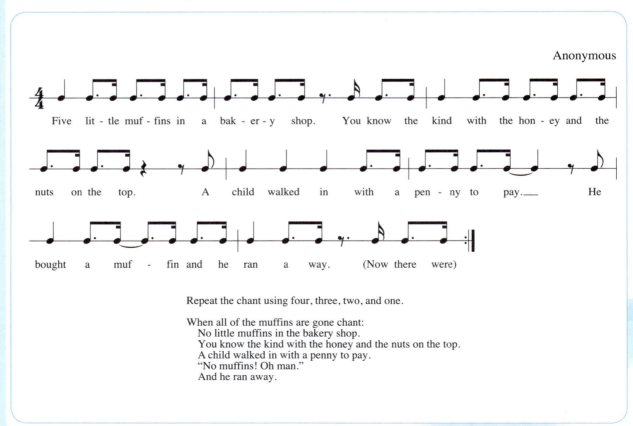

Anonymous

Five little muffins in a bakery shop. You know the kind with the honey and the nuts on the top. A child walked in with a penny to pay. He bought a muffin and he ran away. (Now there were)

Repeat the chant using four, three, two, and one.

When all of the muffins are gone chant:
  No little muffins in the bakery shop.
  You know the kind with the honey and the nuts on the top.
  A child walked in with a penny to pay.
  "No muffins! Oh man."
  And he ran away.

Move

Perform the chant again with the hand motions and demonstrate performing macrobeats in your feet by swaying back and forth as you chant. Ask the student to stand and copy your movements. Invite students to perform the chant with you as soon as they know it.

> **CONNECTION TO LITERATURE**
>
> Read *If You Give a Moose a Muffin* by Laura Joffe Numeroff (Harper Collins 1991). Discuss the events of the story, and list them on the board. Even though most students will not be able to read what is written, they will have the opportunity to see language and reflect on and articulate a plot line.

JUMP RIGHT IN: THE MUSIC CURRICULUM

MOS MOS (CAT SONG)

Activity Type: Movement

Tonality: Major

Resting Tone:

Meter: Usual Duple

Macrobeats:

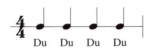

Microbeats:

Keyality: F

Range: d–a

Disc One
Track 35

Piano Bk
Page 86

Materials Needed: Enough space for everyone to move comfortably.

Purpose:
1. To help students increase body awareness.
2. To give students experience moving in a continuous, fluid style in locomotor self space.

TEACHING PLAN
Everyone should be seated in self space.

Spinal Awareness
Have the students come to their hands and knees in table-top position in self space. Ask them to inhale as they take their noses and tailbones to the ceiling. Tell them that their backs should look like saggy old cows.

70

Then have the students exhale and arch their backs high to the ceiling, letting their heads and tailbones move toward the floor. Tell them that they should resemble angry cats.

Repeat the "cow" movement with an inhalation. Repeat the "angry cat" movement with an exhalation. Move gently between the two positions several times.

Listen
Ask the students to sit with crossed legs and listen to the recording, paying special attention to the "meows."

Locomotor Movement
Have the students come to their hands and knees again. Tell them that they will crawl forward to empty spaces when they hear the recording. If the recording pauses, they will freeze. When they hear the "meows," they will perform at least one cat and one cow movement as they learned earlier in the Teaching Plan. They should perform them at their own paces during the "meows."

Play the recording. Pause the recording only when necessary for classroom management. Remind the students as needed when to make their cat and cow shapes. Repeat the activity, having the students crawl backward.

FOR THE MUSIC TEACHER
This Teaching Plan focuses on several types of movement. Crawling helps to encourage continuous, fluid movement. Cat and cow positions are drawn from the practice of yoga, which is helpful in developing spine flexibility and in coordinating breath with movement.

JUMP RIGHT IN: THE MUSIC CURRICULUM

TWO LITTLE SAUSAGES

Activity Type: Chanting, Movement

 Disc One Track 36   Piano Bk Page 146

Meter: Usual Duple

Macrobeats:

Microbeats:

Materials Needed: Enough space for everyone to move freely.

Purpose:
1. To help students identify rhythm patterns as being the same or different.
2. To help students learn to anticipate and predict.
3. To give students experience with continuous, fluid movement with pulsations.

TEACHING PLAN
Everyone should be seated in self space.

Learn the Chant
Perform the chant, moving your arms in a continuous, fluid way while pulsating your hands to macrobeats. Ask the students to describe your movements. They should comment both on the flowing nature of the movement as well as the pulsations. Perform the chant again, and ask the students to move with you.

Perform the chant again, this time flowing with pulsations during the first phrase, clapping on the word "pop," and hitting the ground on the word "bam." Ask the students to describe your movements again, this time associating the specific movements with the words in the chant. As soon as they are able to describe the movements, invite them to perform the movements with you as you perform the chant again.

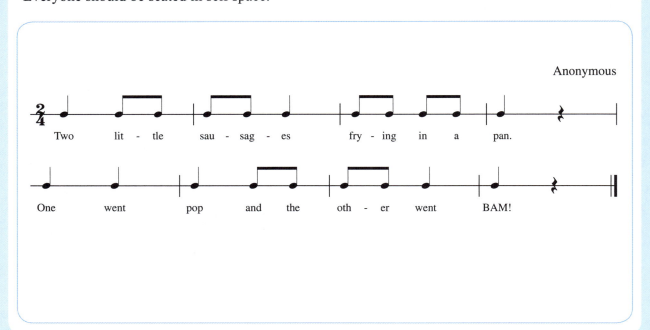

72

Tell the students that they are in charge of the "pop" and the "bam." When you get to that point in the chant, they should say the appropriate word and perform the appropriate movement with the word. Perform the chant several times with the students saying and moving to "pop" and "bam." Then invite the students to perform the entire chant without you.

Same and Different Rhythm Patterns

Tell the students that at the end of the chant you will chant two patterns that are either the same as or different from one another. They should show you whether the two patterns are the same or different by holding out their hands. If the two patterns are the same, they should hold out two fists so that their two hands are the same. If the two patterns are different, they should hold out one fist and one open hand so that their two hands look different.

Tell them that you are going to give them a chance to practice. Hold up one finger, and chant a four-macrobeat pattern using the syllable "pop" or "bam" for the entire pattern. Then, in tempo and without a break, hold up two fingers, and chant a different four-macrobeat pattern using the same syllable. Ask the students to show you whether they are the same or different using their hands. Tell the students that the patterns were different, and show them how their hands should have looked. Practice several more times with different patterns, sometimes using "pop" and sometimes using "bam," making sure to demonstrate patterns that are the same and patterns that are different.

Perform Patterns after the Chant

Put this activity back in the context of the chant. First, have the students perform the chant. Then perform two four-macrobeat patterns that are the same or two patterns that are different, and have the students show you whether they are the same or different using their hands.

Create Rhythm Patterns

After the students are mostly successful with the Teaching Plan, you can have the students create their own four-macrobeat patterns. Tell the students that after you perform the chant you will perform a four-macrobeat pattern. Then you will gesture to a student, who should either imitate your pattern or create a new one. The students should show you whether the two patterns were the same or different using their hands. Ask for a volunteer to demonstrate same and different again for the class.

Perform the chant several times, followed by performing a pattern and gesturing to a student to perform a "same" or "different" pattern from your pattern. Check the students' hands to make sure they are responding correctly to "same" and "different." Repeat the chant several times, and choose a different student to perform a pattern each time you perform the chant.

JUMP RIGHT IN: THE MUSIC CURRICULUM

SLEEP, MY BABE *(DORS, DORS 'TIT BÉBÉ)*

Activity Type: Singing, Solo Singing, Movement

Tonality: Harmonic Minor

Resting Tone:

Meter: Usual Duple

Macrobeats:

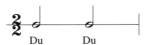

Microbeats:

 Disc Two Track 1

 Piano Bk Page 123

Keyality: G

Range: d–b-flat

Materials Needed: Recording. Enough space for everyone to move comfortably.

Purpose:
1. To sing tonic and dominant patterns in Harmonic Minor tonality.
2. To sing Harmonic Minor patterns alone and in a group.

TEACHING PLAN

Everyone should be seated in self space in a circle.

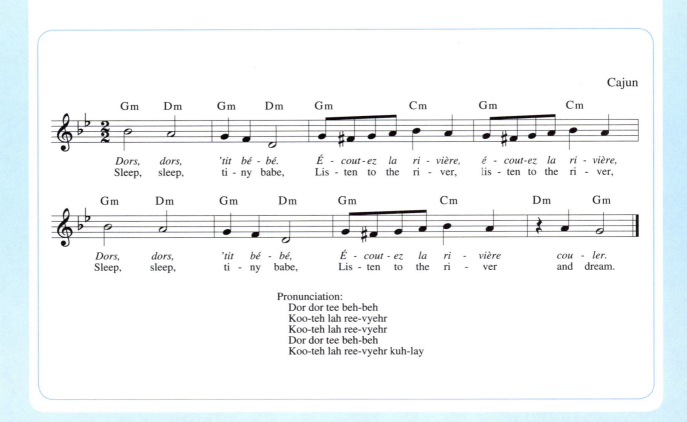

74

TEACHER'S EDITION • KINDERGARTEN

Listen and Move

Play the recording or sing "Sleep, My Babe," and move your upper body and arms in a continuous, fluid motion. Ask the students to imitate your movements.

Focus on Patterns

Sing a tonic pattern in Harmonic Minor tonality to the students using the neutral syllable BUM, and then give them a preparatory breath and gesture to indicate that you want them to imitate your pattern. Sing another tonic pattern, and have the students imitate you. Then sing a dominant pattern in Harmonic Minor tonality, and have students imitate you. Practice performing tonic and dominant patterns by having the students, as a class and in solo, imitate the patterns you perform.

Play the recording or sing the song again several times, and use continuous, fluid movement during each performance. Have the class and individuals echo tonic and dominant patterns in Harmonic Minor tonality after each repetition of the song.

TEACHING TIP

If you have difficulty getting some of the students to respond in solo, use a puppet when singing tonic and dominant patterns to individuals. Some students respond better to a puppet than to an adult because they focus on the puppet rather than on their uneasiness about singing in solo.

FOR THE MUSIC TEACHER

This activity can also be used as an opportunity for students to create tonal patterns. As soon as the majority of the students are comfortable imitating your tonic and dominant patterns in Harmonic Minor tonality, have them create new tonal patterns using BUM after each repetition of the song. Have the class imitate the pattern each student creates.

75

JUMP RIGHT IN: THE MUSIC CURRICULUM

THE ELEPHANT SONG

Activity Type: Singing, Movement

Tonality: Major

Resting Tone:

Meter: Usual Duple

Macrobeats:

Microbeats:

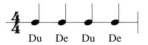

Keyality: D

Range: d–d'

Materials Needed: Enough space everyone to move comfortably.

 Disc Two Track 2

 Piano Bk Page 42

Purpose:
1. To help students discriminate between same and different tonal patterns in Major tonality.
2. To give students an opportunity to move with strong and gentle weight.

TEACHING PLAN

Everyone should be seated in self space.

Sing and Move

Sing the song for the students, and ask them to tell you about the words of the song. They should identify that elephants are walking on a spider's web. Ask the students what would happen if an elephant, even a small one, really walked on a spider's web. (Answer: The elephant would crash through the web.)

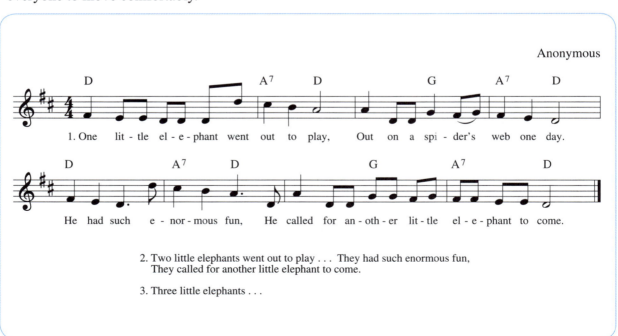

2. Two little elephants went out to play . . . They had such enormous fun,
   They called for another little elephant to come.

3. Three little elephants . . .

Tell the students that they are going to pretend to be elephants walking on a spider's web. Remind them that they should walk as gently as possible so that they do not break through the spider's web. Also, remind them to stay in self space. Sing the song as the students gently walk around the room.

Then tell the students that you will sing the song again, and this time they should move like heavy elephants, shaking the ground with each of their steps. Sing the song again as they move with strength. Then tell the students that they can choose, for this repetition of the song, whether they want to be strong or gentle movers, but by the end of the song, everyone should be back in their seats. Sing as the students move, watching to see how well they are able to move with strength or gentleness.

Play a Game
Tell the students that you are going to play a game. You are going to be the lead elephant and walk around the room like an elephant as you sing the song. At the end of the song, you will walk up to a student and sing two tonal patterns. Those patterns will either be the same or different from one another. If the patterns are the same, the student should show you two hands that are the same. (They should hold out two fists or two open hands.) If the patterns are different, the student should hold out two hands that are different (one fist and one open hand).

Then the student should choose whether the elephants will pretend to be big elephants or elephants who are light enough to walk on a spider's web. As you sing the song, the student should join hands with you and follow you around the room, either moving with strong or gentle weight. After each repetition of the song, perform two patterns for a student, and have that student join the line and choose the type of movement for the next repetition of the song.

FOR THE MUSIC TEACHER
This game helps you get responses from individual students in the class. Because the individual responses are solicited in the context of a game, students who are normally reticent to respond will often do so freely.

The game can be varied in many ways. You could chant rhythm patterns rather than singing tonal patterns after each repetition of the song. You could also perform a single tonal or rhythm pattern and ask the student to echo your pattern, rather than having the student identify a pattern as the same or different.

MY LITTLE DUCKLINGS

Activity Type: Movement

Tonality: Major

Resting Tone:

Meter: Usual Duple

Macrobeats:

Microbeats:

Keyality: F

Range: f–d'

Disc Two
Track 3

Piano Bk
Page 87

Materials Needed: Enough space for everyone to move comfortably.

Purpose: To give students an opportunity to explore pathways through movement.

TEACHING PLAN
Everyone should be seated in self space.

Model Movement
Tell the students that you are going to move and that they should be ready to describe your movement at the end of the song. Walk around the room to macrobeats in a curvy line as you sing the song. At the end of the song, ask the children to describe your movement. They should notice that you were walking to beat and that the pathway in which you walked was curvy

TEACHER'S EDITION • KINDERGARTEN

or squiggly. Then tell them that you are going to model movement again, but this time the movement will be different in some way. Sing the song again while walking to macrobeats in a straight line. When you are done, ask the students to describe this movement. Guide them to notice that everything was the same except the pathway.

Move
Ask the students to stand. Tell them that you will sing the song and that you want them to walk behind you like ducklings following their mother in curvy pathways to macrobeats as you sing. Remind them that they need to stay in self space, which means that they do not touch anyone else as they walk. Sing the song and move. Then, while they are still standing, ask them to follow your next pathway. This time, walk in a straight pathway as you sing the song. You will need to plan your movement carefully, and you may need to take small steps to prevent turning a corner before the end of the song. After you have finished singing and moving, ask the students to describe the pathway. Repeat, this time moving in a straight pathway for the first phrase of the song and a curvy pathway for the second phrase of the song. Again, ask the students to describe the pathways.

Then select individual students to lead the duckling line in straight and curvy pathways. At first, whisper in the leader's ear the type of pathway he or she should use, and have the class guess what you whispered after they have moved. After students are confident with the activity, let them choose their own type of pathway when they are the leaders.

TEACHING TIP
Locomotor movement to beat is more difficult than movement in place to beat. If your students have difficulty walking to macrobeats, you can gently play a hand drum to reinforce the macrobeats as they move. However, the main focus of the activity is pathways, so if students do not walk consistently to macrobeats, that is not a serious problem in this context.

FOR THE MUSIC TEACHER
This activity can be extended by using other locomotor movements as the basis for movement in straight or curvy pathways. For example, the students could hop on one foot or crawl in straight or curvy pathways as you sing the song.

CONNECTION TO LITERATURE
Read the book *Make Way for Ducklings* by Robert McCloskey (Viking Kestral Picture Books 1941). This children's classic describes ducklings following their mother around Boston, looking for a place to live. As you read, ask the students to look at the pictures of the ducklings and describe their pathways. Because the ducklings cross streets, the book also provides an opportunity to talk about traffic safety.

JUMP RIGHT IN: THE MUSIC CURRICULUM

ZION'S CHILDREN

Activity Type: Movement, Audiation

Tonality: Major

Resting Tone:

Do

Meter: Usual Duple

Macrobeats:

Du   Du

Microbeats:

Du De Du De

Keyality: F

Range: c–d'

Disc Two
Track 4

Piano Bk
Page 157

Materials Needed: Recording. Two pom-poms for each student. Enough space for everyone to move comfortably.

Purpose:
1. To help students audiate same and different rhythm patterns in Usual Duple meter.
2. To give students an opportunity experience continuous, fluid movement with pulsations.

TEACHING PLAN
Everyone should be seated in self space.

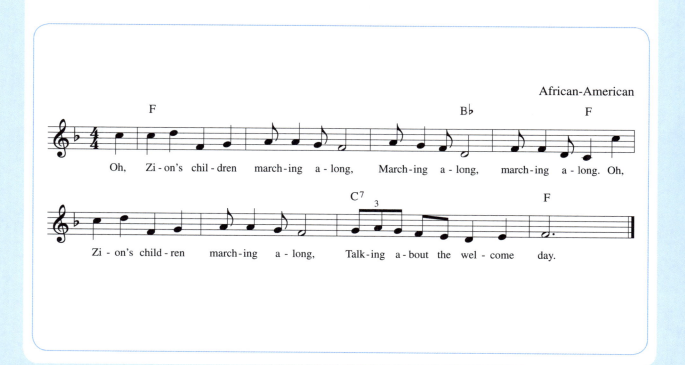

80

TEACHER'S EDITION • KINDERGARTEN

Flow with Pulsations

Ask the students to observe your movement and to be prepared to describe it when the song is finished. Stand and hold a pom-pom in each hand. Then sing the song without text, or play the recording, moving your arms with flow and pulsating the pom-poms to microbeats. Use both high and low space in your movements. Guide the discussion of your movement so that the students realize you were both flowing and pulsating to microbeats. Also, help them to realize that the movement was in place; your feet did not move.

Ask the students to stand, and give two pom-poms to each student. Then ask them to move in place with flow and pulsations to microbeats as you sing or play the song again.

Same and Different

Tell the students that after each performance of the song you will perform two rhythm patterns. If the patterns are the same, they should hold out both pom-poms. If the patterns are different, they should drop a pom-pom and hold out one empty fist and one pom-pom. Sing the song while the students move. Then chant two patterns that are the same, holding up one finger while performing the first pattern and two fingers while performing the second pattern; the students should hold out both pom-poms because the patterns were the same. Repeat this process multiple times. Sometimes perform two patterns that are the same, and sometimes perform two patterns that are different. The students should move with flow and pulsations each time you sing the song.

> **TEACHING TIP**
>
> If students are successful with the Teaching Plan, you can extend the activity by asking them to echo the patterns immediately after you perform them. After they echo each pattern, they can show you "same" or "different" with the pom-poms.
>
> You could also make this a locomotor movement activity by having the students march to microbeats while pulsating and moving their arms with flow.

JUMP RIGHT IN: THE MUSIC CURRICULUM

IN THE WINDOW

Activity Type: Singing, Movement

Tonality: Harmonic Minor

Resting Tone:

La

Meter: Usual Triple

Macrobeats:

Du   Du

Microbeats:

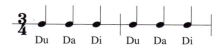
Du Da Di Du Da Di

Keyality: G

Range: d–d'

Disc Two Track 5

Piano Bk Page 71

Materials Needed: Bean bag. Bass xylophone and mallets. Enough space for everyone to move comfortably.

Purpose:
1. To help students audiate resting tone in Harmonic Minor tonality.
2. To give students experience with continuous, fluid movement with microbeat pulsations in Usual Triple meter.
3. To develop students' harmonic audiation.

TEACHING PLAN
Everyone should be seated in self space.

Flow and Flow with Pulsations
Ask the students to listen to the song and to watch you move. Sing the song for the students while you move with continuous flow. In your movement, be certain to use high, medium, and

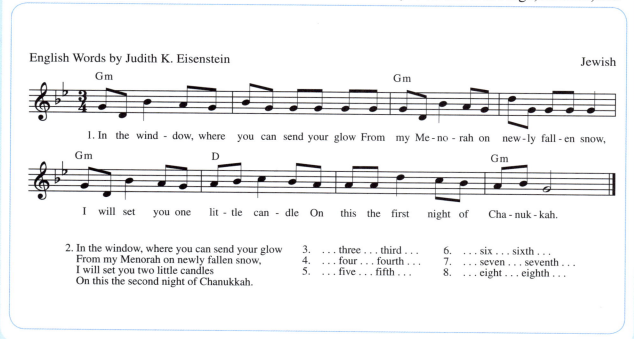

82

low space as well as the space in front of and behind you. Ask the students to stand and move like you did as you sing the song again.

Then ask the students to watch your movement as you sing the song again. Tell them to pay attention to what is the same and what is different about your movement this time. Sing the song and move with continuous flow with pulsations in your hands to microbeats. As before, be certain to use high, medium, and low space as well as the space in front of and behind you. This will mean you never pulsate in the same place twice. At the end of the song, ask the students what was the same and what was different about your movements. Guide the discussion so that they notice you still moved with continuous flow throughout all levels of space but that you added microbeat pulsations. Ask them to move like you did as you sing the song again.

Singing the Resting Tone

On a different day, focus on the tonal elements of the song. With everyone seated in self space, sing the song. Then sing the resting tone for the students, and have them imitate you. Give them a breath gesture as a cue for when to sing.

Tell the students that you want them to audiate that pitch, which means that they will continue to think it as you sing the song and that they should sing the resting tone whenever you drop the bean bag. Sing the song, and pause every several measures to drop the bean bag as a cue for the students to sing the resting tone.

Play Chord Roots

When students are comfortable singing the resting tone, tell them to listen to you sing the song and play the chord roots on a bass xylophone. Tell them that after they have listened you will ask them to select the resting tone from the two pitches you played on the bass xylophone. Play the chord roots on macrobeats as you sing the song using the chord symbols notated in the song as a guide. Then show the students the two bars you played, and engage them in a discussion to have them figure out which one is the resting tone. You may need to have them sing the resting tone again as part of that process.

FOR THE MUSIC TEACHER

Although kindergarten students probably are not ready to sing in harmony, they benefit from hearing chord roots played or sung to the melodies that they are hearing and learning to sing. In fact, researchers have found that young students who regularly hear chord root accompaniments are able to improvise better tonally.

JUMP RIGHT IN: THE MUSIC CURRICULUM

POPCORN

Activity Type: Listening, Movement, Chanting

Tonality: Major

Resting Tone:

Do

Meter: Usual Triple

Macrobeats:

Du Du

Microbeats:

Du Da Di Du Da Di

Keyality: D

Range: d–a

 Disc Two Track 6

 Piano Bk Page 108

Materials Needed: Enough space for everyone to move comfortably.

Purpose:
1. To help students learn to listen and move.
2. To give students an opportunity to move in a continuous, fluid style with pulsations.

TEACHING PLAN

Everyone should be seated in self space with crossed legs.

Listen and Move While Seated

Tell the students that they will be listeners and movers. Remind them that listening is the most important job of each musician.

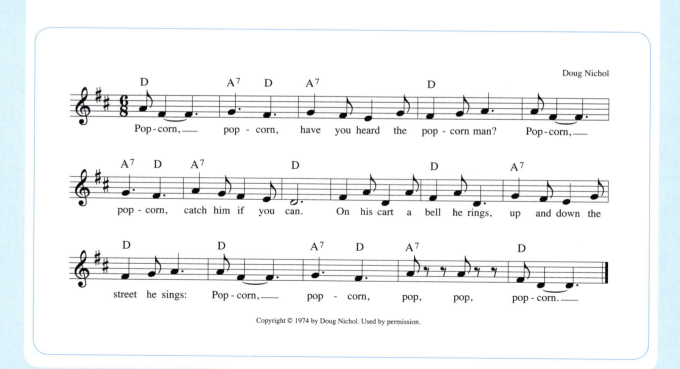

Copyright © 1974 by Doug Nichol. Used by permission.

Have the students copy your movements as you perform the song, moving your hands in bilateral microbeat pulsations. Never perform the microbeat pulsations in the same place twice in a row. Keep moving them all around on the floor, on your legs, and in the air. Use your spine to assist your use of continuous flow, being certain to keep the movement relaxed and fluid. Repeat the song. This time, move with bilateral macrobeat pulsations, and again, have the students imitate your movements.

Next, have the students copy your bilateral microbeat pulsations while they chant TUH to microbeats to help coordinate their tongues with their body movements. Sing the song again as they move. Repeat the song, this time having the students copy your bilateral macrobeat pulsations while they chant BAH to macrobeats to help them feel the difference between microbeats and macrobeats.

Stand and Rock
When students become comfortable with each type of seated movement above, have them stand and rock from side to side to macrobeats and simultaneously chant BAH on the macrobeats. Make sure that the students use their weight. They should stand on the balls of their feet and raise their heels alternately as they rock.

Stand and Pulsate
Have the students copy your bilateral microbeat hand pulsations while they chant TUH to microbeats to coordinate their tongues with their body movements. Again, never perform the microbeat pulsations in the same place twice in a row. Keep moving them around on your legs and in the air. Use spine movement to assist your use of continuous flow, being certain to keep the movement relaxed and fluid.

FOR THE MUSIC TEACHER
The use of TUH and BAH as neutral syllables for microbeats and macrobeats will serve as readiness for chanting using rhythm syllables at a later time. Both of these syllables are forward in the mouth, making them easy to perform. Chanting in this way helps the students coordinate their bodies with their audiation.

JUMP RIGHT IN: THE MUSIC CURRICULUM

PERSONENT HODIE (CELEBRATE JOYOUSLY)

Activity Type: Movement, Singing

Tonality: Dorian

Resting Tone:

Meter: Usual Duple

Macrobeats:

Microbeats:

 Disc Two Track 7

 Piano Bk Page 107

Keyality: D

Range: c–d'

Materials Needed: Recording. Enough space for everyone to move comfortably.

Purpose:
1. To help students develop body awareness using continuous, fluid movement.
2. To give students an opportunity to respond to sound and silence through moving and freezing.
3. To help students audiate the resting tone and characteristic patterns in Dorian tonality.

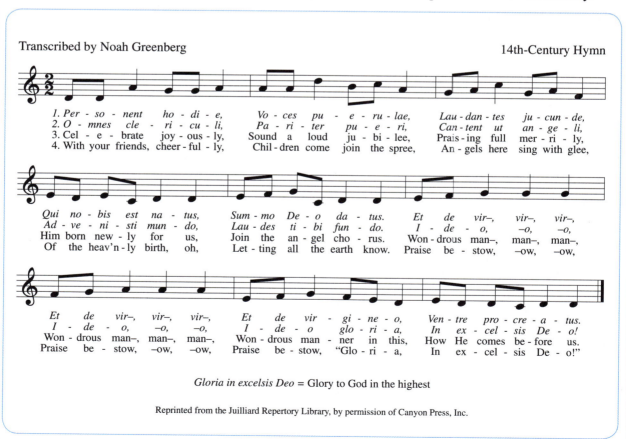

Transcribed by Noah Greenberg — 14th-Century Hymn

1. Per - so - nent ho - di - e, Vo - ces pu - e - ru - lae, Lau - dan - tes ju - cun - de,
2. O - mnes cle - ri - cu - li, Pa - ri - ter pu - e - ri, Can - tent ut an - ge - li,
3. Cel - e - brate joy - ous - ly, Sound a loud ju - bi - lee, Prais - ing full mer - ri - ly,
4. With your friends, cheer - ful - ly, Chil - dren come join the spree, An - gels here sing with glee,

Qui no - bis est na - tus, Sum - mo De - o da - tus. Et de vir–, vir–, vir–,
Ad - ve - ni - sti mun - do, Lau - des ti - bi fun - do. I - de - o, –o, –o,
Him born new - ly for us, Join the an - gel cho - rus. Won - drous man–, man–, man–,
Of the heav'n - ly birth, oh, Let - ting all the earth know. Praise be - stow, –ow, –ow,

Et de vir–, vir–, vir–, Et de vir - gi - ne - o, Ven - tre pro - cre - a - tus.
I - de - o, –o, –o, I - de - o glo - ri - a, In ex - cel - sis De - o!
Won - drous man–, man–, man–, Won - drous man - ner in this, How He comes be - fore us.
Praise be - stow, –ow, –ow, Praise be - stow, "Glo - ri - a, In ex - cel - sis De - o!"

Gloria in excelsis Deo = Glory to God in the highest

Reprinted from the Juilliard Repertory Library, by permission of Canyon Press, Inc.

TEACHING PLAN
Everyone should be standing in stationary self space.

Introduce the Melody
Tell students you are going to play a recording. Ask students to imitate your movement. Before you begin, remind them to stay in stationary self space.

Dance for a Part of the Body
As you play the recording, model continuous, fluid movement. Emphasize one part of the body, such as your hips, your wrist, or your back as you move. Draw circles in the air, being certain to use your whole body as you move. Change to another part of the body each time a new phrase begins (note that measure five is part of the previous phrase). Observe the students as you model movement. Notice students who are coordinating themselves as they move and are able to engage the whole body while emphasizing one body part.

Establish Tonality with a Neutral Syllable
Establish tonality by singing the sequence of tones notated below using BUM. Then sing the resting tone and give the students a breath gesture for them to echo.

Move and Freeze, Freeze and Move
After the students have had several opportunities to move, invite them to play a game of move and freeze. Tell them that when you sing the melody they should move as before. If you stop singing, they should freeze. Model the movement as you sing.

Follow the directions on this page for establishing tonality and inviting the students to sing the resting tone. Tell them that you will sing the melody. This time, when they hear the melody they should freeze and audiate the resting tone. When they hear silence, they should continue to audiate the resting tone, move with continuous flow, and watch you. You will give them the gesture to sing the resting tone they are audiating as they continue to move. When you resume the melody, they should freeze again.

Sing Patterns
On a different day, invite the students to play another game using this melody. Sing the melody once for them. At the end of the melody, invite them to breathe and sing these tonal patterns:

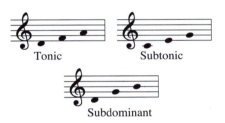

Play freeze and move again. This time, instead of singing the resting tone as they move, you will sing patterns using the functions above and invite students to echo. Observe students who are coordinating their breathing, movement, and singing.

JUMP RIGHT IN: THE MUSIC CURRICULUM

AMERICA

Activity Type: Listening, Movement, Singing

Tonality: Major

Resting Tone:

Do

Meter: Usual Triple

Macrobeats:

Du Du

Microbeats:

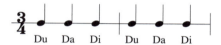
Du Da Di Du Da Di

Keyality: G

Range: f-sharp–e'

 Disc Two Track 8

 Piano Bk Page 5

Materials Needed: Recording. Enough space for everyone to move comfortably.

Purpose:
1. To give students experience listening and moving.
2. To give students experience moving in a continuous, fluid style with pulsations.
3. To give students experience singing the resting tone.

TEACHING PLAN

Everyone should be seated in self space.

Listen and Move with Pulsations

Tell the students that they will be listeners and movers. Remind them that listening is the most important job for each musician.

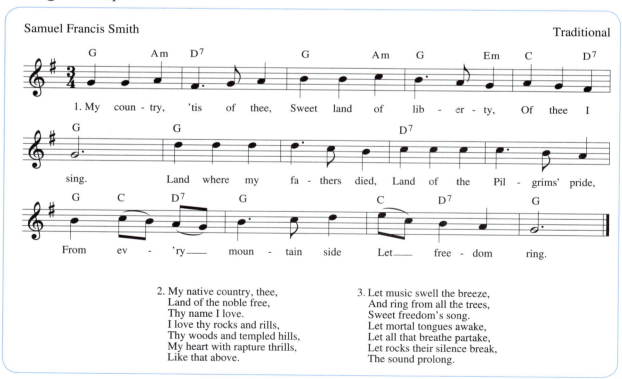

88

TEACHER'S EDITION • KINDERGARTEN

AMERICA

Have the students sit with crossed legs and copy your movements as you perform the song or play the recording. Sing or start the recording, and perform bilateral microbeat pulsations with your hands. Never perform the microbeat pulsations in the same place twice in a row. Keep moving them all around on the floor, on your legs, and in the air. Use your spine to assist your use of continuous flow, being certain to keep the movement relaxed and fluid.

Sing or play the song again. This time, move with bilateral macrobeat pulsations, and have the students copy your movements.

Move and Chant
Sing or play the song a third time, and perform bilateral microbeat pulsations again. Now have the students copy your bilateral microbeat pulsations while they chant TUH to microbeats to help coordinate their tongues with their body movements.

Sing or play the song again while pulsing macrobeats again. Have the students copy your bilateral macrobeat pulsations while they chant BAH to develop their awareness of the differences between microbeats and macrobeats and to help them audiate meter.

Sing the Resting Tone
Say, "Listen to this pitch." Sing the resting tone using the neutral syllable BUM.

Sing on the resting tone, "Watch my hands; they will tell you when to breathe. Now, think that pitch." Give the students a moment to think the pitch. Sing, "Watch my hands. Take a breath and sing the pitch you were thinking." Give a clear breath gesture as you breathe and sing the pitch with the students. Sing, "Your job is to remember that pitch."

Sing, "I am going to sing the song again. Sometimes I will pause. Then I will show you when to breathe and sing the pitch you were thinking." Perform the song, and pause every two measures to give the breath gesture and sing the resting tone with the students.

COORDINATION WITH INSTRUMENTAL MUSIC

Play the solo oboe recording of "America" from *Jump Right In: The Instrumental Music Series* (J229CD, track 2). Show the students a picture of the oboe using Instrument Card 8. Tell the students the name of the instrument and that it is a wind instrument because it makes a sound when you blow into it.

Play a grow-and-shrink game with the recording. Tell the students that you want them to start in a completely closed position on the floor, meaning that they should crunch themselves into as small a shape as possible. Ask several students to demonstrate their closed shapes, and talk about them with the class. Ask them, "Is there a way to make that shape even more closed?" Then tell the students that they will all start with a closed shape and gradually grow to the most open shape possible by the end of the recording. Have several students demonstrate open shapes and discuss them. Then have the students take their starting closed position. When you play the recording, they will gradually change shape, becoming more and more open. When the recording is over, they should hold their open shapes. Play the recording again; this time the students should gradually move from their open shapes back to their closed shapes by the end of the song.

89

JUMP RIGHT IN: THE MUSIC CURRICULUM

BALOO, LAMMY

Activity Type: Movement

Tonality: Major

Resting Tone:

Meter: Usual Triple

Macrobeats:

Microbeats:

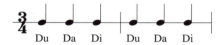

Keyality: E-flat

Range: e-flat–d-flat'

 Disc Two Track 9

 Piano Bk Page 16

Materials Needed: Recording. Enough space for everyone to move comfortably.

Purpose:
1. To help students increase their body awareness.
2. To help students learn to move parts of the body in isolation.
3. To give students experience moving quickly and slowly.

TEACHING PLAN

Everyone should be seated in self space.

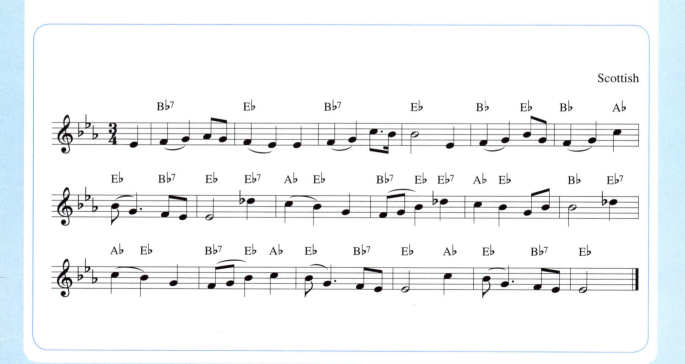

90

Teacher's Edition • Kindergarten

Body Part Isolations and Time
Have the students sit with crossed legs in a circle and copy your movements as you play the recording. (If your students are adept at using self space, you may have them stand for this activity.) Begin by moving only one thumb as slowly as you can during the first two phrases of the song. Pause and move that thumb as quickly as you can during the next two phrases. Replay the recording, and repeat the slow and quick movements with your other thumb. Make sure the students copy your movements.

Repeat the activity using the following parts of the body: elbows, shoulders, and hips. Be sure to use individual body parts so that the students gain experience isolating them. You can label these as "body part solos."

Discuss how it feels to move parts of the body in isolation. Your students will discover that it is easier to move some body parts by themselves than it is to move others. That is the beginning of body awareness.

Finish the lesson by allowing individual students to be the movement leaders. Ask a student to select a part of the body and a quick or slow starting tempo. All other students will follow the leader's movement and tempo. Play the recording, and allow the student to lead the movement. After the first two phrases of the recording, instruct the student to switch tempos. (If the student started with a quick tempo, he or she will switch to a slow tempo and vice versa.)

Repeat the activity with several different leaders. Be sure to have the students select different parts of the body. Discuss how it feels to move each of the body parts slowly or quickly.

FOR THE MUSIC TEACHER
You can extend this activity to develop body awareness and coordination more fully. On another day, repeat the activity using pairs of body parts, so both parts of the body will be moving at the same time and in the same tempo. You can label these "body part duets."

COVENTRY CAROL

Activity Type: Movement, Chanting, Rhythm Creativity

Tonality: Harmonic Minor

Resting Tone:

La

Meter: Usual Triple

Macrobeats:

Du Du

Microbeats:

Du Da Di Du Da Di

Keyality: G

Disc Two
Track 10

Piano Bk
Page 31

Range: f-sharp–d'

Materials Needed: Enough space for everyone to move comfortably.

Purpose:
1. To move using continuous, fluid movement with pulsations.
2. To create rhythm patterns in Usual Triple meter.

TEACHING PLAN

Everyone should be seated in self space.

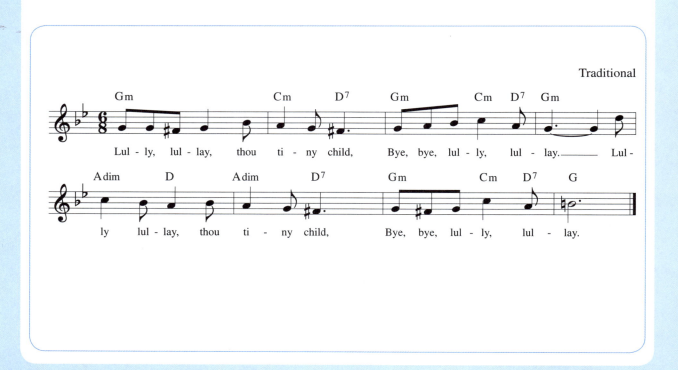

TEACHER'S EDITION • KINDERGARTEN

Listen and Move

Have the students sit with crossed legs and copy your movements as you review the differences between microbeats and macrobeats. Perform the song with continuous, fluid movement with bilateral microbeat pulsations. Ask the students to copy your flow and bilateral microbeat pulsations while they chant TUH to coordinate their tongues with their body movements. Then sing the song again, and move with flow and bilateral pulsations to macrobeats. Have the students copy your bilateral macrobeat pulsations while they chant BAH.

Imitate and Identify Different Rhythm Patterns

Now tell the students you are going to perform two rhythm patterns that are different from each other. Chant each of the following rhythm patterns using BAH. Pause between the patterns, and hold up one finger for the first pattern and two fingers for the second pattern to allow the students to identify each pattern.

Then have the students chant and bilaterally pat each rhythm pattern several times. Tell the students those two rhythm patterns can be used to accompany the song.

Rhythm Pattern Repetition and Ostinato

Have the students chant and pat the first rhythm pattern four times successively. Make sure that the students are using the neutral syllable BAH and patting bilaterally. Have them sway their spines fluidly as they chant, repeating the pattern four more times as you sing.

Next, have the students chant and pat the second rhythm pattern four times successively. Make sure that the students are using the neutral syllable BAH and patting bilaterally. Have them sway their spines fluidly as they chant, repeating the pattern four more times as you sing the song.

Tell the students that a short, repeated pattern is called an ostinato.

COORDINATION WITH INSTRUMENTAL MUSIC

Play the solo bassoon recording of "Coventry Carol" from *Jump Right In: The Instrumental Music Series* (J229CD, track 88). Show the students a picture of the bassoon using Instrument Card 13. Tell them that the instrument is taller than even the tallest student in the class and that it can play very low notes because it is so long. Also tell the students that it is a wind instrument because it makes a sound when you blow into it.

Give each student a scarf. Tell the students to drape their scarves over one of their hands so that it is completely covered. Ask the students to stand, being careful to prevent their scarves from falling. Then tell them that when you play the bassoon recording, you want them to give their scarves a continuous, flowing ride around the room. When the song is over, they should freeze. At the end of the recording, choose a new part of the body to drape with the scarf, and give the scarf a flowing ride. Play the recording again each time that the students choose a new part of the body.

JUMP RIGHT IN: THE MUSIC CURRICULUM

AS JOSEPH WAS A-WALKING

Activity Type: Listening, Movement

Tonality: Major

Resting Tone:

Do

Meter: Usual Triple

Macrobeats:

Microbeats:

Keyality: F

Range: c–d'

 Disc Two Track 11   Piano Bk Page 11

Materials Needed: Recorder. Enough space for everyone to move comfortably.

Purpose:
1. To give students experience with continuous, fluid movement.
2. To help students develop body awareness.
3. To help students learn to audiate phrases.
4. To give students experience hearing characteristic tone quality on a recorder.

TEACHING PLAN
Everyone should be seated in self space on the floor.

94

Listen to the Song

Tell the students that you are going to play a song on the recorder and that they should listen and determine what type of movement best fits the song. Ask them if the movement would be smooth or bumpy. Have the students close their eyes as they listen. Then play the melody of the song on the recorder, paying special attention to making the melody as smooth as possible.

At the end of the song, ask the students to open their eyes, and help them to determine that the melody was smooth and flowing. Guide them to make smooth and flowing movements.

Move with Flow in a Seated Position

Invite a student to choose a part of the body for the class to move with flow as you perform the song on recorder again. Perform the song while the students move. Repeat, having students choose different parts of the body to move using continuous, fluid motion for each repetition of the song.

Move with Flow through Space

Ask the students to stand in self space. Tell them that you are going to play the song but that this time they should move with flow through space. Ask a student who moves particularly well to demonstrate what that would look like. Then play the song as the students move around the room in a continuous, fluid style. Remind the students that they should use all levels of space, meaning that they should sometimes be moving high, sometimes be moving low, and sometimes be moving in the middle. Play the song again so that they can practice using all of the levels.

Moving and Freezing

Explain that you are going to add one more thing to their movement. This time when they hear the song, they should move, and when you pause, they should freeze their movements. Remind them that when they freeze they should not move at all. Play the song several times on the recorder. This time, pause at the end of each phrase while the students freeze. If needed, remind them that they should be using multiple levels in their movement. While they are frozen, comment on the levels that you see in the students' body positions.

TEACHING TIP

If the classroom is small, making it difficult for all of the students to move at the same time, have half of the students (perhaps dividing the class by gender) freeze in a standing position, and ask the other half to move with flow around those who are "frozen." Then have the class switch roles.

TEACHING TIP

If your recorder skills are not strong, you can perform this same Teaching Plan using the recording of the song rather than playing the song on the recorder.

JUMP RIGHT IN: THE MUSIC CURRICULUM

I WONDER AS I WANDER

Activity Type: Movement

Tonality: Aeolian

Resting Tone:

Meter: Usual Triple

Macrobeats:

Microbeats:

Keyality: A

Range: c–e'

 Disc Two Track 12 Piano Bk Page 69

Materials Needed: Recording. Enough space for everyone to move comfortably.

Purpose:
1. To help students audiate Aeolian tonality.
2. To demonstrate and give students experience with body awareness using continuous, fluid movement.
3. To help students learn to sustain the resting tone as harmonic accompaniment to a song.

TEACHING PLAN

Everyone should be seated in scattered formation and in self space.

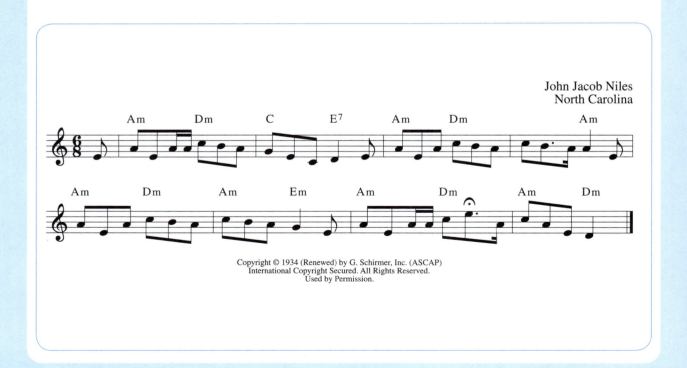

John Jacob Niles
North Carolina

Copyright © 1934 (Renewed) by G. Schirmer, Inc. (ASCAP)
International Copyright Secured. All Rights Reserved.
Used by Permission.

Introduce the Melody
Establish tonality by singing the sequence of tones notated below using a neutral syllable.

Then sing the resting tone using BUM. Invite the students to sing the resting tone after you by giving them a breath gesture.

Tell the students you are going to play a recording for them. Ask them to continue to audiate the pitch that they just sang silently. Tell them you will invite them to sing the resting tone again when the melody ends.

Play the recording (or sing the melody using neutral syllables) for the students. At the end, give the breath gesture and sing the resting tone with them.

Sing on the resting tone, "I am sprinkling this sound in the room. When I sprinkle this sound on you, take a breath and sing the sound." Pantomime gentle, continuous flow using your whole body, and sustain the resting tone as you move to a student. When you sprinkle the resting tone on a student, pantomime a breath gesture. Make a note of who is able to breathe and sing the resting tone.

Dance for One Part of the Body
Stand in a spot in the room where the students can see you. Remind them of the movement vocabulary that they are using at this point. Invite them to stand in self space. Tell them that you will be doing a dance for one part of the body and that they should imitate you. Say to them that you will know who has figured out which part of the body you are moving because, if they know, they will be moving just like you.

Play the recording, or sing the melody several times. Move your whole body with gentle, continuous flow, but emphasize one part of the body during each repetition. Be certain that the chosen part of the body moves through a lot of space, above, behind, and to the front and sides of you. Remember to model space at high, medium, and low levels. Keep your knees flexible as you move to encourage whole-body movement.

Sustain the Resting Tone
Invite students to sing the resting tone while they dance one body part and listen to the melody. Gesture for them to breathe at the end of each phrase. Ask them whether the melody ends on their sound. Only listen to their answers; do not expect correct answers.

JUMP RIGHT IN: THE MUSIC CURRICULUM

O LITTLE TOWN OF BETHLEHEM

Activity Type: Movement, Singing

Tonality: Major

Resting Tone:

Meter: Usual Duple

Macrobeats:

Microbeats:

 Disc Two Track 13

 Piano Bk Page 92

Keyality: F

Range: c–d'

Materials Needed: Enough space for everyone to move comfortably.

Purpose:
1. To help students learn to discriminate between same and different with movement.
2. To give students experience moving using straight (direct) and curvy (indirect) pathways in locomotor self space.

98

TEACHING PLAN
Everyone should be standing in stationary self space.

Introduce the Song
Invite the students to audiate the song and copy your movement while you sing. Sing the song while moving with continuous flow. After the students have had opportunities to hear the melody several times, change your movements to macrobeats. Ask them to continue audiating and moving the same way you move and sing the song. Change macrobeat movements for each phrase of the song. Notice which students coordinate their movements and anticipate that their movements will change at the beginnings of phrases.

Same and Different
On a different day, review the movements described above. Then invite the students to play a game. Tell them that you will sing the melody. If you move with continuous flow, they should move to beat in stationary self space. If you move to beat, they should move in stationary self space with continuous flow.

After the students experience success with you leading the movement, invite a student who is coordinated while moving to lead movement for the game. Have him or her select another leader who was successful moving differently.

Straight Pathways
Ask students to tell you what locomotor means (to travel from one spot to another). Tell them that today they will travel to new places in the room in one of two ways. Model walking using a pathway that is straight, taking you directly to another spot. Label that as a straight pathway.

Tell students that when they hear you sing the song, they should use locomotor and self space movement, using straight pathways. Remind them that every time you stop singing they should freeze. Show them how they can use straight pathways to turn corners when they run out of space as they travel in one direction. Sing the song, and observe their movements, modeling straight pathways as you sing.

Curvy Pathways
Repeat the sequence for straight pathways, this time modeling and moving in curvy pathways.

Same and Different Again!
On a different day, repeat the first same and different activity near the beginning of the Teaching Plan. Substitute locomotor, self space, or straight and curvy pathways as models for stationary, self space continuous flow and steady-beat movement. On yet a different day, you can invite students to lead the game.

JUMP RIGHT IN: THE MUSIC CURRICULUM

AWAY IN A MANAGER

Activity Type: Movement

Tonality: Major

Resting Tone:

Do

Meter: Usual Triple

Macrobeats:

Du Du

Microbeats:

Du Da Di Du Da Di

Keyality: G

Range: d–d'

Disc Two
Track 14

Piano Bk
Page 12

Materials Needed: Enough space for everyone to move comfortably.

Purpose: To help students audiate, move to, and chant macrobeats and microbeats in Usual Triple meter.

TEACHING PLAN
Everyone should be seated in self space.

Identify Macrobeats
Ask the students to listen to the song and watch as you move. Sing the song for the students while patting your lap in parallel motion to macrobeats. In your beat motion, use lots of flow and space. Tell the students that you are patting to the macrobeats of the song.

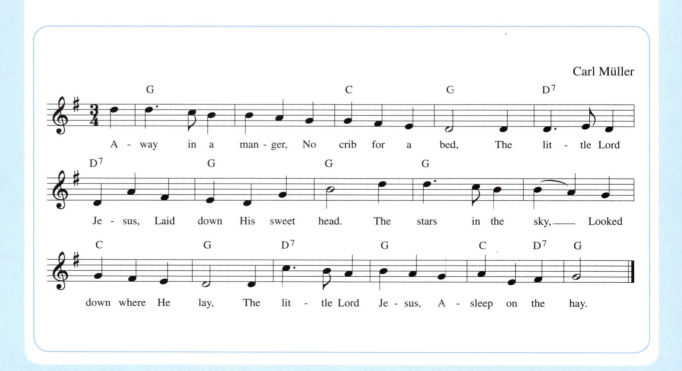

Carl Müller

A-way in a man-ger, No crib for a bed, The lit-tle Lord Je-sus, Laid down His sweet head. The stars in the sky, Looked down where He lay, The lit-tle Lord Je-sus, A-sleep on the hay.

TEACHER'S EDITION • KINDERGARTEN

Move to Macrobeats

Stand and sing the song while swaying to macrobeats. After you have completed the song, sing the following directions on the resting tone and in meter while you continue to sway: "[Insert four to five student names], please join me and sway." The students should stand beside you on either side, forming a connected line by linking elbows with the persons on either side. Continue swaying, and sing the song again. After each repetition of the song, invite more students to join the line, until the entire class is swaying in a single line in unison.

Add Microbeats

Once all of the students are swaying in unison, begin chanting microbeats using BAH as you continue to sway to macrobeats. Ask the students to continue swaying and join you in chanting. Then sing the song as the students move and chant.

FOR THE MUSIC TEACHER

In the next class period, explore whether the students can move to macrobeats and chant microbeats without being physically connected to others. Ask the students to stand and move to self space. Then ask them to sway to macrobeats as you sing the song. Watch to see which students are able to move with accuracy.

If most of the students are able to move to macrobeats with accuracy, add the chanting of microbeats using TUH, and sing the song again. If many students are struggling to move to macrobeats with accuracy, you can either provide them with an aural macrobeat cue, such as performing macrobeats gently on a hand drum, or you can ask them to sway in pairs. Place rhythmically strong students with those who are still learning to audiate and move to macrobeats.

COORDINATION WITH INSTRUMENTAL MUSIC

Play the solo flute recording of "Away in a Manger" from *Jump Right In: The Instrumental Music Series* (J199CD, track 25). Ask the students if they can identify the instrument that they heard on the recording. Then show them a picture of a flute using Instrument Card 8, and talk about the instrument. Ask the students if anyone knows how to make a sound on the flute. They should identify that it is necessary to blow into it to make a sound, which is why it is called a wind instrument.

Place a large parachute on the floor, and ask the students to stand around the outside of the parachute and hold on to its edge with both hands. Tell the students that you are going to slowly lift and lower the parachute and that they should pay careful attention to the direction that you are moving and imitate your movements. Play the flute recording, and gently guide the parachute up and down to correspond to the lengths of the phrases of the song, starting with the parachute on the ground. As each new phrase begins, you should change the direction of the movement.

SOFTLY

Activity Type: Listening, Movement

Tonality: Major

Resting Tone:

Meter: Usual Triple

Macrobeats:

Microbeats:

Keyality: D

Range: d–f-sharp

Disc Two
Track 15

Piano Bk
Page 125

Materials Needed: Enough space for everyone to move comfortably.

Purpose:
1. To help students listen.
2. To give students experience moving in a continuous, fluid style while pulsating macrobeats and microbeats in Usual Triple meter.

TEACHING PLAN

Everyone should be seated with crossed legs in self space.

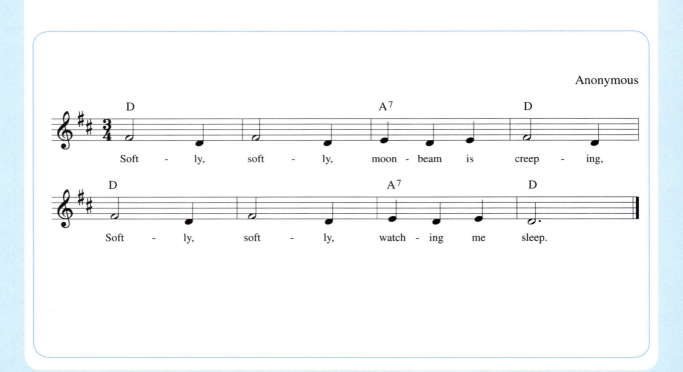

TEACHER'S EDITION • KINDERGARTEN

Listen and Move with Pulsations

Have the students copy your movements as you perform the song and bilateral microbeat pulsations with your hands. Never perform the microbeat pulsations in the same place twice in a row. Keep moving them all around on the floor, on your legs, and in the air. Use your spine to assist your use of continuous flow, being certain to keep the movement relaxed and fluid.

Repeat the song. This time, have the students copy your bilateral macrobeat pulsations.

Repeat the song. Now have the students copy your bilateral microbeat pulsations while they chant TUH to microbeats to help coordinate their tongues with their body movements. Repeat the song again, having the students copy your bilateral macrobeat pulsations while they chant BAH to aid their feeling of the difference between microbeats and macrobeats.

Bound Flow Locomotor Movement

Now tell the students to copy your tiptoe movements. Tiptoe carefully to microbeats. Have the students join you and chant TUH on each microbeat as you sing the song.

Next tell the students to copy your tiptoe movements. Tell the students that your feet are going to be getting stuck in the moonbeams. Step on the macrobeats to demonstrate how to move when your feet are getting stuck. Have the students join you by copying your movements, chanting BAH on each macrobeat as they move and as you sing the song.

Ask the students how it felt when they were tiptoeing carefully. Remind them that, when we are being careful, we are using bound flow because it is easy to stop our movements. Ask the students how it felt to move when their feet were getting stuck. Remind them that, when we are getting stuck, we are also using bound flow because it is easy to stop our movements.

JUMP RIGHT IN: THE MUSIC CURRICULUM

CHILDREN'S LULLABY

Activity Type: Singing, Solo Singing, Movement

 Disc Two Track 16

 Piano Bk Page 29

Tonality: Major

Resting Tone:

Meter: Multimetric (Usual Duple, Usual Triple)

Macrobeats:

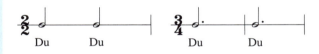

Microbeats:

Keyality: G

Range: d–b

Materials Needed: Enough space for everyone to move comfortably.

Purpose:
1. To help students audiate resting tone in Major tonality.
2. To give students an opportunity to use continuous, fluid movement.
3. To help students develop body awareness.

TEACHING PLAN

Everyone should be seated in self space.

104

TEACHER'S EDITION • KINDERGARTEN

Move with Flow

Ask the students to listen to the song and watch you move. Sing the song for them while moving your arms with flow. Ask the students to describe your movement, helping them to focus both on what body parts are moving and the quality of the movement. Ask the students to move their arms with continuous, fluid movement as you sing the song. Ask individual students to suggest a new part of the body that could be moved with flow for each repetition of the song.

Hum the Resting Tone

Hum the resting tone, and gesture for the students to join you in your humming. Sing to them that they can take a breath whenever they need one and that they should join back in with the humming. As soon as they are successfully sustaining their humming, gesture for them to continue humming as you sing the song.

Ask individual students or small groups of students to hum the resting tone while you sing the song. When doing this, make sure to adjust the volume of your voice to match that of the students.

TEACHING TIP

This Teaching Plan can be spread over two class periods. During the first class period, you can perform the movement. In the second class period, you can introduce humming on the resting tone.

TEACHING TIP

If the students have difficulty sustaining the resting tone, softly play a resting tone tremolo on an alto metallophone as an aural reference for the students. This also gives them an opportunity to observe correct tonebar instrument performance techniques and will provide readiness for their playing tonebar instruments at a later time.

105

OH, I'LL BUILD A SNOWMAN

Activity Type: Movement

Tonality: Harmonic Minor

Resting Tone:

La

Meter: Usual Triple

Macrobeats:

Du   Du

Microbeats:

Du Da Di Du Da Di

 Disc Two Track 17   Piano Bk Page 94

Keyality: D

Range: d–d'

Materials Needed: Recording. Enough space for everyone to move comfortably.

Purpose: To help students coordinate continuous, pulsating flow and chanting microbeats in Usual Triple meter.

TEACHING PLAN

Set the scene for playing in the snow. Everyone should be in standing self space in scattered formation.

Copyright © 1978 by Doug Nichol. Used by permission.

Introduce the Song, Move to Macrobeats

Ask the students to move gently like light, airy, falling snowflakes as they imitate your movements. Sing or play the recording of "Oh, I'll Build a Snowman" as you move to macrobeats. The following are suggestions for macrobeat movements: twist, rock side to side, rock front to back, push and pull, stretch up high, bend knees, or pat legs. Observe students' movements, and notice which students are bending knees and moving hips and body parts independently with flow as they audiate silently.

Move to Microbeats

Tell students that, while they have been moving to macrobeats, it has begun to snow again. Invite them to touch snowflakes with their fingertips. Ask them to audiate silently and move as you move. Chant microbeats in the tempo of the song, and move using continuous, fluid movement with pulsations to microbeats. Tell them that, each time they reach for a snowflake, they should reach in a different place in space.

Chant Microbeats

After students can coordinate their continuous, fluid movements with pulsations to microbeats to your chanting, ask them to make snowflake sounds to the microbeats. Model soft and expressive chanting, using the syllable TUH to each microbeat. Once they can chant TUH while moving, continue your movements. Change your expressive chanting to the syllable BAH to macrobeats. If they are able to chant their part while you chant BAH, have them continue as you sing the song. If necessary, play the recording and model movement without joining in the chanting.

JUMP RIGHT IN: THE MUSIC CURRICULUM

I'M A LITTLE SNOWFLAKE

Activity Type: Chanting, Solo Chanting, Movement, Rhythm Creativity

 Disc Two Track 18

 Piano Bk Page 70

Meter: Usual Duple

Macrobeats:

Microbeats:

Materials Needed: Recording. Enough space for everyone to move comfortably.

Purpose:
1. To give students experience with continuous, fluid movement.
2. To give students experience with gentle movement.
3. To allow students to explore high, middle, and low levels of space.

TEACHING PLAN
Everyone should be standing in self space.

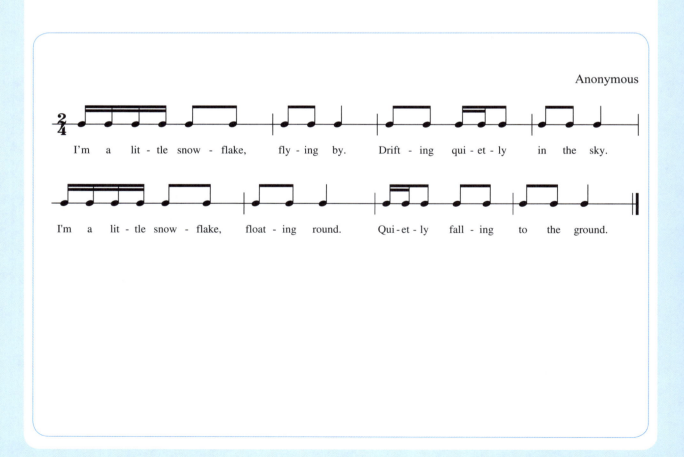

Anonymous

I'm a lit-tle snow-flake, fly-ing by. Drift-ing qui-et-ly in the sky.
I'm a lit-tle snow-flake, float-ing round. Qui-et-ly fall-ing to the ground.

Teacher's Edition • KINDERGARTEN

Listen and Discuss

Play the recording of "I'm a Little Snowflake." Discuss how a snowflake moves gently through the air and that no two snowflakes look the same. Play the recording again, and invite the students to move like snowflakes as they listen, moving with continuous, fluid movement around the classroom. Ask the students what happens to the snowflake at the end of the chant. How would they float to the ground? Would it happen suddenly or gradually? Invite the students to demonstrate how they would float to the ground. Perform the chant again, and invite students to add the new movement to the chant.

Same/Different Discrimination and Rhythm Improvisation

To extend the activity, play a same and different game at the end of the chant. Teach the students the hand signs for same (two open hands) and different (one open hand and one closed fist). Chant a duple rhythm pattern, and show a same hand sign, inviting students to chant the same pattern. Then chant another duple rhythm pattern and show a different hand sign, inviting students to improvise a pattern different from yours. Repeat the activity with the students several times. You may also give rhythm patterns to individual students and allow them to choose whether they will chant a same or different pattern.

JUMP RIGHT IN: THE MUSIC CURRICULUM

WALKING WITH MY MOM

Activity Type: Movement

Meter: Usual Duple

Macrobeats:

Microbeats:

Materials Needed: Recording. Enough space for everyone to move comfortably.

Purpose:
1. To give students experience moving in locomotor self and shared space.
2. To help students learn to discriminate whether rhythms are the same or different.

 Disc Two Track 19

 Piano Bk Page 148

TEACHING PLAN
Everyone should be seated in self space, prepared to move to standing self and shared space.

Teach or Review Labels
Stand in a place where you are not touching anyone or any object (including your book, chalk, or other item). Say, "I am standing in self space." Then move to lean against a wall or a desk and say, "I am not standing in self space." Find a new spot on the floor, again in self space. Say, "I am standing in self space." Finally, move to a place where your shoulder is touching another person's shoulder. Say, "I am not standing in self space." Then ask the students to raise their hands if they can define "self space." Encourage them to use the definition that self

Edwin E. Gordon

TEACHER'S EDITION • KINDERGARTEN

space is a place in which you are not touching anything (except the floor or the chair, your own clothes, and the air around you) or anyone (with no exceptions).

Play the Recording

Ask the students to close their eyes and listen to the recording. Ask them to audiate so they will be able to describe what they have heard. When the recording is complete, listen to students' descriptions. Guide them to realize that there are two adult voices on the recording.

Move in Locomotor Self and Shared Space

Divide the class into four groups. Invite each group, one at a time, to move in locomotor self space and then locomotor shared space. For this activity, do not use any music. Instead, observe whether students coordinate themselves and understand how to use locomotor movements in self and shared space. When students are comfortable, introduce the next partner activity.

Same and Different

Assign each student a partner. Select as many partners as you have space for movement, and invite them to stand. Tell them to move side by side in locomotor shared space when they hear the two voices on the recording.

Ask the seated students to observe their movements. After pairs are successful, invite them to decide how they would like to move to the recording. First, ask them to use only self or shared locomotor space as their choices. After all students have had an opportunity to move using that vocabulary, invite the students to show same and different using other movement vocabulary they have experienced, such as continuous flow, continuous flow with pulsations, stationary space, open and closed shapes, and quick and slow continuous flow.

JUMP RIGHT IN: THE MUSIC CURRICULUM

DARLING, GOODNIGHT

Activity Type: Singing, Solo Singing, Movement

Tonality: Aeolian

Resting Tone:

Meter: Usual Duple

Macrobeats:

Microbeats:

Keyality: E

Range: e–d'

 Disc Two Track 20

 Piano Bk Page 34

Materials Needed: Scarves. Enough space for everyone to move comfortably.

Purpose:
1. To help students audiate resting tone in Aeolian tonality.
2. To give students an opportunity to perform a tonal pattern in solo.
3. To give students experience with continuous, fluid movement, both in place and through space.

TEACHING PLAN

Everyone should be standing in self space.

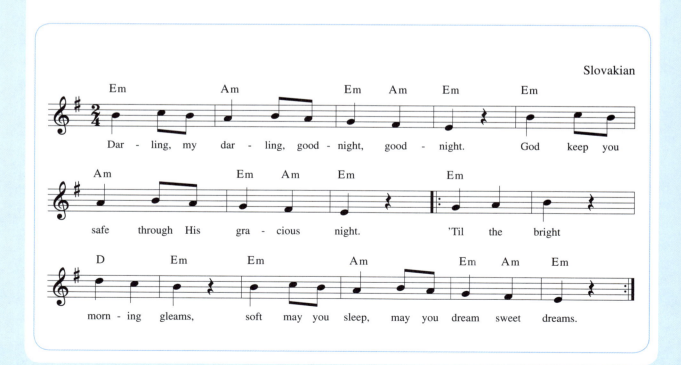

TEACHER'S EDITION • KINDERGARTEN

Move with Flow

Give every student a scarf. Tell the students that, without moving their feet, they should move their scarves with flow as you sing the song. Encourage them to use all of the space around them, including high space, low space, the space in front of them, and the space behind them. Sing the song using a neutral syllable as they move. At the end of the song, throw your scarf in the air, and sing the dominant. When the scarf lands on the ground, sing the resting tone. Ask the students to do the same. Then pick up your scarf, and repeat the entire process, this time without giving instructions.

Tell the students that now, instead of staying in one place and moving with flow, they should move with flow around the room. Demonstrate locomotor flow with a scarf for the students. Remind them that they should freeze as soon as they are done with the song. Sing the song as they move. At the end of the song, everyone should throw their scarves up and sing the dominant; when they land, they should sing resting tone as before. Repeat this process several times.

Echoing Patterns in Solo

After the students are comfortable with locomotor movement with flow, tell them that you are going to add one more thing to the activity. After all of the scarves are on the ground, you are going to tap a student gently on the shoulder. That student should echo your tonal pattern. Demonstrate with a student who you know will be successful. Your patterns should either be tonic or subtonic. Some possible patterns are notated below.

Sing the song, moving around the room with scarves as before and reinforcing resting tone at the end of the song by throwing scarves. You should move around the room with the students, positioning yourself so that, by the end of the song, you are standing near the student you would like to have sing a pattern. Gently tap that student on the shoulder, and sing a pattern. That student should echo your pattern. Repeat several times, and between each repetition of the song, have one or several students echo patterns individually.

TEACHING TIP

Allowing students opportunities to respond individually serves several purposes. First, young children sing with more accuracy when they sing alone. Second, children develop their singing voices and tonal skills more quickly if they have opportunities to hear themselves in solo. Often, children are surprised at how they sound and will adjust their solo performances to match those of the teacher. Finally, only through having children sing in solo can teachers accurately evaluate their students' singing and tonal skills. When singing with others, children can engage in split-second imitation of those singing around them. When singing alone, this is not possible, and they need to rely on their own audiation skills.

JUMP RIGHT IN: THE MUSIC CURRICULUM

YOU'LL SOUND AS WEIRD AS ME

Activity Type: Listening, Movement

Tonality: Multitonal

Resting Tone:

Meter: Usual Triple

Macrobeats:

Microbeats:

Keyality: Multikeyal

Range: d–c-sharp'

 Disc Two Track 21   Piano Bk Page 156

Materials Needed: Enough space for everyone to move comfortably.

Purpose:
1. To help students learn to listen.
2. To give students experience moving in a continuous, fluid style while pulsating microbeats in Usual Triple meter.

TEACHING PLAN
Everyone should be seated with crossed legs in self space.

Listen and Move While Seated
Tell the students that they will be listeners and movers. Remind them that listening is the most important job of each musician.

Have the students copy your movements as you perform the song or play the recording and perform bilateral microbeat pulsations with your hands. Never perform the microbeat pulsations

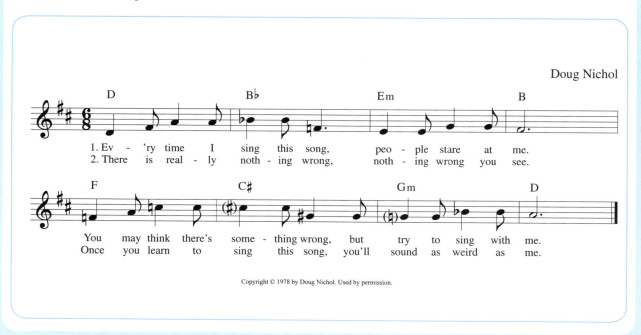

114

in the same place twice in a row. Keep moving them all around on the floor, on your legs, and in the air. Use your spine to assist your use of continuous flow, being certain to keep the movement relaxed and fluid.

Repeat the song. This time, have the students copy your bilateral macrobeat pulsations as you sing the song again.

Repeat the song again. This time as you sing the song, have the students copy your bilateral microbeat pulsations while they chant TUH to microbeats to coordinate their tongues with their body movements.

Repeat the song. Now have the students copy your bilateral macrobeat pulsations while they chant BAH to macrobeats to help them feel the differences between microbeats and macrobeats.

Stand and Rock
When students become comfortable with each type of seated movement, have them stand and rock from side to side and simultaneously chant BAH on the macrobeats. Make sure the students place the weight of their bodies on the balls of their feet and raise their heels alternately as they rock.

Stand and Pulsate
Now, as you sing the song, have the students copy your bilateral microbeat pulsations while they chant TUH to microbeats to help them coordinate their tongues with their body movements. Again, never perform the microbeat pulsations in the same place twice in a row. Keep moving them around on your legs and in the air, and use your spine to assist your use of continuous flow.

> **FOR THE MUSIC TEACHER**
> The use of TUH and BAH as neutral syllables for microbeats and macrobeats will serve as readiness for chanting using rhythm syllables at a later time. Both of these syllables are forward in the mouth, making them easy to perform. Chanting in this way helps the students coordinate their bodies with their audiation.

JUMP RIGHT IN: THE MUSIC CURRICULUM

BÍ, BÍ, OG BLAKA (FLIP, FLAP, AND FLUTT'RING)

Activity Type: Singing, Movement

Tonality: Major

Resting Tone:

Do

Meter:

Macrobeats:

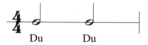
Du Du

Microbeats:

Du De Du De

Keyality: F

Range: e–d'

Disc Two
Track 22

Piano Bk
Page 20

Materials Needed: One bean bag for each student. Enough room for everyone to move comfortably.

Purpose:
1. To help students audiate resting tone in Major tonality.
2. To help students develop body awareness.

TEACHING PLAN
Everyone should be seated in self space in a circle.

Singing Resting Tone
Sing the song for the students. At the end, sing the resting tone. Breathe and gesture for the students to echo you. Tell the students that you are going to sing parts of the song and that you

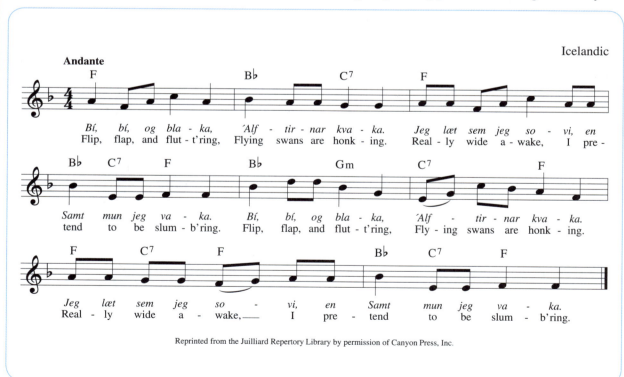

Reprinted from the Juilliard Repertory Library by permission of Canyon Press, Inc.

will pause. During the pause, you will throw a bean bag to a student and then sing the resting tone. The student who caught the bean bag should watch you for your breath and preparatory gesture. When you gesture, the student should sing the resting tone and then place the bean bag on the floor in front of him or her.

Then sing the song, pausing every two measures. During each pause, throw a bean bag to a student, sing the resting tone, gesture for the student to sing the resting tone, and continue while that student places the bean bag on the floor. Keep going until all students have a bean bag on the floor.

Moving with Bean Bags
Without speaking, gesture for the students to pick up their bean bags and place them on the back of one of their hands. Sing the first two measures of the song, moving your hand with flow, being careful not to let the bean bag fall. Then pause, take a preparatory breath, drop the bean bag on the floor, and sing the resting tone when the bean bag lands. The students should also drop their bean bags and sing the resting tone.

Silently pick up your bean bag and place it on another part of the body. Sing the next two measures of the song, pause, breathe, and drop the bean bag again, singing the resting tone when it lands. Continue singing the song, using another part of the body every two measures, and singing the resting tone each time you drop the bean bag. During the entire activity, the students should be moving and singing the resting tone like you do. However, they should not be expected to sing the song.

After you have performed the whole song in this way, you can choose students to be the leaders. They should silently show the class where to balance the bean bag for each two-measure phrase. You should still sing, breathe, and drop. However, after dropping the bean bag, you and the class will watch the leader for where the bean bag should go next.

TEACHING TIP
Using preparatory breath in music class is essential. During the preparatory breath, a musician begins to audiate what he or she is about to perform. As a result, the performance is more musical and accurate. That is why good conductors breathe with their preparatory gestures and encourage their ensembles to breathe as well. That is also why pianists and string players, although they do not play wind instruments, breathe in tempo before they begin to perform. By helping students learn to respond to a preparatory breath cue and by habituating this response, you are helping them develop their audiation skills and their overall musicianship.

JUMP RIGHT IN: THE MUSIC CURRICULUM

DANCE FROM ZALONGOU

Activity Type: Movement

Tonality: Multitonal (Natural Minor, Dorian)

Resting Tone:

Meter: Unusual Unpaired

Macrobeats:

Microbeats:

Keyality: E

Range: c-sharp–d'

 Disc Two Track 23

 Piano Bk Page 32

Materials Needed: Enough space for everyone to move comfortably.

Purpose:
1. To give students experience moving using strong and gentle, continuous flow.
2. To give students experience moving in a continuous, fluid style with macrobeat pulsations in Unusual Unpaired meter.

TEACHING PLAN

Everyone should be standing in stationary self space.

Set the Scene

Tell students that you will play a recording for them and ask them to listen and move their whole bodies using continuous flow. Remind them to stay in stationary self space.

Observe the students as they move, and notice which students are able to initiate energy from a variety of parts of the body. Compliment these students for their use of flow, staying in self space, and staying in one place. Especially compliment students who use their hips, backs, and shoulders and keep a lot of space above and behind them as they move.

Change the Air
Tell the students that the air around them is going to change into bubbles that are very fragile, and when they hear music, they should move using gentle and careful continuous flow so the bubbles will not pop. Play the recording, modeling gentle, continuous flow using your whole body. If students are not coordinating themselves, remind them to watch you and move as you are moving.

Change the air again. This time, tell the students that they are moving through oatmeal. Ask them whether they think gentle movements will help them flow through oatmeal. Tell them you will move with them using strong, continuous flow. Play the recording again. Notice the students who are not coordinating themselves as they move. If most are having difficulties, return to gentle, continuous flow.

Continue to change the air to substances such as peanut butter, mud, pudding, or sand for strong, continuous movement. Suggest sprinkled feathers, clouds, stardust, or falling snowflakes to encourage the use of gentle, continuous flow. Play the recording or perform the melody each time they move. Remind them to audiate as they move.

Continuous Flow with Pulsations
After students coordinate themselves using strong and gentle continuous, fluid movement, ask them to observe you. Sing the melody or play the recording, and move using continuous, fluid movement with pulsations of your hands to macrobeats. Invite the students to audiate the music silently and move as you move. Observe their movements as you model, and return to this activity several times on different days.

When you model pulsations, be certain not to interrupt the continuous movement. Pulsations happen through space in different places in space and can be moved to different parts of the body.

JUMP RIGHT IN: THE MUSIC CURRICULUM

THE STAR–SPANGLED BANNER

Activity Type: Listening, Movement, Singing

Tonality: Major

Resting Tone:

Meter: Usual Triple

 Disc Two Track 24

 Piano Bk Page 129

Macrobeats:

Microbeats:

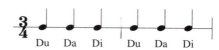

Keyality: A-flat

Range: A-flat–e-flat'

Materials Needed: Enough space for everyone to move comfortably.

Purpose:
1. To help students listen with comprehension.
2. To give students experience moving in a continuous, fluid style while pulsating to macrobeats and microbeats in Usual Triple meter.
3. To give students an opportunity to sing the resting tone.

TEACHING PLAN

Everyone should be seated with crossed legs in self space.

Listen and Move

Tell the students that they will be listeners and movers. Remind them that listening is the most important job of each musician.

Have the students copy your movements as you perform the song or play the recording and perform bilateral microbeat pulsations with your hands. Never perform the microbeat pulsations in the same place twice in a row. Keep moving them all around on the floor, on your legs, and in the air. Use your spine to assist your use of continuous flow, being certain to keep the movement relaxed and fluid.

Repeat the song. This time, have the students copy your bilateral macrobeat pulsations as you sing the song again.

Repeat the song for a third time. This time, as you sing the song, have the students copy your bilateral microbeat pulsations while they chant TUH to microbeats to help coordinate their tongues with their body movements.

Repeat the song. Now have the students copy your bilateral macrobeat pulsations while they chant BAH to macrobeats to help them feel the differences between microbeats and macrobeats.

Sing the Resting Tone

Say, "Listen to this pitch." Sing the resting tone using BUM. Sing on the resting tone, "Watch my hands, they will tell you when to breathe. Take a breath, and sing that pitch." Give the students a breath gesture for them to sing the resting tone. Sing, "Now, think that pitch." Give the students a moment to think the pitch. Sing, "Watch my hands. Take a breath and sing the pitch that you were thinking." Again, give a clear breath gesture and sing the pitch with the students. Say, "Your job is to remember that pitch."

Say, "I am going to sing the song again. Sometimes I will pause. Then I will show you when to breathe and sing the pitch you were thinking." Perform the song, and pause every few measures to give the breath gesture for the students to sing the resting tone.

COORDINATION WITH INSTRUMENTAL MUSIC

Play the solo trumpet recording of "The Star-Spangled Banner" from *Jump Right In: The Instrumental Series* (J199CD, final track). Ask the students if, without looking at the picture of the instrument, they can identify the instrument that they heard. If a student is able, ask that student how he or she knew. If they are unable to identify the instrument, show them a picture of the trumpet using Instrument Card 19. Tell the students that the trumpet is called a wind instrument because it makes a sound when you blow into it. Ask the students if they can name any other wind instruments.

Repeat the Listen and Move portion of the Teaching Plan using the trumpet rather than the vocal recording of the song.

LONDON BRIDGE

Activity Type: Singing, Solo Singing, Movement

Tonality: Major

Resting Tone:

Do

Meter: Usual Duple

Macrobeats:

Du Du

Microbeats:

Du De Du De

Keyality: D

Range: d–b

Disc Two
Track 25

Piano Bk
Page 83

Materials Needed: Hand drum. Enough space so that everyone can move comfortably.

Purpose:
1. To teach students a traditional game song.
2. To give students an opportunity to perform a tonal pattern in solo.
3. To help students audiate macrobeats in Usual Duple meter.

TEACHING PLAN
Everyone should be seated in self space.

Identify Macrobeats
Ask the students to listen to the song and watch you move. Sing the song for the students while patting your lap in bilateral motion to macrobeats. Tell the students that you are patting to the macrobeats of the song. Ask the students to join

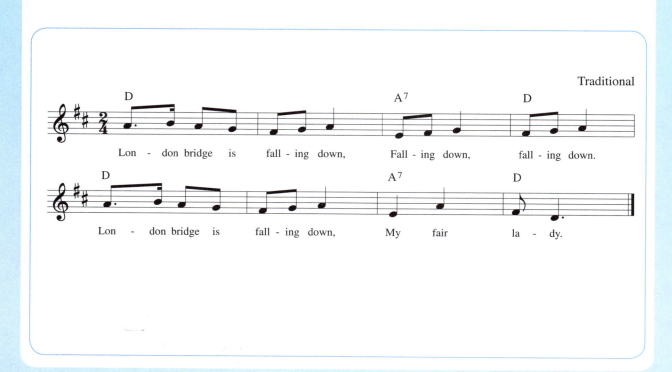

you in patting macrobeats as you sing the song again. Ask one student where else to pat macrobeats. Sing the song several more times while incorporating different student suggestions of where else to pat macrobeats.

Demonstrate moving your hands in alternating motion on the floor, as if they are walking, and ask the students to copy your movement. Sing the song again with the new movement. Then ask the students to stand and walk around the room to macrobeats, staying in self space. Lightly play the hand drum as you sing and they walk.

Play the Game
Choose two students to form a bridge by standing about two feet apart, facing one another and joining hands above their heads. Help the other students form a line on one side of the bridge, and tell them that you will lead the line. Sing the song, leading the line by walking to macrobeats under the bridge and back around so that the students are ready to go under the bridge again. This may take several times through the song and will result in the class forming a circle that walks under the bridge.

Tell the two students who form the bridge that their bridge should fall (their hands should lower) on the word "lady" and capture a student between their arms. You should sing a tonic or dominant pattern, and the student who is captured should echo that pattern and replace one of the students forming the bridge. The student being replaced should join the line going under the bridge. For each repetition of the song, a different student should be captured, sing, and take his or her place as part of the bridge.

FOR THE MUSIC TEACHER
This activity can be used for several purposes. The student who is caught could echo a four-macrobeat rhythm pattern rather than echoing a tonal pattern. The student could also sing the resting tone.

This activity can also be used as a means of having students create tonal patterns. You could ask the student who is captured to sing a tonal pattern that is different from yours rather than echoing you. Another option is to sing a short antecedent phrase in Major tonality with the student singing a short consequent phrase. If you choose to do this, tell the students that you will start the song and that the caught student should finish it.

JUMP RIGHT IN: THE MUSIC CURRICULUM

TOSS AND CATCH

Activity Type: Movement, Singing

Tonality: Aeolian

Resting Tone:

La

Meter: Usual Duple

Macrobeats:

Microbeats:

Keyality: D

Range: c–d'

 Disc Two Track 26

 Piano Bk Page 142

Materials Needed: Enough space for everyone to move comfortably.

Purpose:
1. To give students experience moving in a continuous, fluid style while pulsating microbeats.
2. To help students discriminate between tonal patterns that are the same or different.

TEACHING PLAN
Everyone should be seated in self space.

Listen and Move
Sing the song a few times, and have the students copy your movements as you sing and perform bilateral microbeat pulsations with your hands. Never perform the microbeat pulsations in the

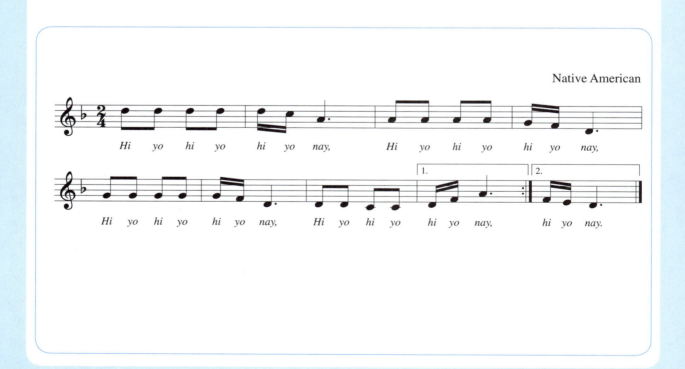

124

same place twice in a row. Keep moving them all around on the floor, on your legs, and in the air. Use your spine to assist your use of continuous flow, being certain to keep the movement relaxed and fluid.

Imitate and Identify Same and Different Tonal Patterns

Sing the following tonal pattern on BUM. Give the students a breath gesture, and have them repeat the pattern.

Sing the following tonal pattern using BUM. Give the students a breath gesture, and have them repeat the pattern.

Tell the students to listen as you sing the first pattern and the second pattern again. Tell the students that the two patterns are different. Have the students hold up two hands that are different (one open and one closed) and repeat the word "different."

Sing the first pattern, and then repeat it. Tell the students the two patterns are the same. Have the students hold up two hands that are same (both open or both closed), and repeat the word "same."

Play a same or different game using the two patterns. Have the students show you with their hands whether the two patterns you perform are the same or different.

Tell the students that the tonal patterns are in the song you sang earlier. The first pattern is heard at the end of the first repetition. Instruct the students that you will sing the song for them, but it will be their responsibility to sing the first pattern when you gesture to them to sing. Sing the song, and give the breath gesture when the first pattern occurs in the song. Repeat this process with the second pattern.

FIVE LITTLE SPECKLED FROGS

Activity Type: Singing, Movement, Tonal Creativity

Tonality: Major

Resting Tone:

Meter: Usual Duple

Macrobeats:

Microbeats:

Keyality: D

Range: d–e'

 Disc Two Track 27

 Piano Bk Page 54

Materials Needed: Frog puppet. Recording. Enough space for everyone to move comfortably.

Purpose:
1. To help students audiate and sing resting tone in Major tonality.
2. To model an audiation breath.
3. To give students an opportunity to improvise tonal patterns in Major tonality.

TEACHING PLAN

Everyone should be standing in self space.

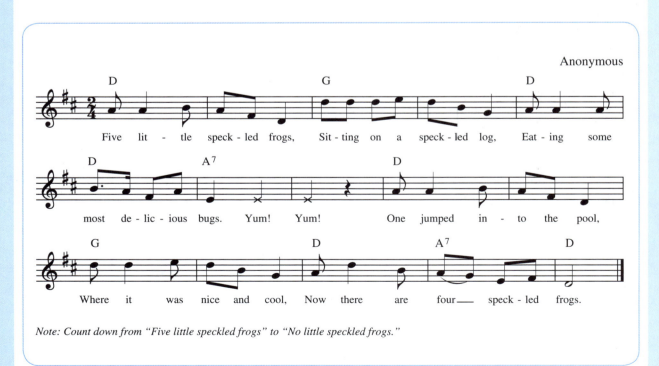

Note: Count down from "Five little speckled frogs" to "No little speckled frogs."

TEACHER'S EDITION • KINDERGARTEN

Singing and Jumping

Play the recording of "Five Little Speckled Frogs." Model patting microbeats on your thighs in bilateral motion for the students. Play the recording again, and invite them to pat microbeats along with you. At the end of the song, take a big jump while singing the fifth scale degree, and then sing the resting tone when you land. Be sure to model taking a breath before jumping. Invite the students to do the same at the end of each repetition of the song.

Resting Tone

To extend the activity, use a frog puppet or stuffed animal. Sing the song again, and stop in the middle. Using the puppet, model singing the resting tone in the middle of the song. Invite the students to sing the resting tone with the frog puppet each time the song stops. Be sure to model taking a breath before singing the resting tone.

Tonal Improvisation

At the end of the song, sing various tonic and dominant patterns in Major tonality. Use the frog puppet to model the same and different tonal patterns by having the frog sing to you. Following each pattern that "the frog performs," either create a pattern or imitate the pattern that was performed by the frog. Invite your students to sing patterns back to the frog also. Allow them to choose whether they will sing a same or different tonal pattern. Invite the class to discriminate whether an individual student sang the same or a different tonal pattern by using hand signs (two open hands for same, and one open and one closed hand for different).

127

HORSES

Activity Type: Singing, Movement

Tonality: Major

Resting Tone:

Meter: Multimetric (Usual Duple, Usual Triple)

Macrobeats:

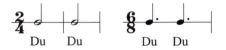

Microbeats:

Disc Two
Track 28

Piano Bk
Page 66

Keyality: G

Range: d–d'

Materials Needed: Enough space so that everyone can move comfortably.

Purpose: To help students audiate meter through movement.

TEACHING PLAN
Everyone should be seated in self space.

Identify Macrobeats and Microbeats

Sing the song for the students, patting your lap in parallel motion to macrobeats. Ask the students whether the macrobeat stays the same or changes. They should discover that the macrobeat stays constant throughout the song. Invite the students to pat their laps to microbeats as you perform the song again. Then ask the students to determine whether the microbeats stay the same or change. Sing the song again, patting your lap to microbeats. The students should discover that they change. (They are faster in the triple meter portion of the song.) Ask the students to pat their laps to microbeats as you sing the song again.

Move in Space

Ask the students, "What kinds of movements are made by the horses in the song?" They should identify walking and galloping. Ask the students to stand and walk to macrobeats during the first part of the song and to gallop during the second part of the song. Remind them that, although they are moving around the room, they should remain in self space. This means that they should not touch anyone. Sing the song through several times, with the students changing their movements at the appropriate time. Sing the song without the text, and see if the students still change their movements at the appropriate point in the song.

TEACHING TIP

If the students have begun using rhythm syllables, you can have them chant the microbeats of the song using syllables while they pat their laps to microbeats. You also can identify the meters that are used in the song and remind them that when they are audiating Du De as microbeats they are in Usual Duple meter, and when they are audiating Du Da Di as microbeats, they are in Usual Triple meter.

JUMP RIGHT IN: THE MUSIC CURRICULUM

EVERYBODY DO THIS!

Activity Type: Movement, Singing, Chanting

Tonality: Major

Resting Tone:

Meter: Usual Duple

Macrobeats:

Microbeats:

Keyality: G

Range: d–b

 Disc Two Track 29

 Piano Bk Page 47

Materials Needed: Enough space for everyone to move comfortably.

Purpose:
1. To help the students learn to coordinate movement with teacher's music.
2. To help the students learn to coordinate movement with their own singing.

TEACHING PLAN
Everyone should be in standing self space.

Introduce the Song
Tell the students that you will sing the song several times. Invite them to audiate silently and copy your movement. Tell them to watch for changes in the movements each time you begin the song.

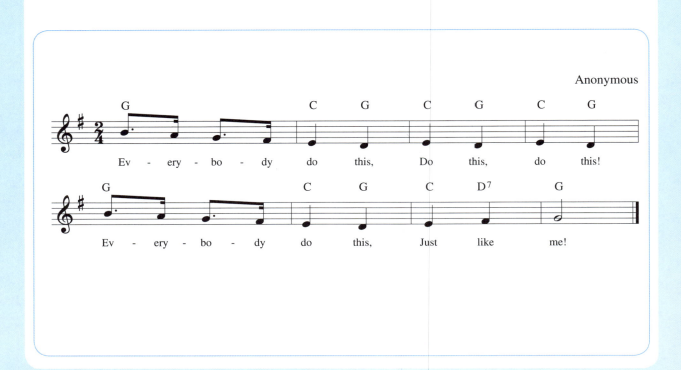

Sing and move using the suggested order, changing the movement quality with each repetition of the song: continuous flow, continuous flow with pulsations to microbeats, large movement to macrobeats (twist, stretch, bend, bounce, rock, push/pull), small movement only to macrobeats (put macrobeats in your heels), small movement only to microbeats (put microbeats in your fingertips as you pat your thighs), and movement to macrobeats and microbeats together.

Observe which students are coordinating the different types of movements. If students have difficulties with a certain type of movement, return to this activity on a different day and model all of the movements suggested previous to the troublesome one. You can use this sequence of movements to other music, too.

Sing and Move

After the students have heard the song many times, invite them to sing the melody as they move. Sing the preparatory sequence notated on this page, and give a breath gesture on the final macrobeat of the sequence. Do not sing with students.

Bum Bum Bum   Read-y Sing

Model continuous flow using your whole body while the students sing. If they have difficulties singing alone, compliment their efforts, but do not drill and practice the melody. Come back to it another day.

If students are singing well as they move with continuous flow, invite them to add pulsations to their flow as they sing. Continue through the list of suggested movements on different days. Notice which students are able to coordinate their moving, their breathing, and their singing.

SWING A LADY

Activity Type: Circle Game

Tonality: Mixolydian

Resting Tone:

So

Meter: Usual Duple

Macrobeats:

Du   Du

Microbeats:

Du De Du De

Keyality: F

Disc Two
Track 30

Piano Bk
Page 134

Range: c–e-flat'

Materials Needed: Enough space for everyone to stand in a circle.

Purpose:
1. To give students experience moving to macrobeats in Usual Duple meter.
2. To give students an opportunity to participate in a circle game.
3. To give students experience with Mixolydian tonality.

TEACHING PLAN

Everyone should be standing in a circle.

Play the Game

Ask the students to stand in a circle with one arm extended in front of them, making a fist with the extended arm. Walk around the inside of the circle, tapping each student's fist to macrobeats while singing the song. At the conclusion of the refrain, touch the fists of the two students closest to you. Those two students will need to sit down in place in the circle until the conclusion of the game. However, before they sit down, gesture for each to breathe and echo a four-macrobeat rhythm pattern in solo.

Repeat this process, eliminating two students for each performance of the song. Continue until you have one or two students left or you want to move on to another activity. The students left standing are the winners of the game.

TEACHING TIP

You can provide a reward to the winners. For example, the winners of the game might be allowed to choose an instrument at the end of class to play while everyone else is lining up at the door. Alternately, the winners may be given a special task, such as collecting rhythm sticks or bean bags in another activity.

JUMP RIGHT IN: THE MUSIC CURRICULUM

DANCING BEAR

Activity Type: Listening, Movement

Tonality: Major

Resting Tone:

Do

Meter: Usual Duple

Macrobeats:

Microbeats:

Keyality: D

Range: c-sharp–b

 Disc Two Track 31

 Piano Bk Page 32

Materials Needed: Recording. Enough space for everyone to move comfortably.

Purpose:
1. To give students experience with macrobeats and microbeats in Usual Triple meter.
2. To give students an opportunity to explore high, middle, and low levels of space.
3. To identify and label ABA form.

TEACHING PLAN

Everyone should be seated in self space.

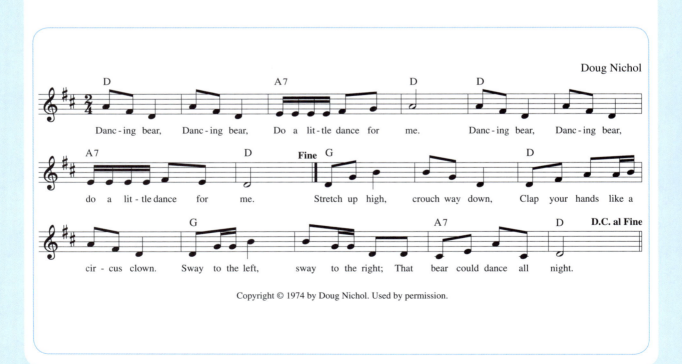

Copyright © 1974 by Doug Nichol. Used by permission.

134

Listen and Identify

Play the recording of "Dancing Bear." Tell the students that there are two sections of the song. If students demonstrate readiness, you may label the two sections as A and B. Play the recording again, and ask which of the two sections is repeated. Guide students to identify the pattern (form) in the song as ABA.

Move

Sing the song for students while quietly patting the microbeats throughout the A section. Invite students to pat the microbeats with you. Ask the students what movements the bear might make in the B section. Ask the students to demonstrate how they would stretch high or crouch down low. Invite the students to make the same movements as the bear in the B section. Ask them to predict what movement they will do when the A section returns. Sing the song again to allow the students to perform the movements for each section of the song.

LISTENING LESSON

Everyone should be seated in self space. Tell the students that you are going to play a recording and that they should listen and be prepared to describe how the music sounds when the recording is over. Play the instrumental recording of "Dance of the Jesters" by Piotor Tchaikovsky (Disc Two, Track 32), arranged by Ray Cramer. After listening to the recording, lead the class discussion through listening and questioning to help the students realize that the music is fast, bouncy, and light.

This discussion can be far-ranging, including instrumentation, mood, tempo, volume, and any other aspects of the music the children notice. Write key music vocabulary words on the board as they arise in the discussion. Even though kindergarten students may not have sophisticated vocabulary, engaging in musical discussions will help them learn how to talk about music.

Ask the students to move to standing self space. Tell them that you want them to move with continuous flow with their bodies and flick their hands to macrobeats as they move. Demonstrate this movement, being certain to engage your whole body in the continuous flow. Play the recording, and watch the students move to see which students are able to coordinate their movements with the music.

YANGTZE BOATMEN'S CHANTEY

Activity Type: Movement, Singing

Tonality: Aeolian

Resting Tone:

La

Meter: Usual Duple

Macrobeats:

Du Du

Microbeats:

Du De Du De

Keyality: G

Range: g–d'

Disc Two
Track 33

Piano Bk
Page 155

Materials Needed: A long rope. Enough space for everyone to move comfortably.

Purpose:
1. To give students an opportunity to experience Aeolian tonality.
2. To help students audiate and sing the resting tone in Aeolian tonality.
3. To give students an opportunity to feel macrobeats in Usual Duple meter.

TEACHING PLAN

Everyone should be sitting in self space in a circle.

Singing Resting Tone

Slowly and with heaviness, sing the song using the English text. Then sing the resting tone. Take a preparatory breath as you gesture for the students to echo you. Then tell the students that you want them to remember the resting tone

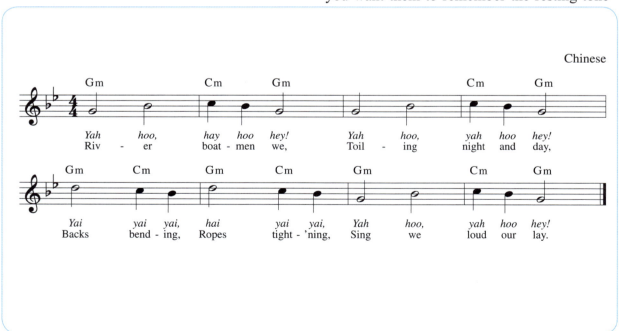

because you are going to ask them to sing it again when you finish singing the song. Sing the song again in the same style, and then breathe and gesture for the students to sing the resting tone. If they need help, model it for them again and repeat the process. Make sure most of the students can do this before continuing with the Teaching Plan.

Movement

Place a thick rope at the center of the circle, and hold one end of it with both hands. (Ideally, the rope will be the thickness of gymnasium climbing rope.) Place one foot in front of the other for stability, and rock forward and backward to macrobeats as you sing the song. Ask the students to describe your movement. Then tell them that you are going to ask them to join you in moving with the rope.

At the end of the song, you will walk around and gesture for individual students to sing the resting tone. After singing the resting tone, each one should stand behind you and hold the rope. When you begin singing again, they should copy your rocking movement. Sing the song several times, and have several students sing the resting tone individually and join the students holding the rope between each performance of the song. Eventually, all of the students should be in a line, holding the rope and rocking forward and backward to macrobeats (with you as the leader at the front of the rope) as you sing the song.

TEACHING TIP

If students have difficulty singing the resting tone individually or as a group, you can adapt the Teaching Plan slightly to provide more support. Rather than having students remember the resting tone and sing it from audiation, you could sing it for them each time immediately before asking them to sing it. This way, they will have the opportunity to imitate it rather than audiate it, and imitation is readiness for audiation. Also, when asking individuals to sing the resting tone, you can sing along with them when they echo you so that they can simultaneously compare their performance with yours.

TEACHING TIP

If you cannot find a rope for this activity, you can still teach it by placing students in seated pairs, each holding the ends of two rhythm sticks, one in each hand. Then, instead of rocking in one long standing line, the students would rock in seated pairs. As you will not be sharing a rope with the students, you may want to play macrobeats lightly on a hand drum to provide rhythmic support. Also, you should pair rhythmically weaker students with those who are rhythmically strong so that each pair is successful.

BLOW THE MAN DOWN

Activity Type: Movement

Tonality: Major

Resting Tone:

Meter: Usual Triple

Macrobeats:

Microbeats:

Keyality: D

 Disc Two Track 34

 Piano Bk Page 24

Range: c-sharp–b

Materials Needed: Recording. Enough space for everyone to move comfortably.

Purpose:
1. To give students experience with macrobeats and microbeats in Usual Triple meter.
2. To give students an opportunity to move in shared space.
3. To give students an opportunity to create macrobeat movement in shared space.

TEACHING PLAN

Everyone should be seated in self space.

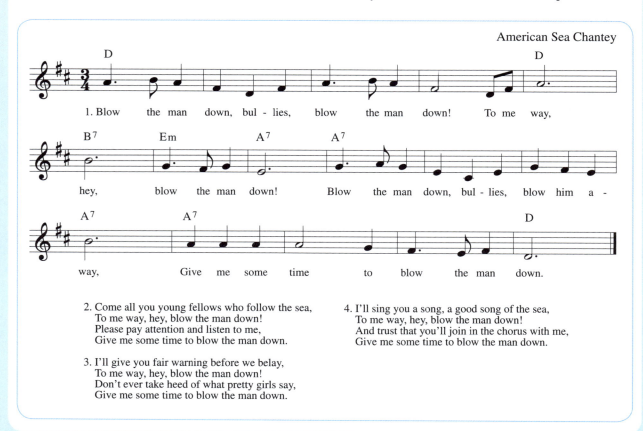

American Sea Chantey

1. Blow the man down, bul-lies, blow the man down! To me way, hey, blow the man down! Blow the man down, bul-lies, blow him a-way, Give me some time to blow the man down.

2. Come all you young fellows who follow the sea,
   To me way, hey, blow the man down!
   Please pay attention and listen to me,
   Give me some time to blow the man down.

3. I'll give you fair warning before we belay,
   To me way, hey, blow the man down!
   Don't ever take heed of what pretty girls say,
   Give me some time to blow the man down.

4. I'll sing you a song, a good song of the sea,
   To me way, hey, blow the man down!
   And trust that you'll join in the chorus with me,
   Give me some time to blow the man down.

TEACHER'S EDITION • KINDERGARTEN

Model and Move
Play the recording of the "Blow the Man Down." Model patting microbeats quietly on your lap. Play the song again, and invite students to pat the microbeats to the song. At the conclusion of the song, tell the students you are going to move to a different beat. If the students demonstrate readiness, you may choose to label them as the macrobeats. Play or sing the song again, and pat the macrobeats on your lap. Invite the students to pat the macrobeats with you.

Move with a Partner
To extend the activity, tell the students they are going to move to macrobeats again, but this time using a different movement. Using a student or classroom assistant as your partner, model rowing back and forth to macrobeats. Invite the students to pair up with a partner and move the same way. Sing the song again while the students move. After several repetitions, invite the students to create their own macrobeat movements with their partners.

COORDINATION WITH INSTRUMENTAL MUSIC
Play the solo trombone recording of "Blow the Man Down" from *Jump Right In: The Instrumental Series* (J299CD, track 28). Ask the students if any of them can identify the instrument on the recording. Show them a picture of the trombone using Instrument Card 23. Talk about the instrument with the students. Help them discover that it is made of metal, which is why it is a member of the brass family, and that it makes a sound when you blow into it, which is why it is called a wind instrument.

Repeat the Teaching Plan, this time using the trombone recording rather than the vocal recording of the song.

JUMP RIGHT IN: THE MUSIC CURRICULUM

BLOW THE WINDS SOUTHERLY

Activity Type: Singing, Solo Singing, Movement

Tonality: Major

Resting Tone:

Do

Meter: Usual Triple

Macrobeats:

Du   Du

Microbeats:

Du Da Di Du Da Di

Keyality: F

Range: f–c'

 Disc Two Track 35   Piano Bk Page 26

Materials Needed: Co-op band. Enough space so that everyone can move comfortably.

Purpose:
1. To give students experience with macrobeats in Usual Triple meter.
2. To give students an opportunity to sing in solo.
3. To help students audiate tonic and dominant pitches in Major tonality.

TEACHING PLAN
Everyone should be seated in self space in a circle.

140

Sing Resting Tone

Using a neutral syllable, sing the song for the students. Then sing the resting tone; give the students a preparatory breath and gesture for them to echo you. Tell them that you are going to sing the song again, but during the song you will stop and gesture for either all of the students or just one student to sing the resting tone. Sing the song, and pause after two measures. Using two hands, gesture to the entire class to sing the resting tone. Then, at the end of the song, gesture, using a single hand, for a student to sing the resting tone. Repeat this several times, using two hands to indicate that all students should sing and one hand to indicate that one student should sing.

Use the Co-op (Stretchy) Band

Put the co-op band in the middle of the circle, and ask everyone to hold on, stretching the band so that everyone uses both hands. Sing the song, and move the co-op band in small circles toward and away from your body, with one revolution per macrobeat. If they have not done so already, ask the students to join you in performing the macrobeat movement as you sing the song again. At the end of the song, lean back and stretch the co-op band while you sing the dominant. Sit back straight, and sing the resting tone. Repeat several times.

TEACHING TIP

The co-op band, which is a large stretchy band that forms a loop, is an excellent teaching tool, both tonally and rhythmically. Rhythmically, you can use it to connect students physically as in the Teaching Plan so that those who do not feel the beat are helped along by those who do. Tonally, the tension and release created by stretching the co-op band and then releasing it mirrors the tonal tension and release that is created when resolving dominant function to tonic.

FOR THE MUSIC TEACHER

This song can also be used to help students explore their use of breath. Ask the students to lie on their backs on the floor. After each performance of the song, ask the students to take as big a breath as they can when you say "breathe." Then, when you say "exhale," they should hiss to let their breath out until they are completely empty of breath. Before the students try this, you may want to demonstrate. You can accompany their exhalation with a rain stick to help them get a sense of the sustained sound that you want. Repeat several times, singing the song between each breath.

TSAMICO DANCE

Activity Type: Movement, Singing, Rhythm Creativity, Chanting

Tonality: Hungarian Minor

Resting Tone:

Meter: Usual Triple

Macrobeats:

Microbeats:

Keyality: A

Range: e–e'

Disc Two Track 36
Piano Bk Page 142

Materials Needed: Enough space for everyone to move comfortably.

Purpose:
1. To experience a song from Greece.
2. To create rhythm patterns in Usual Triple meter.
3. To experience an unusual tonality.
4. To experience macrobeats and microbeats in Usual Triple meter.

TEACHING PLAN

Everyone should be standing in self space.

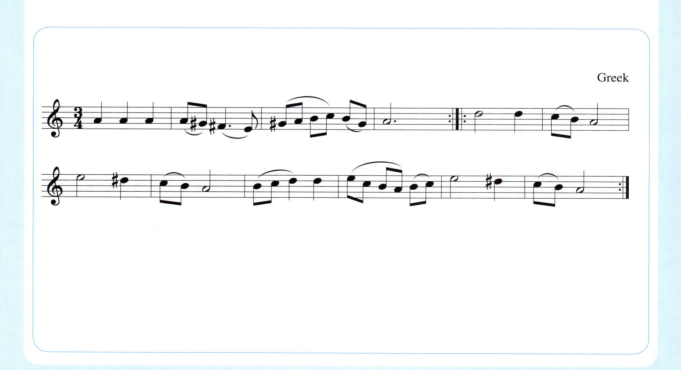

Move and Listen
Sing the song, and sway to macrobeats. Ask the students to imitate your movements.

While swaying again, sing the song and use "spider fingers" on your legs to tap to microbeats. Ask the students to imitate your movements.

Imitate Patterns
Using BAH, chant a four-beat rhythm pattern in Usual Triple meter in the tempo of the song and gesture for the students to imitate your pattern. Chant two or three different four-macrobeat rhythm patterns, and have the students imitate you. Then chant additional patterns, and gesture to individuals to imitate your rhythm patterns. Following are some sample patterns.

TEACHING TIP
Move continuously as you chant patterns, and encourage students to do the same. This will help them to keep a consistent tempo and feel the length of the space between macrobeats.

Create Patterns
Sing the song again. Tell them that you are going to ask them to make up a pattern that is not the same as your pattern. Perform a four-beat rhythm pattern, and have the students create new rhythm patterns in response. They will all be chanting different patterns at the same time, which, although a bit confusing, will give them the safety of not being heard. Then call on individuals to perform the rhythm patterns that they have created.

Sing the song again. Have individual students create a new rhythm pattern using BAH after each repetition of the song. The entire class should imitate each student's created pattern.

JUMP RIGHT IN: THE MUSIC CURRICULUM

WILL WINTER END?

Activity Type: Movement, Singing

Tonality: Phrygian

Resting Tone:

Meter: Usual Duple

Macrobeats:

Microbeats:

Range: d–e-flat'

Materials Needed: Two scarves or streamers per person. Enough space for everyone to move comfortably.

 Disc Two Track 37

 Piano Bk Page 154

Purpose:
1. To give students experience with moving to a place in standing self space.
2. To give students experience moving using strong and gentle continuous flow.
3. To help students audiate the resting tone and tonal patterns in Phrygian tonality.

TEACHING PLAN
Everyone should be seated in self space.

Find an Empty Spot on the Floor
Tell the students to use their eyes to find an empty spot on the floor while you sing a song for them. Remind them that an empty spot has no furniture, no people, and no objects in it and has room only to be filled by one person. Tell the students that, if they have found an empty spot on the floor when you reach the end of the song, they should make an open shape (see "The Squirrel" for the definition of open

Cheryl Meade

Cold, ic-y winds blow a-cross my nose, I'm real-ly froz-en down to my toes. Right now I'm read-y for the spring, 'Til then I'll have this song to sing.

144

and closed shapes) as they are seated. Remind the students that someone else may have already selected that space and that they should then remain in self space and move to an alternate spot.

Move to Standing, Stationary Self Space

Tell the students that when you begin singing they are to move to their empty spots on the floor as if they were walking through a cold, icy wind. Ask them to use strong, continuous flow as they move. (If this is the first time students have done this, you might consider asking only a few students to move at a time.) For management purposes, tell them that if you stop singing at any time, they are to freeze, even if they are not yet in their spots. When they are frozen, you can repeat your instructions or help them as needed.

Establish Tonality

When all students are seated in their spots, ask them to audiate silently. Establish tonality using the sequence of tones notated below. Then sing the resting tone using BUM, and gesture for students to breathe and sing it after you.

Ask students to imitate your movement and listen to the words of the song. When you finish, sing questions about the lyrics of the song on the resting tone. Structure your questions so that the answers are one word. Gesture for the class to breathe and sing their answers. Breathe and sing the answer on the resting tone. For example, you might sing, "Is the weather hot in the song?" Then you would breathe and sing "No" with them on the resting tone. Or you might ask, "Is the wind blowing in this song?" in which case you would breathe and sing "Yes" with them on the resting tone.

Distribute Scarves with Resting Tones or Patterns

Tell the students that it has begun to snow scarves. Ask them to keep the scarves snowing by moving them with gentle, continuous flow. Sing the song, stopping the song to sing the resting tone as you drop a scarf on a student.

Prepare the students for three possibilities: At the end of the song, you might (1) sing the resting tone and gesture for everyone to sing, (2) sing the resting tone and gesture for only one person to sing, or (3) sing patterns for everyone to audiate silently. Remind them to watch you so they will know what to do. In any case, remind the students to audiate, move, and breathe. Breathe and gesture each time you finish the song.

ROLL THAT BIG BALL DOWN TO TOWN

Activity Type: Movement, Singing

Tonality: Major

Resting Tone:

Do

Meter: Usual Duple

Macrobeats:

Du   Du

Microbeats:

Du De Du De

Keyality: G

Range: d–d'

Materials Needed: Enough space for everyone to move comfortably.

Disc Three
Track 1

Piano Bk
Page 111

Purpose:
1. To give students experience moving in a continuous, fluid style while pulsating microbeats.
2. To give students an opportunity to imitate tonal patterns.

TEACHING PLAN ONE
Everyone should be seated in self space.

Listen and Move
Sing the song without words, and ask the students to copy your movements. While you sing, use your hands to pulsate microbeats. Never perform them in the same place twice. Keep moving them all around on the floor, on your legs, and in the air. Sing the song once more without words, and have the students copy your macrobeat movements. Use your spine to assist your use of continuous flow, keeping the movement relaxed and fluid.

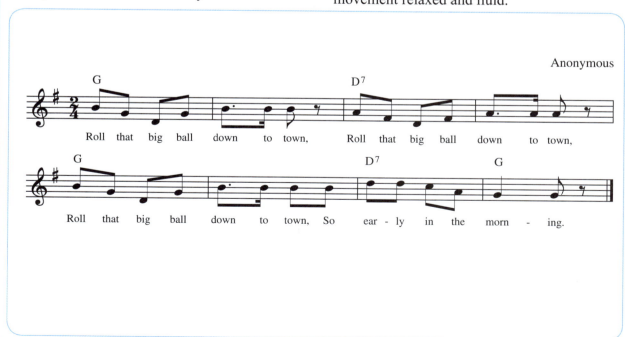

Imitate and Identify Tonal Patterns

Sing the following tonal pattern using the neutral syllable BUM. Give the students a breath gesture and, have them repeat the pattern.

Tell the students that this is the first tonal pattern of the song. Sing the tonal pattern again. Give the students a breath gesture, and have them repeat the tonal pattern again.

Sing the following tonal pattern using the neutral syllable BUM. Give the students a breath gesture, and have them repeat the pattern.

Tell the students that this pattern is the first tonal pattern of the second phrase. Sing the second tonal pattern again. Give the students a breath gesture, and have them repeat the second pattern again.

Tell the students you will sing the song again without words and that you will show them when the first tonal pattern and the second tonal pattern appear. You will hold up one finger for the first tonal pattern and two fingers for the second tonal pattern. Tell the students to copy your hand signs. Tell them that the first tonal pattern will appear twice. Challenge them to predict its second appearance.

Sing the song without words. Hold up one finger as you sing the first and fifth measures. Hold up two fingers as you sing the third measure.

Finish by having the students sing the song without words.

ROLL THAT BIG BALL DOWN TO TOWN (continued)

TEACHING PLAN TWO

Activity Type: Movement

Materials Needed: Enough space for everyone to move comfortably.

Purpose:
1. To move give students experiencing moving in a continuous, fluid style while pulsating microbeats.
2. To give students experience with strong and gentle movement.

Everyone should be seated in self space.

Listen and Move

Sing the song without words, and have the students copy your movements. While you sing, use your hands to pulsate microbeats. Never perform them in the same place twice. Keep moving them all around on the floor, on your legs, and in the air. Use your spine to assist your use of continuous flow, being certain to keep the movement relaxed and fluid. Sing the song again without words, and have the students copy your microbeat movements.

Add the Effort of Shape

The song lyrics tell students to "Roll that big ball down to town." Create a big, imaginary ball out of space as if you were a pantomime artist. Have the students copy your movements so that each student will have his or her own big ball. Now, in self space, ask the students to roll their imaginary balls each time you sing the word "roll" in the song. Lift the imaginary balls high into the air as you sing the last phrase, "So early in the morning." Repeat your singing and the movement.

Now ask the students to create a tiny imaginary ball. Have the students copy your movements so that each student will have his or her own tiny ball. Now, in self space, roll those imaginary balls each time you sing the word "roll." Lift the imaginary balls high into the air as you sing the last phrase, "So early in the morning." Repeat your singing and the movement.

Add the Effort of Weight

Recreate the imaginary big balls. Tell the students that this time they will be really heavy. Ask them to use all of their strength to roll their imaginary balls each time you sing the word "roll." Tell them they will need even more strength to lift their imaginary balls high into the air as you sing the last phrase, "So early in the morning." Repeat.

Recreate their imaginary tiny balls. Tell them that this time their balls will be really light. Without needing to be strong, they should roll their tiny imaginary balls each time you sing the word "roll." Tell them that they should lift their imaginary balls high into the air easily as you sing the last phrase, "So early in the morning." Repeat.

Repeat the activity, this time creating big imaginary balls that are very light. Then repeat the activity imagining tiny balls that are very heavy.

JUMP RIGHT IN: THE MUSIC CURRICULUM

HANI KOUNI

Activity Type: Movement, Singing

Tonality: Aeolian

Resting Tone:

Meter: Usual Duple

Macrobeats:

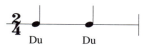

Microbeats:

Keyality: D

Range: c–a

Disc Three
Track 2

Piano Bk
Page 62

Materials Needed: Enough space for everyone to move comfortably.

Purpose:
1. To give students experience with continuous, fluid movement.
2. To give students experience moving to macrobeats and microbeats in Usual Duple meter.
3. To share a Native American song.
4. To share a song with repeated phrases.

TEACHING PLAN

Everyone should be standing in stationary self space.

TEACHER'S EDITION • KINDERGARTEN

Sing and Move

Tell the students to observe and copy your movements. Although you will be using locomotor space, ask the students to remain in stationary space. Sing the song several times as you move among the students using continuous, fluid movement. Remember to flow with body parts other than arms only.

When you have finished the song, stand in stationary space. Sing the song again, and move to microbeats. Tap your thighs with your fingertips.

When you finish the second repetition of the song, sing it a third time, and move with continuous flow through locomotor space as you did before. Alternate between flow and beat in the subsequent repetitions of the song.

Extend the Activity

The following are several ways you can extend the activity in subsequent class periods.

1. Tell students that during the first continuous, fluid movement section you will tap a few students on their shoulders as you pass. They should be prepared to join you in locomotor movement using continuous, fluid movement the next time you travel using that movement style (for example, third, fifth, seventh repetitions of the song). Continue until all students have had a turn moving with continuous flow. Everyone should move to microbeats with you on the even repetitions of the song.

2. Instead of moving to microbeats during the second repetition, move to macrobeats using large and then bilateral stationary movements.

3. If the students coordinate themselves during microbeat and macrobeat movement, model simultaneous microbeat and macro-beat movement during the alternate repetitions. Put macrobeats in your heels and microbeats in your fingertips as you pat your thighs.

4. Invite a student to select which kind of movements to perform during the second repetition. Also, when students are ready, invite them to move using locomotor space when they move with continuous flow during alternate sections.

Sing the Song

After the students have heard the song and moved to it several times (on different days), invite them to be your echoes. Because the song has repeated phrases, you can "share the song" with them. Sing the first phrase, giving the students a breath gesture on the final macrobeat of that phrase. Continue this for each of the three phrases. If the students are audiating your phrases, later invite them to begin the phrases so you can be their echo.

151

SCANDINAVIAN FOLK SONG

Activity Type: Movement

Tonality: Harmonic Minor

Resting Tone:

La

Meter: Usual Triple

Macrobeats:

Du   Du

Microbeats:

Du Da Di Du Da Di

Keyality: G

Range: d–d'

Disc Three
Track 3

Piano Bk
Page 114

Materials Needed: Enough space for everyone to move comfortably.

Purpose:
To give students experience moving to macrobeats and microbeats in Usual Triple meter.

TEACHING PLAN
Everyone should be standing in self space.

Listen and Move
Sing the song, or play the recording. Sway from side to side to macrobeats as you and the students listen. Ask the students to imitate your movements. Then sing the song or play the recording again, and walk to microbeats. Ask the students to imitate your movements.

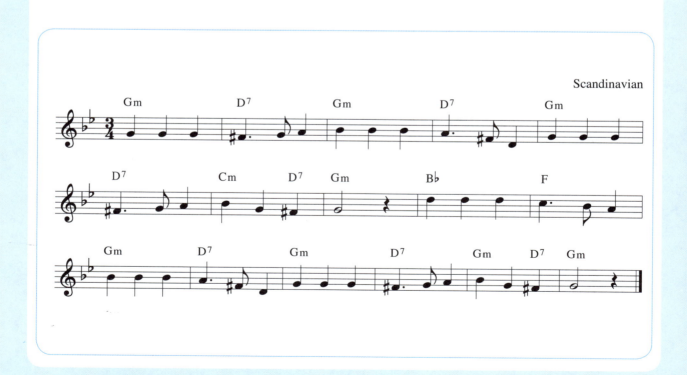
Scandinavian

Tell the students that you are going to play the Switch Game, which requires them to alternate between swaying and walking when you say the word "switch." Play the recording again, and sway to macrobeats. Halfway through the song, say "switch," and walk to macrobeats.

Play the recording again, and switch between swaying and walking at the end of every four-measure phrase.

TEACHING TIP
You can use this activity to introduce students to the timbres of small percussion instruments. Instead of saying "switch," use an unpitched instrument (tambourine or woodblock) to indicate when to switch.

FOR THE MUSIC TEACHER
This activity can be used to evaluate the feeling of phrase.

Play the recording, and switch at the end of each phrase from swaying to walking. Then do not have them switch at the end of a phrase, and watch the students to determine which ones were expecting you to switch. Keep a record of those students who were able to anticipate the feeling of phrase.

After switching at the ends of four-measure phrases several times through the song, you could also ask the students to switch without telling them when to determine whether they have internalized the phrases of the song.

JUMP RIGHT IN: THE MUSIC CURRICULUM

CITY LINE AVENUE

Activity Type: Singing, Movement

Tonality: Mixolydian

Resting Tone:

So

Meter: Usual Duple

Macrobeats:

Microbeats:

Keyality: F

Range: c–f'

Disc Three Track 4   Piano Bk Page 29

Materials Needed: Enough space so that everyone can move comfortably.

Purpose:
1. To help students audiate resting tone in Mixolydian tonality.
2. To give students an opportunity to move in space to microbeats.

TEACHING PLAN
Identify Macrobeats and Microbeats
Everyone should be seated in self space. Ask the students to listen to the song, close their eyes, and pat macrobeats lightly so that they make no sound. Then have them open their eyes and pat their laps to microbeats as you perform

Jennifer Bailey

TEACHER'S EDITION • KINDERGARTEN

the song again. Call attention to students who are responding to different levels of beat, and tell the students that both are right, depending upon how one audiates the song. Move to quarter-note microbeats, and tell the students that for this activity you are demonstrating microbeats. Then ask the students to move to macrobeats. Sing the song for the students while patting your lap in parallel motion to macrobeats. The students should imitate your movements.

Walk to Microbeats

Ask the students to stand and walk in place to microbeats. Sing the song while you and the students walk in place to microbeats. Then tell the students that they should walk around the room to microbeats, being careful to stay in self space. Remind them that being in self space means that they are not touching anyone else. Sing the song, walking around the room to microbeats.

Reinforce Resting Tone

Tell the students that they are going to pretend that they are driving cars around the room as they walk to microbeats. Have them hold their imaginary steering wheels and walk while you sing the song. On the quarter-note rests in the second, fourth, and final measures, sing "Beep, Beep" on the resting tone while pushing on an imaginary car horn.

After you have completed the song and movement, ask the students, "What car noise did you hear? Did I say it or did I sing it?" Then ask the students to join you by singing "Beep, Beep" at the appropriate times, while everyone moves around the room to microbeats and you sing the song. Ask the students to create other car noises that could be sung on the resting tone, along with hand motions to accompany the sound. Sing the song again, using the new sounds and motions that were created by the students.

TEACHING TIP

You can use this activity as a way of helping students to explore their singing voices. Instead of singing "Beep, Beep," they can pretend to be in a police car and make a siren noise. Using light head voice, start above the break and perform a vocal slide that goes down and then up. It is essential to start the vocal slide solidly in the upper head voice for this voice exploration to be successful. By doing so, students set their vocal mechanisms for singing rather than for speaking. Demonstrate the up-to-down direction of the sound by moving your hand up and down with the sound. Ask the students to follow your hand and make the sound with you. Then perform the song again, making siren sounds in the rest.

JUMP RIGHT IN: THE MUSIC CURRICULUM

ELEPHANTS AND KITTY CATS

Activity Type: Movement

Tonality: Dorian

Resting Tone:

Re

Meter: Usual Duple

Macrobeats:

Microbeats:

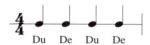

 Disc Three Track 5

 Piano Bk Page 44

Keyality: E

Range: d–e'

Materials Needed: Recording. Enough space for everyone to move comfortably.

Purpose:
1. To give students experience with Dorian tonality.
2. To give students and opportunity to explore strong and gentle weight through movement.

Grace Olin Jordon and Alice Ricky

When el-e-phants walk, they walk like this, Clump, clump, clump. They're ver-y heav-y and ver-y slow, This is the way that el-e-phants go, Clump, clump, clump. When kit-ty cats walk, they walk like this, Pit-pat, pit-pat, pit-pat. They're soft as silk and el-e-gant, not at all like an el-e-phant, Pit-pat, pit-pat, pit-pat.

156

TEACHER'S EDITION • KINDERGARTEN

TEACHING PLAN

Everyone should be seated in self space.

Move and Discuss

Play the recording of "Elephants and Kitty Cats." Ask the students which two animals are mentioned in the song. Ask the students to describe how an elephant moves, and invite individuals to demonstrate. Model moving like an elephant using strong, heavy movements. Ask the students to describe how a kitty cat moves, and invite individual students to demonstrate. Model moving like a kitty cat using gentle, light movements. Ask the students to compare how they moved differently as an elephant versus a kitty cat. Play the recording of "Elephants and Kitty Cats" again, and invite your students to move throughout the room like elephants or kitty cats at the appropriate time in the song.

JUMP RIGHT IN: THE MUSIC CURRICULUM

HIGH BIRD

Activity Type: Movement

Tonality: Phrygian

Resting Tone:

Meter: Usual Duple

Macrobeats:

Microbeats:

Keyality: E

Range: d–b

 Disc Three Track 6

 Piano Bk Page 65

Materials Needed: Recording. Enough space for everyone to move comfortably.

Purpose:
1. To give students experience moving using locomotor self space.
2. To give students experience with low, middle, and high space.

TEACHING PLAN

Everyone should be seated in self space.

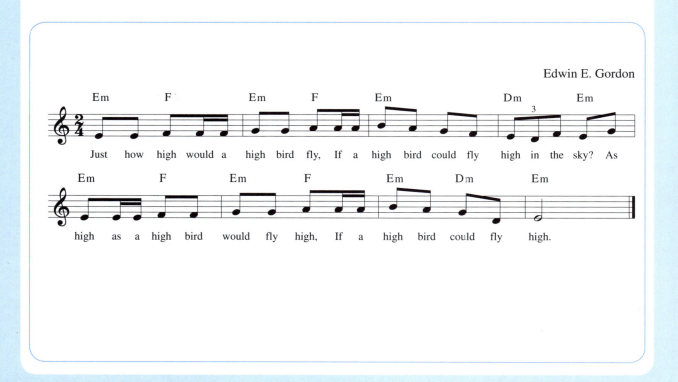

Edwin E. Gordon

Just how high would a high bird fly, If a high bird could fly high in the sky? As high as a high bird would fly high, If a high bird could fly high.

158

Low, Middle, and High Body Shapes

Ask the students to make body shapes that are very low and in self space. Then ask them to make body shapes that are very high and in self space. Finally, ask them to make shapes in self space that are in the middle, between low and high. Be sure to have the students look around at the shapes their peers make at each level.

Listen, Move, and Freeze

Ask the students to stand in self space. Tell them they will be listeners and movers and that they will travel to empty spaces using locomotor self space when they hear the recording. Remind them that, when they are in self space, they may not touch another person. When they hear the recording pause, they will freeze in low shapes.

Start the recording. Make sure the students move toward empty spaces while using self space. Pause the recording. Make sure the students freeze in low shapes. Repeat several times so that the students become comfortable with low space.

Now practice the activity, having the students freeze in high shapes. Repeat several times so that the students become comfortable with high space.

Next, practice the activity having the students freeze in middle shapes. Repeat several times so that the students become comfortable with middle space.

Choose Levels

Finish by asking the students to choose the type of space they would like to use for freezing. First, have the students choose for the entire class. Then have them choose individually so that they will be freezing at multiple levels at the same time. Be sure to allow the students several opportunities to experience each level of space.

Have the students discuss the body-shape levels that they enjoyed the most and the least. Discuss which were easiest and most difficult to demonstrate.

BARNACLE BILL

Activity Type: Movement, Singing

Tonality: Major

Resting Tone:

Meter: Usual Triple

Macrobeats:

Microbeats:

Keyality: G

Disc Three
Track 7

Piano Bk
Page 18

Range: d–e'

Materials Needed: Recording. Enough space for everyone to move comfortably.

Purpose:
1. To model taking an audiation breath for students.
2. To sing the resting tone in Major tonality.
3. To identify and label AB form.

TEACHING PLAN
Everyone should be seated in self space.

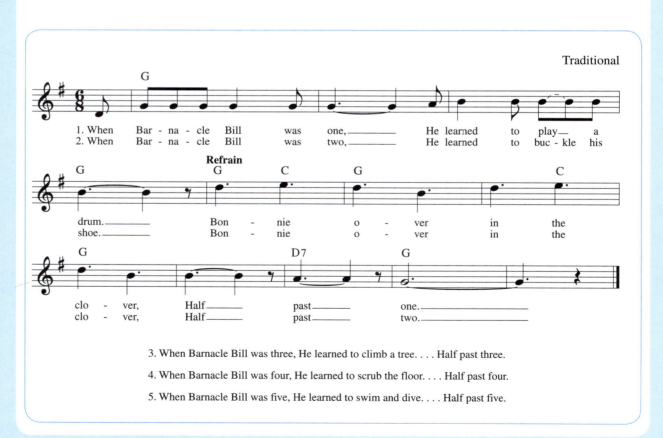

3. When Barnacle Bill was three, He learned to climb a tree.... Half past three.

4. When Barnacle Bill was four, He learned to scrub the floor.... Half past four.

5. When Barnacle Bill was five, He learned to swim and dive.... Half past five.

TEACHER'S EDITION • KINDERGARTEN

Listen and Move

Play the recording of "Barnacle Bill." As students listen, model patting macrobeats quietly on your lap in bilateral motion. Invite the students to move to the macrobeats with you. Tell them that there are two sections to this song. Play the recording again, and ask them to identify the two different sections. If your students demonstrate readiness, you may label them as section A and section B.

Focus on the Resting Tone and Breath Cue

Sing the song for the students. Tell them that you may stop the song at any time, and when you do, you would like them to sing the resting tone. (Use BUM for resting tone.) Tell the students to watch you, because you will give them a special cue to tell them when to take a breath before they sing. Model this by using your hands to gesture taking a breath and then singing the resting tone on BUM. Practice the cue and gesture with your students several times before presenting it in the song. Sing the song for the students, inserting the cue and gesture for the breath and resting tone.

Sing on Macrobeats

To extend the activity, model singing the resting tone on the macrobeats. Invite the students to sing the resting tone with you. Then invite them to sing the resting tone while you sing the A section of the song. If it is difficult for students to maintain the resting tone independent of the melody, use a bass bar or xylophone to reinforce the resting tone pitch.

LISTENING LESSON

Play the recording of "American Overture for Band," a band piece by Joseph Willcox Jenkins (Disc Three, Track 8). This piece has a very steady beat that is conducive to movement. Place a large co-op band on the floor, and ask the students to hold on to the band with both hands. Play the recording, and bounce the co-op band to the macrobeats. Generally, if you are in the circle moving with the students, they are able to maintain the beat. However, if the students have difficulty feeling the beat, chant "bounce, bounce, bounce" to the beats to guide their movements. If you do not own a co-op band, this activity can be done with the students standing in a circle, holding hands and bouncing to the beat by bending their knees and swinging arms to macrobeats.

161

JUMP RIGHT IN: THE MUSIC CURRICULUM

SEE HOW I'M JUMPING

Activity Type: Singing, Movement, Chanting

Tonality: Aeolian

Resting Tone:

La

Meter: Usual Duple

Macrobeats:

Du   Du

Microbeats:

Du De Du De

Keyality: E

Range: d–b'

Disc Three Track 9   Piano Bk Page 118

TEACHING PLAN ONE

Materials Needed: Enough space for everyone to move comfortably.

Purpose:
1. To help students learn to jump in locomotor pathways.
2. To encourage students to breathe before moving and singing.
3. To give students an opportunity to imitate tonal patterns.

Everyone should be standing in self space.

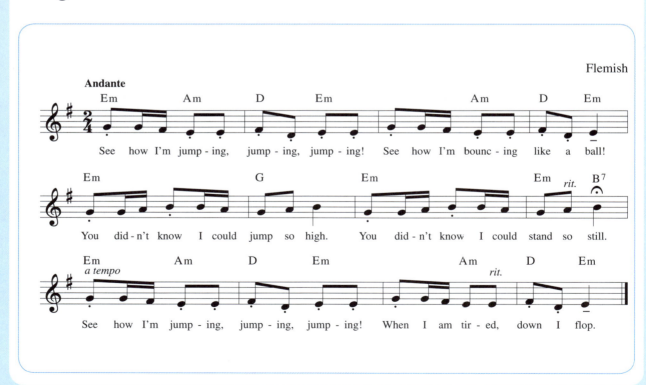

Breathe, Swing, Jump, and Freeze in Locomotor Pathways

Tell the students that they will be traveling to empty spaces by way of jumping, but before they jump, they will need to swing their arms. Have the students bend their knees and prepare their arms by placing their fists at about eye level. They should swing their arms backward, take a deep breath, swing their arms forward, and jump to empty spaces. Practice this several times. Have the students chant the following phrase to guide their movements. Use the same tempo as you will for the song.

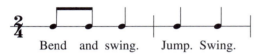

Next, sing the song for the students, and have them notice the words "still" and "flop." Have the students freeze in a high-body shape on the word "still. Then have them demonstrate safe flopping in self space by making low-body shapes on the word "flop." During all other parts of the song, students may jump when they please, as long as they are jumping to empty spaces. Remind them to bend their knees, breathe, and swing their arms each time that they jump. Tell the students that you will pause on the words "still" and "flop," but you may also pause in other places, so they should be ready to pause at any time.

Begin singing the song. Pause, if necessary, for classroom management. Pause on the words "still" and "flop."

Tonal Pattern Imitation

Have the students imitate the following tonal patterns. Before each pattern, prepare and perform a jump, landing as you sing the first pitch of each pattern. Jumping will ensure that students breathe before they sing.

SEE HOW I'M JUMPING (continued)

TEACHING PLAN TWO

Activity Type: Movement, Chanting, Rhythm Creativity

Materials Needed: Enough space for everyone to move comfortably.

Purpose:
1. To give students experience moving in a continuous, fluid style while pulsating macrobeats and microbeats.
2. To give students and opportunity to create rhythm patterns.

Everyone should be seated in self space with crossed legs.

Listen and Move

Perform the song while pulsating microbeats bilaterally. Ask the students to copy your movements. Then ask the students to copy your bilateral microbeat pulsations while they chant TUH to microbeats. Help them coordinate their tongues with their body movements.

Repeat the song, and have the students copy your bilateral macrobeat pulsations while they chant BAH to macrobeats.

Imitate and Identify Different Rhythm Patterns

Now, tell the students you are going to perform two rhythm patterns that are different from each other. Perform each of the following rhythm patterns using BAH. Pause between the patterns.

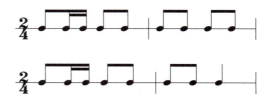

Then have the students imitate each rhythm pattern several times. Tell the students those two rhythm patterns are the only two rhythm patterns in the first and last phrases of the song.

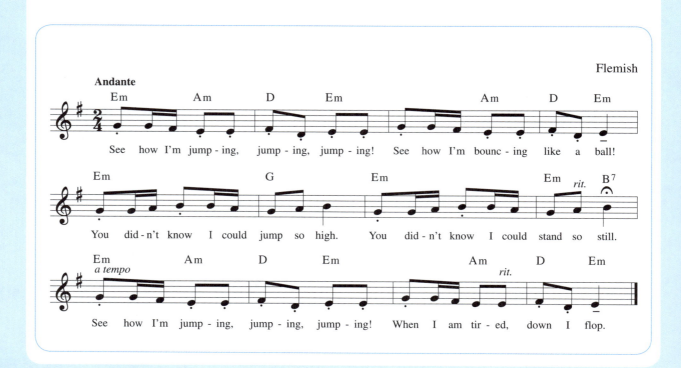

Teacher's Edition • Kindergarten

Rhythm Pattern Creation

Tell the students that you are going to perform a rhythm pattern and that they will get to perform a rhythm pattern that is different from yours. Ask for a volunteer to demonstrate. Perform one of the rhythm patterns. Gesture for the volunteer to breathe and perform his or her pattern. Then have the class imitate the student's pattern and determine if it was the same as or different from yours. They can show you their decisions by using their "same" (both hands closed or both hands open) or "different" hands (one hand closed and one hand open).

Accept all student attempts to be different from you in this lesson. If the student's rhythm pattern is different from yours, say, "Yes, that was different." Be sure to have the class repeat each student's rhythm pattern for reinforcement. The point of the lesson is to make it safe to be different. In their first conscious attempts to be different, students may not be able to stay in tempo. With opportunity and practice, accuracy will increase.

If the student's rhythm pattern is the same as yours, say, "Thank you. That was the same pattern as mine. Here is a pattern that is different." Then demonstrate a different rhythm pattern, and have everyone imitate that pattern.

SHALOM CHAVERIM

Activity Type: Movement, Singing

Tonality: Aeolian

Resting Tone

Meter: Usual Duple

Macrobeats:

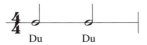

Microbeats:

Keyality: E

Range: B–e'

Materials Needed: Enough space for everyone to move comfortably.

 Disc Three Track 10   Piano Bk Page 120

Purpose: To help students coordinate movement and singing using continuous flow and tonal patterns.

TEACHING PLAN

Everyone should be standing in stationary self space. Later, everyone will move to standing, stationary, shared space with a partner.

Introduce the Song

Establish tonality by singing the sequence of tones notated below using a neutral syllable.

Sing the song and model continuous, fluid movement. As you model, pretend that you are facing one other person and that you are holding hands with him or her. Hold your hands out, and move gently and continuously. As you breathe

TEACHER'S EDITION • KINDERGARTEN

to sing a phrase, show the breath in your body movement.

Observe students who are moving like you and coordinating their movement as you sing. Continue singing, and approach a coordinated student. Extend your hands to that student and non-verbally invite him or her to share space by holding hands as you move. As you sing, move your hands in circular pathways with that student.

Invite Partners to Share Space

Assign the students partners to move like you moved with the student. If some students have difficulty coordinating their continuous flow, try to pair them with students whose movements seem coordinated. Sing the melody twice as you observe their shared space movement.

Sing Patterns

Invite the students to turn with their partners so that everyone can see you. Ask them to continue moving with continuous flow in shared space while looking at their partners, as they were doing before, each time they hear you sing the melody. However, when you stop singing, they should drop their hands and continue to move with flow but in self space. Sing the song, and at the end of the song have them drop their partners' hands and move with flow. Ask them to watch you as they continue to move. Move with continuous flow, and sing tonal patterns in Harmonic Minor. Gesture for the students to breathe and echo your patterns. Pause briefly after you sing each pattern. The students should move with continuous flow the entire time. Then, when you return to singing the song, they should return to their movement in shared space.

On a different day, ask the students to move to a different partner after pattern dialogue. Because the students will be familiar with the tonal pattern portion of the activity, they should be able to watch you for the breath gesture, regardless of where you are when you sing patterns. During the melody, join your hands with a set of partners' hands to form a trio. Stay next to those partners when you drop hands and move in self space. This will allow you to hear their responses. At first, indicate that everyone should continue to echo patterns. On yet a different day, indicate that only the pair whose movement you joined should echo your patterns. After each pair echoes, move to another set of partners.

COORDINATION WITH INSTRUMENTAL MUSIC

Play the tenor saxophone recording of *Shalom Chaverim* from *Jump Right In: The Instrumental Series* (J299CD, track 76). Show the students a picture of a tenor saxophone using Instrument Card 17. Ask the students to imitate your movement as they audiate and listen to the recording. Move with continuous flow, and pulsate your hands to macrobeats as you flow. Be certain to use high, medium, and low space, as well as the space in front and in back of you as you move. You should never pulsate in the same place twice.

167

JUMP RIGHT IN: THE MUSIC CURRICULUM

THE GREENLAND WHALE FISHERY

Activity Type: Listening, Singing, Movement

Tonality: Mixolydian

Resting Tone:

Meter: Usual Duple

Macrobeats:

Microbeats:

 Disc Three Track 11

 Piano Bk Page 61

Keyality: G

Range: d–d'

Materials Needed: Recording. Enough space for everyone to move comfortably.

Purpose:
1. To give students experience with a song in Mixolydian tonality.
2. To give students experience moving to macrobeats and microbeats.
3. To give students experience with strong, continuous, fluid movement.

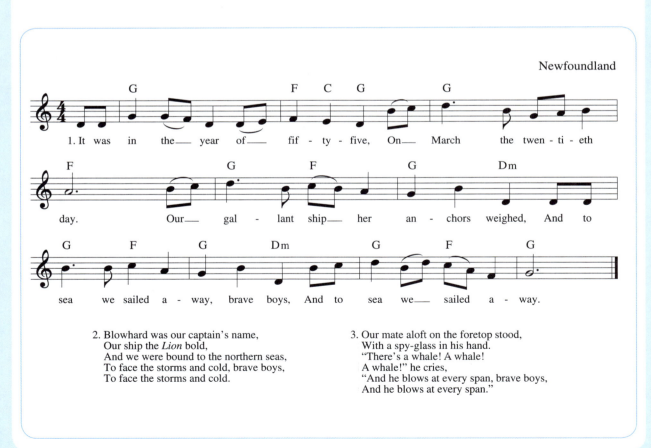

2. Blowhard was our captain's name,
   Our ship the *Lion* bold,
   And we were bound to the northern seas,
   To face the storms and cold, brave boys,
   To face the storms and cold.

3. Our mate aloft on the foretop stood,
   With a spy-glass in his hand.
   "There's a whale! A whale!
   A whale!" he cries,
   "And he blows at every span, brave boys,
   And he blows at every span."

TEACHER'S EDITION • KINDERGARTEN

TEACHING PLAN
Everyone should be seated in self space. Later, students will move to standing.

Introduce the Song
Remind the students that the words to songs often tell the audience a story. Invite the students to be your audience, and tell them that you will ask them what the song is about after they listen to it. Play the recording, or sing the song with all of the verses for the students.

Sing Parts of the Story
When students tell you what they heard, improvise questions about the story using pitches from the characteristic functions of tonic and subtonic in Mixolydian tonality. Invite individuals to answer. Any answer (verbal or musical) is acceptable. For example:

Was there a ship? Yes, there was a ship!
Was there a shark? No, not a shark!
Was there a canoe? No, not a canoe!

Gesture for the students to continue audiating silently. Sing the following patterns for students, and gesture for them to be your echoes.

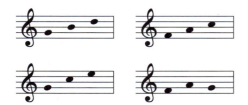

Model Beat Movement During Song
Invite the students to stand in stationary self space. Ask them to imitate your movement as you sing the song. During the verse, model macrobeat movements. In later repetitions of the song, model microbeat movements. As the students improve their coordination, model macrobeat movement in your heels and microbeat movement in your fingertips.

Continuous Flow During Patterns
When a verse (or a repetition of the melody) is complete, sing patterns from each of the characteristic functions in Mixolydian tonality, having the students echo each pattern by giving them a breath gesture as a cue. Before you perform a pattern, breathe while moving with continuous flow, modeling a lot of space (even though you remain in stationary self space). Continue to flow while singing the patterns. Encourage their breath with facial expressions, breathing, and movement. Remind students to imitate both your movement and your singing when they echo the patterns.

Move with Strong Continuous Flow
Review the action that develops in the verses of the song. Help the students pantomime by providing strong movements to accompany the song. They can animate the action of the story; they can be an anchor, a storm, waves, cold air, or the whale.

FIRE HOUSE

Activity Type: Movement, Vocal Exploration, Circle Dance

Tonality: Harmonic Minor

Resting Tone:

La

Meter: Usual Duple

Macrobeats:

Du   Du

Microbeats:

Du De Du De

Keyality: D

Range: d–a

Disc Three
Track 12

Piano Bk
Page 49

Materials Needed: Streamers. Recording. Enough space for everyone to move comfortably.

Purpose:
1. To engage students in vocal exploration to help them find head voice.
2. To give students experience moving to microbeats in Usual Duple meter.
3. To give students experience with a circle dance.

TEACHING PLAN

Everyone should be seated in self space.

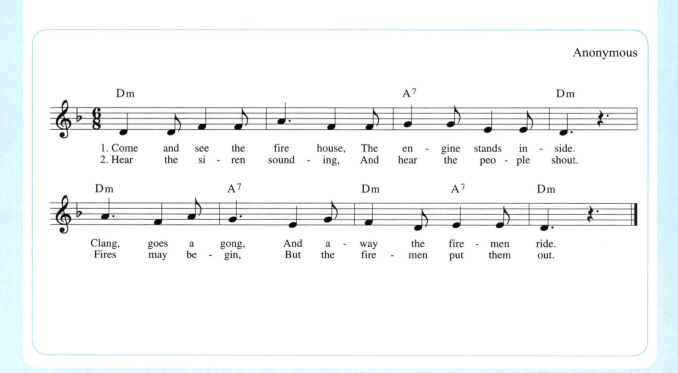

Anonymous

1. Come and see the fire house, The en - gine stands in - side.
   Clang, goes a gong, And a - way the fire - men ride.
2. Hear the si - ren sound - ing, And hear the peo - ple shout.
   Fires may be - gin, But the fire - men put them out.

Move to Microbeats

Play the recording of "Fire House" for the students. Model microbeats by patting gently using a bilateral motion on your legs. Play the recording again, and invite the students to pat microbeats with you. Ask the students for suggestions as to what other parts of the body they could move to microbeats. Repeat the song several times using students' suggestions and microbeat movement. Invite the students to stand and move to microbeats. Model rocking from side to side, making sure to displace your body weight from one foot to the other as you rock. Invite the students to move to microbeats in the same way while you sing the song.

Vocal Exploration

To extend the activity, ask the students what kind of sounds they hear when a fire truck goes by. Model making a siren sound using your head voice. Encourage the students to explore their own "siren voices" to sensate head voice.

Move with Streamers

Invite the students to stand, and make a circle formation. Give each fireperson in your circle a streamer to use as a fire hose. Model putting the heavy fire hose over your shoulder. Invite the students to make their siren sounds as they prepare to move in a circle. Sing the song for the students, and move around the circle to microbeats. At the end of the first verse, take a big breath and blow it out, putting out the fire with your fire hose. Sing the second verse, and move around the circle in the opposite direction, walking to microbeats.

FOR THE MUSIC TEACHER

Because of the fast tempo of this song, children will usually audiate the microbeats in twos rather than threes as indicated in the song information. Meter should be identified based on how a song is audiated rather than notated. Therefore, this song is in Usual Duple meter, even though it is notated in 6/8.

WILD DOG ON OUR FARM

Activity Type: Movement

Tonality: Mixolydian

Resting Tone:

So

Meter: Usual Duple

Macrobeats:

Du Du

Microbeats:

Du De Du De

Keyality: E

Range: B–e'

Disc Three
Track 13

Piano Bk
Page 152

Materials Needed: Rhythm sticks.

Purpose:
1. To help students imitate and perhaps audiate macrobeats in Usual Duple meter.
2. To give students experience with Mixolydian tonality.

TEACHING PLAN
Everyone should be seated in self space.

Identify Macrobeats
Ask the students listen to the song and watch you move. Sing the song for the students while patting your lap in parallel motion to macrobeats. Tell the students that you are patting to the macrobeats of the song. Have the students join you in patting macrobeats as you sing the song

again. Ask a student where else to pat macrobeats. Sing the song several more times while incorporating different student suggestions for macrobeat placement.

Use the Rhythm Sticks

Give each student two rhythm sticks. Tell the students that they will be performing the macrobeats using rhythm sticks. Sing the song, or play the recording, and tap the rhythm sticks in bilateral motion to macrobeats. Ask for student suggestions for how to perform the macrobeats using rhythm sticks. Have them use the sticks differently for each repetition of the song. At some point, ask the students to make a more complicated motion—alternately tapping the floor and clicking the sticks together to macrobeats.

If a few of the students are able to make this more complicated motion with rhythmic accuracy, increase the difficulty level by having them tap, click, and then shake them in the air twice, making a four-macrobeat pattern. You may want to chant "floor, click, shake, shake" to reinforce this movement if you are using the recording. End the activity with an easier macrobeat movement so that many of the students will be able to perform it with accuracy.

TEACHING TIP

Although few, if any of your students, will be able to perform the four-beat pattern in the Teaching Plan successfully, students should still be given the opportunity to try. If most students can do what the teacher asks on the first try, the more advanced students in class probably are not being sufficiently challenged. In every lesson plan, try to include something that challenges even the strongest students in your class. This will ensure that all students are learning and will prevent the most advanced students from becoming bored.

FUNNY PUPPY

Activity Type: Singing, Solo Singing, Movement

Tonality: Harmonic Minor

Resting Tone:

La

Meter: Usual Duple

Macrobeats:

Microbeats:

Keyality: D

Range: d–b

 Disc Three Track 14

 Piano Bk Page 57

Materials Needed: Dog puppet. Recording. Enough space for everyone to move comfortably.

Purpose:
1. To give students experience with macrobeats and microbeats in Usual Duple meter.
2. To give students experience with Minor tonality.
3. To give students experience discriminating between tonal patterns that are the same and different.

TEACHING PLAN

Everyone should be seated in self space.

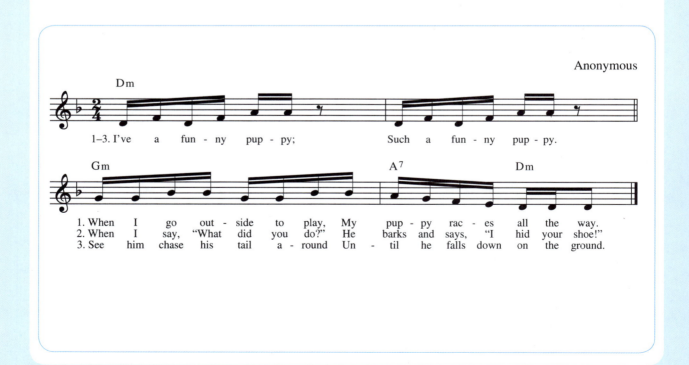

174

Move to Microbeats and Macrobeats

Play the recording of "Funny Puppy." As the students listen, model microbeat movement on your lap by patting in bilateral motion. Invite the students to move to microbeats with you. Play the recording again, this time modeling macrobeat movement. Invite your students to move to macrobeats with you. Once the students can pat macrobeats and microbeats independently, invite them to pat the microbeats while you pat the macrobeats, and vice versa.

Echo Patterns

To extend the activity, use a dog puppet. Sing the song for the students. At the end of the song, tell the students that your dog is special because he sings. Use the puppet to sing Minor tonic and dominant patterns using a neutral syllable. Invite the students to echo the tonal patterns. Sing the song again for the students to re-establish minor tonality for them.

At the end of the song, use the puppet to demonstrate same and different patterns. Sing a minor tonic pattern, and have the puppet echo a minor dominant pattern. Ask the students whether the "dog" sang the same pattern as yours or a different one. Sing minor tonal patterns, and invite individual students to sing either the same or a different tonal pattern.

JUMP RIGHT IN: THE MUSIC CURRICULUM

SIDEWALK TALK

Activity Type: Listening, Movement

Meter: Usual Duple

Macrobeats:

Microbeats:

 Disc Three Track 15

 Piano Bk Page 121

Materials Needed: Enough space for everyone to move comfortably.

Purpose:
1. To give students an opportunity to listen and move.
2. To give students experience moving in a continuous, fluid style while pulsating macrobeats and microbeats.

TEACHING PLAN
Everyone should be seated with crossed legs in self space.

Listen and Move with Pulsations
Though this chant begs for the use of locomotor movement, for optimal success, begin with stationary movement. Tell the students that they will be listeners and movers. Remind them that listening is the most important job of each musician.

Have the students copy your movements as you perform the chant and bilateral microbeat pulsations with your hands. Never perform the microbeat pulsations in the same place twice in a row. Keep moving them all around on the floor, on your legs, and in the air. Use your spine to assist your use of continuous flow, being certain to keep the movement relaxed and fluid.

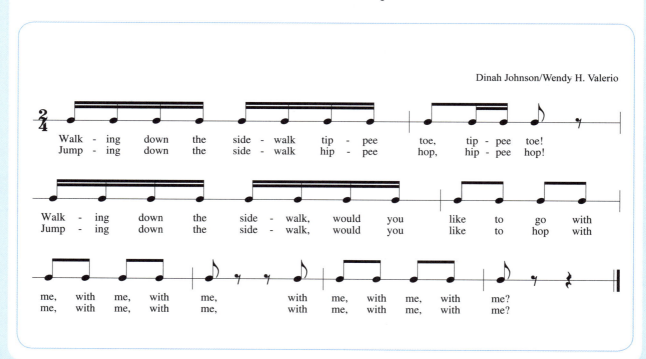

Dinah Johnson/Wendy H. Valerio

Repeat the chant. This time, have the students copy your bilateral macrobeat pulsations.

Repeat the chant, now having the students copy your bilateral microbeat pulsations while they chant TUH to microbeats to coordinate their tongues with their body movements. Then repeat the chant again, now having the students copy your bilateral macrobeat pulsations while they chant BAH to help them feel the difference between microbeats and macrobeats. When students become comfortable with the movements, encourage them to perform the chant as they move.

TEACHING PLAN TWO

Activity Type: Movement

Materials Needed: Enough space for everyone to move comfortably.

Purpose:
1. To help students move using locomotor self space.
2. To give students experience moving with bound and free flow.

Use this plan after students have been successful with self space in Teaching Plan One of "Sidewalk Talk." Everyone should be standing in self space.

Listen and Move with Bound Flow
Tell the students to pretend that they are standing on a sidewalk puddle that froze overnight. Tell them that they may travel by tiptoe to an empty space on the puddle when they hear you perform the chant, but that they must "freeze" when you are not chanting. When tiptoeing, the students should be careful, as if they are trying to not crack the ice of the frozen puddle.

Remind the students that empty spaces are places on the floor with no one and nothing in them. Also remind them that they will be traveling in self space.

Perform the chant. Check to be sure that all students are tiptoeing carefully. Pause frequently to allow the students to practice their listening and "freezing" skills.

Now tell the students to copy your tiptoe movements. Tiptoe on the microbeats. Have the students join you, chanting TUH on each microbeat as they tiptoe while you perform the chant.

Next, tell the students to copy your tiptoe movements. Tiptoe on the macrobeats. Have the students join you, chanting BAH on each macrobeat as you perform the chant.

Ask the students how it felt when they were tiptoeing carefully. Remind them that when we are being careful we are using bound flow because it is easy to stop our movements.

Listen and Move with Free Flow
Tell the students to pretend again that they are standing on a sidewalk puddle that froze overnight. Tell them that they may travel to an empty space on the puddle when they hear you perform the chant, but that they must freeze when you are not chanting. This time, when tiptoeing, the students should try not to fall. Tell them to move as if they were slipping and sliding on frozen puddles.

Perform the chant. Check to be sure that all students are slipping and sliding in self space.

Ask the students how it felt to be slipping and sliding. Remind them that when we are slipping and sliding we are using free flow. This makes it difficult for us to stop our movements.

JIM ALONG JOSIE

Activity Type: Singing, Movement

Tonality: Pentatonic

Resting Tone:

Do

Meter: Usual Duple

Macrobeats:

Du   Du

Microbeats:

Du De Du De

Keyality: D

Range: d–a

Materials Needed: Enough space for everyone to move comfortably.

Disc Three Track 16

Piano Bk Page 73

Purpose:
1. To explore locomotor movement.
2. To help students audiate resting tone in Major Pentatonic.

TEACHING PLAN

Everyone should be seated in self space at the beginning of the lesson. Later, all will move into standing self space.

Singing

Teach the song using the Rote Song Teaching Procedure found in the Reference Manual. Sing the resting tone of the song, and give the students a preparatory breath and gesture for them to echo you. Tell them that they need to be prepared to sing the resting tone, either as a group or in solo, each time you breathe and gesture. Then ask the students to stand in self space for a movement activity with the song.

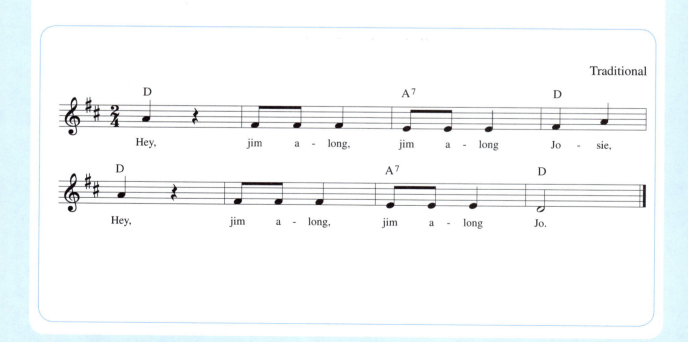

TEACHER'S EDITION • KINDERGARTEN

Move and Sing

Tell the students that you are going to change the words of the song. Change "hey" to "hi." Have students walk in self space and wave to each other when they sing "hi." After the performance of the song, give them a preparatory breath, and gesture for them to sing the resting tone.

Then change "hi" to "jump," having them jump while singing the song. Continue with other verses, such as walk, hop, crawl, and slide. Between each performance of the song, gesture for the students to sing the resting tone.

CONNECTION TO SOCIAL STUDIES

Discuss greetings from other countries with the students. Ask them if they know the way any other cultures say "hello," such as *hola* or *aloha*. Identify as many ways to say hello as possible. Substitute some of these in the song in place of "hey," and perform the locomotor movement, waving each time you sing the greeting.

BRE'R RABBIT, SHAKE IT

Activity Type: Listening, Movement, Singing

Tonality: Pentatonic

Resting Tone:

Meter: Usual Duple

Macrobeats:

Microbeats:

Keyality: G

Range: d–b

Disc Three
Track 17

Piano Bk
Page 27

Materials Needed: Enough space for everyone to move comfortably.

Purpose:
1. To help students listen and experience continuous, fluid movement.
2. To help students isolate different parts of the body.
3. To give students the opportunity to imitate a tonal pattern.
4. To introduce call-and-response song form.

TEACHING PLAN
Everyone should be standing in self space.

Listen and Move
Tell the students that they will be listeners and movers and to copy your movements as you sing a song for them.

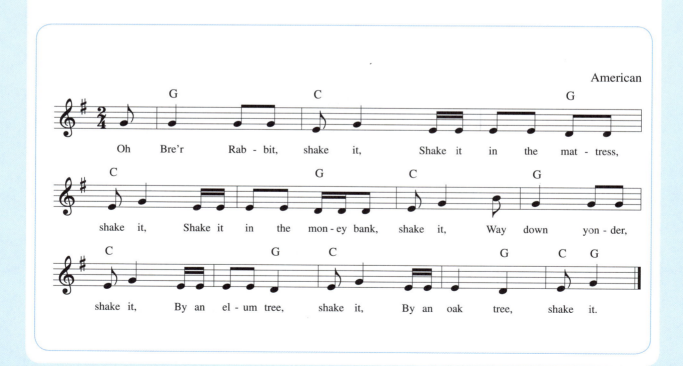

Sing the song with the words. Each time you sing the words "shake it," wiggle your shoulders in a figure-eight movement. Make sure that the students move like you.

Tonal Pattern Imitation
Sing the following tonal pattern using the neutral syllable BUM.

Have the students imitate the tonal pattern. Use a clear breath gesture to start the singing. Tell the students that the tonal pattern is the "shake it" tonal pattern. Have the students repeat the pattern using the words "shake it." Tell the students that the "shake it" part of the song is called the response, and this will be their part. Your part of the song is the call.

Move and Sing
Tell the students that their job will be to sing the response after each call. Sing the song, and gesture clearly for the students to move their shoulders and sing their pattern each time it occurs. Sing the song again, and change the "shake it" movement. This time, have the students move their hips as if hula-hooping. Repeat the song several times, using other parts of the body to move for the response. Include spines, knees, ankles, elbows, heads, necks, and tummies.

Once students are comfortable moving isolated parts of the body, have them continuously roll their forearms and fists during your call and shake the chosen part of the body during the response.

TISKET, A-TASKET

Activity Type: Singing, Movement

Tonality: Pentatonic

Resting Tone:

Do

Meter: Usual Duple

Macrobeats:

Du Du

Microbeats:

Du De Du De

Keyality: F

Range: g–c'

Disc Three Track 18

Piano Bk Page 139

Materials Needed: Parachute. Enough space for everyone to move comfortably.

Purpose:
1. To help students audiate dominant and tonic in Pentatonic tonality.
2. To provide readiness for folk dancing.

TEACHING PLAN
Everyone should be seated in self space.

Identify Macrobeats
Ask the students listen to the song and watch you move. Sing the song for the students while patting your lap in parallel motion to macrobeats. Tell the students that you are patting to the macrobeats of the song. Have them join you in patting macrobeats as you sing the song again. Ask a student where else to pat macrobeats. Sing

the song several more times while incorporating different student suggestions of where else to pat macrobeats.

Move in a Circle
Lay the parachute flat on the floor. Ask the students to hold the edge or handles of the parachute with both hands and lift the parachute to waist level. The students should be standing in a large circle holding the parachute. Ask the students to walk in a circle to macrobeats while holding the parachute. They should try to keep the parachute in a perfectly circular shape at all times as they move.

Reinforce the Dominant and Resting Tones
After singing the song and moving in a circle, lift the parachute to head level and sing the dominant pitch. The students should lift, too. Then lower the parachute and sing the resting tone. Repeat the lifting and lowering, accompanied by singing the dominant and resting tone.

Sing the song again, moving in a circle and reinforcing the dominant and the resting tone again at the end of the song.

> **TEACHING TIP**
> This song does not contain the resting tone, which makes it more difficult to audiate. Also, because pentatonic songs have no half steps, audiating the resting tone is a challenge. Therefore, reinforcing the resting tone in pentatonic songs is particularly useful, as this will allow the students to audiate the fundamental tonal center of the song and to engage in the songs with greater tonal understanding.

> **FOR THE MUSIC TEACHER**
> If you do not have a parachute, you can use scarves in this activity. Ask the students to form a circle, with scarves between the students. Each student should grasp an end of a scarf with each hand, and the students on either side of him or her should grasp the other ends of the same scarf. After singing the song and walking in a circle, the students should jointly raise and lower the scarves at the end of the song (in the place of the parachute).
>
> Asking the students to join hands in a circle without the use of props is another possibility. After singing and walking in a circle, the students can raise their joined hands while singing the dominant pitch and bend and touch their joined hands to the floor while singing the resting tone.

BAA, BAA, BLACK SHEEP

Activity Type: Listening, Movement, Singing

Tonality: Major

Resting Tone:

Meter: Usual Duple

Macrobeats:

Microbeats:

 Disc Three Track 19

 Piano Bk Page 14

Keyality: D

Range: d–b

Materials Needed: Enough space for everyone to move comfortably.

Purpose:
1. To help students learn to listen and move in a continuous, fluid style.
2. To give students an opportunity to imitate a tonal pattern.
3. To help students audiate and sing the resting tone.

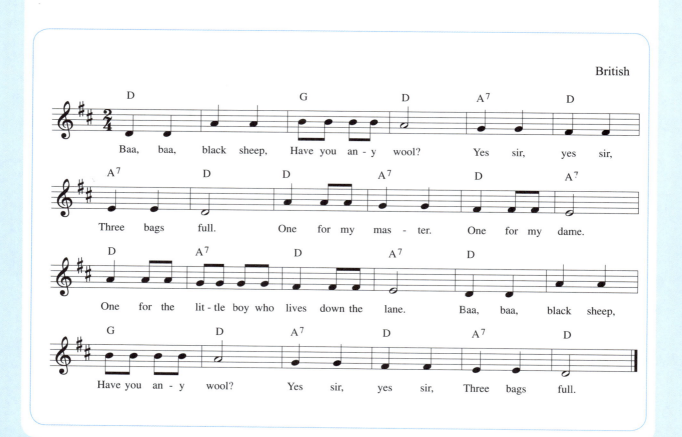

TEACHING PLAN
Everyone should be seated in self space.

Listen and Move Continuously
Tell the students that they will be listeners and movers. Ask them to copy your movements as you sing the song for them without words. Rock from side-to-side, and roll your fists and forearms continuously. Do not worry about keeping a steady beat. Take this chance to move continuously.

Sing and Find a Tonal Pattern
Sing the following tonal pattern using BUM.

Give a clear breath and preparatory gesture, and have the students imitate the tonal pattern.

Tell the students that the tonal pattern is the first tonal pattern of the song. Have the students listen as you sing the beginning of the song again to demonstrate the tonal pattern.

Sing the Resting Tone
Repeat the first listening and moving activity. Then say, "Listen to this pitch." Sing the resting tone using the neutral syllable BUM.

Sing on the resting tone, "Watch my hands; they will tell you when to breathe and sing that pitch." Take a breath, and sing the resting tone with the students. Then say, "Now, think that pitch." Give the students a moment to think the pitch. Say, "Watch my hands. Take a breath, and sing the pitch you were thinking." Again, give a clear breath gesture as you breathe and sing the resting tone with the students. Say, "Your job is to remember that pitch."

Say, "I am going to sing the song again. Sometimes I will pause. Then I will show you when to breathe and sing the pitch you were thinking." Perform the song, and pause every two or four measures to give the breath gesture and sing the resting tone with the students.

JUMP RIGHT IN: THE MUSIC CURRICULUM

SAKURA

Activity Type: Movement, Listening

Tonality: Pentatonic

Resting Tone:

Meter: Usual Duple

Macrobeats:

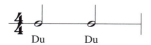

Microbeats:

Keyality: C

Range: d–e-flat'

Disc Three
Track 20

Piano Bk
Page 113

Materials Needed: Recording. Enough space for everyone to move comfortably.

Purpose:
1. To give students experience moving with quick and slow continuous flow.
2. To help students discriminate between same and different tonal patterns in a melodic context.

TEACHING PLAN

Everyone should be standing and ready to use stationary self space.

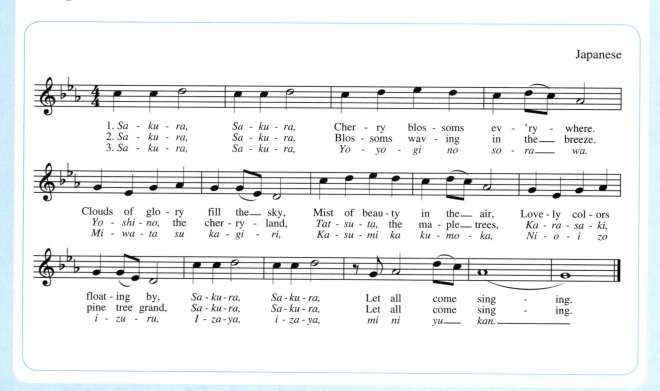

186

Play the Recording and Flow

Ask the students to audiate and imitate your movement while listening to the recording. Model continuous, fluid movement using your whole body, moving at a moderate tempo. At the end of the recording, compliment students who are using their whole bodies while moving with coordinated, continuous flow.

Quick and Slow Flow

Tell the students that you will play the recording again, but that you will move differently than before. Ask the students to imitate this new movement. Tell them that you will ask them to describe two ways in which your movements are different from before.

Play the recording, and move with very slow continuous flow, especially when compared with your first model. Move very slowly during the first phrase. Move very quickly during the middle of the piece, and resume very slow flow when "Sakura" returns during the last phrase. Be certain to explore the space around you, and use your whole body as you model quick and slow continuous flow. Guide students in a discussion that labels your movements as quick or slow while still using continuous flow. Ask the students which way they prefer moving during "Sakura" and why. Just listen to their answers; there is no one correct answer.

Same Tonal Pattern

On a different day, when students have had several opportunities to hear the song, introduce this part of the Teaching Plan.

Gesture for the students to audiate. Sing the patterns in the first two measures without the words. Then invite the students to audiate and listen because the patterns you just sang for them occur again later in the song. Ask them to raise their hands when they hear the "Sakura" pattern repeated. Sing without words, and watch for students to raise their hands. If necessary, sing the song again, and raise your hand when the patterns occur. Return to this activity several times before you continue the Teaching Plan.

Different Tonal Pattern

Tell students you are going to sing "Sakura." Review the opening pattern, and ask the students to sing it. Then invite the students to play a game. Tell them you will sing the song for them with either the same "Sakura" pattern that they know, or a different one. Invite them to describe what they audiated each time you finish singing the song. Always keep the rhythm pattern of "Sakura" the same when you sing a different tonal pattern. Finish the activity with a performance of the original song.

JUMP RIGHT IN: THE MUSIC CURRICULUM

MY NAME IS LITTLE YELLOW BIRD

Activity Type: Singing, Solo Singing, Melodic Creativity, Movement

 Disc Three Track 21

 Piano Bk Page 88

Tonality: Major

Resting Tone:

Do

Materials Needed: Recording. Toy microphone. Enough space for everyone to move comfortably.

Purpose:
1. To help students audiate and perform locomotor movement to macrobeats in Usual Duple meter.
2. To give students an opportunity to create a melodic response.

Meter: Usual Duple

Macrobeats:

Du Du

Microbeats:

Du De Du De

Keyality: D

Range: d–b

TEACHING PLAN

Everyone should be seated in self space.

Identify Macrobeats

Ask the students listen to the song and watch you move. Sing the song, or play the recording for the students while patting your lap in bilateral motion to macrobeats. Tell the students that you

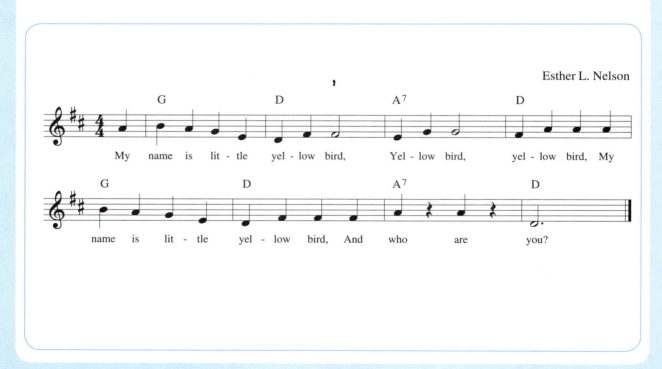

are patting to the macrobeats of the song. Ask them to join you in patting macrobeats as you sing or play the song again. Invite the students to stand in self space. Tell them that this time they should walk to macrobeats as you sing or play the song.

Creating Responses

At the end of the song, create a Duple Major melodic response using the text "I am [insert your name]." Tell the students that you made up what you just sang. Then tell them that they are going to make up their own name melodies. Demonstrate several more times, inserting student names rather than your own. Create a different melody for each demonstration.

Ask the students to freeze their movements at the end of the song. Then when you hold a microphone up to one student, that student should answer the "Who are you?" question at the end of the song with the answer "I am _____."
Sing the song as the students walk to macrobeats. Then hold the microphone for a student to create a name response. Repeat this so that several students have the opportunity to create.

TEACHING TIP

In an activity like that of the Teaching Plan, not every student will have the opportunity to create a solo melody in a single class period. As soon as students seem to be losing interest in this activity, move on to the next one. Then revisit the first activity in a subsequent class period so that more students will have an opportunity to create.

FOR THE MUSIC TEACHER

Listening to students create gives you a "window" into their audiational development. Some students will create in the same keyality and tonality as the song, and others will not. Some will create in the tempo and meter of the song, and others will not. This gives you information about what individuals need from you instructionally in the future. Those who are struggling tonally need more informal exposure to a variety of tonalities and more resting tone activities. They also may benefit from more help in finding their singing voices. Those who are struggling rhythmically need more informal exposure to a variety of meters and more experience with continuous, fluid movement, with and without pulsating beat.

LITTLE TRAIN

Activity Type: Singing, Instrumental Readiness, Movement

Tonality: Pentatonic

Resting Tone:

Do

Meter: Usual Duple

Macrobeats:

Du Du

Microbeats:

Du De Du De

Keyality: F

Range: c–a

 Disc Three Track 22

 Piano Bk Page 81

Materials Needed: Recording. Two rhythm sticks per person. Enough space for everyone to move comfortably.

Purpose: To provide instrumental readiness by using rhythm sticks.

TEACHING PLAN
Everyone should be seated in self space.

Sing and Move
Give each student a pair of rhythm sticks, and ask them to copy your rhythm stick movement. Sing the song or play the recording; model tapping the rhythm sticks in bilateral motion on the floor. Then model other rhythm stick movements (such as tapping them together, tapping them on the floor in alternating motion, tapping your feet, rolling them on the floor, scraping them together), and ask students to copy your movements.

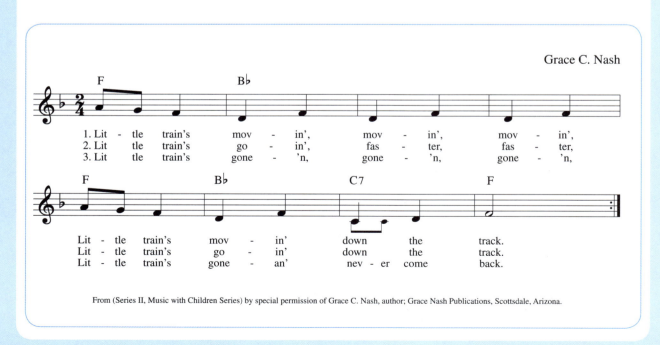

From (Series II, Music with Children Series) by special permission of Grace C. Nash, author; Grace Nash Publications, Scottsdale, Arizona.

Create Movements
Sing the song or play the recording; ask individual students for suggestions of movements with the rhythm sticks.

Sing
Invite students to sing the song with you as soon as they know it.

> **CONNECTION TO LITERATURE**
> Read *The Little Engine That Could* (Penguin Group 2006) by Watty Piper. Discuss how the engine overcomes his fears and weaknesses and learns to trust in himself and succeed.

JUMP RIGHT IN: THE MUSIC CURRICULUM

ENGINE, ENGINE

Activity Type: Movement, Chanting

Meter: Usual Duple

Macrobeats:

Microbeats:

TEACHING PLAN ONE

Materials Needed: Train whistle. Enough space for everyone to move freely.

 Disc Three
Track 23

 Piano Bk
Page 46

Purpose:
1. To help students imitate and begin to audiate macrobeats and microbeats in Usual Duple meter.
2. To help the students explore their voices.
3. To help students experience strong and gentle locomotor movement.
4. To introduce students to a traditional chant.

Blow the train whistle, and ask everyone to stand in self space.

Move in Place

Chant, "Chh, chh, chh, chh," and tap your heels in place on microbeats. Gesture for the students to join you in moving to microbeats with their heels. Once the students are moving to microbeats, perform the chant along with the movement. After the chant is completed, resume chanting microbeats until you blow your train whistle to signal a stop. Repeat the process,

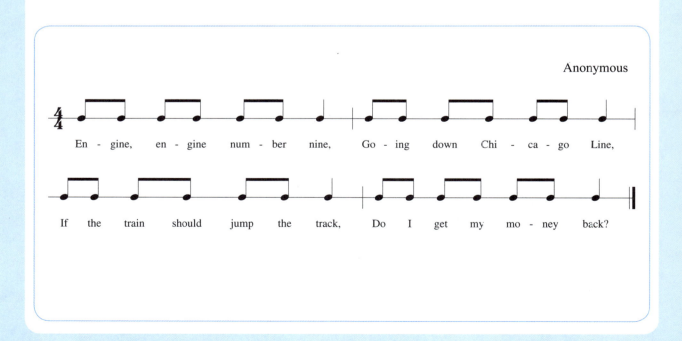

192

moving and chanting to macrobeats instead of microbeats. After the chant, resume chanting macrobeats until you blow the train whistle.

Move in Space
Tell the students that you are going to be a little train moving around the room. Chant, "Chh, chh, chh, chh" to microbeats, taking small, light steps (also to microbeats) as you chant. Gesture for the students to join you. They could move around the outside of the room in a circle, or they could move around the room randomly, being careful to stay in self space. As soon as the students are moving, begin the chant. After the chant is completed, continue moving, and resume chanting to microbeats until you blow the train whistle to signal a stop.

Then tell the students that you are going to be a big train. Repeat the above process, taking heavy steps and chanting to macrobeats. Again, gesture for the students to join you in the movement, and perform the chant as soon as the students are moving well. After the chant is completed, resume chanting macrobeats until you blow the train whistle.

Ask individual students whether they would like to be a big train or a little train and chant either macrobeats or microbeats while making the appropriate movement for each of the student requests. Remind the students that the little train is light and moves gently, whereas the big train shakes the entire track.

Voice Exploration
Ask the students to imitate the sound of your train whistle with their voices. Demonstrate what this would sound like by blowing the train whistle and imitating the sound with your own voice. Use a light vocal quality, and start in head voice. Blow the train whistle, asking the students to imitate you each time. Vary the pitch direction and the speed of pitch change each time you blow the whistle.

FOR THE MUSIC TEACHER
If your students are not able to move to macrobeats, they may need to develop more readiness. By engaging them in many activities that focus on flow with and without pulsations in a variety of meters, you will provide them with the readiness that they need to audiate and eventually to move to macrobeats.

CONNECTION TO LITERATURE
Read *The Little Engine That Could* (Penguin Group 2006) by Watty Piper. This children's classic features updated illustrations.

JUMP RIGHT IN: THE MUSIC CURRICULUM

TEACHING PLAN TWO

Materials Needed: Enough space for everyone to move comfortably.

Purpose:
1. To help students learn to move the whole body with continuous flow.
2. To help students learn to audiate rhythm patterns in Usual Duple Meter.

Everyone should be standing in self space.

Listen and Flow
Ask students to audiate and copy your movement as you move using continuous, fluid movements. Play the recording or perform the chant for students using continuous, fluid movement with your whole body as you audiate or chant. Be certain that you move your hips, shoulders, and back as well as your arms. In this way, you model the exploration of space around you even though you are not using locomotor space. Observe students as they move, making note of those who move as you do, in a coordinated fashion. For students who are having difficulty with balance or using space, consult activities in the Teacher's Edition in which continuous flow is combined with body awareness.

Add Pulsations
If the majority of students can move using continuous flow with their whole bodies, repeat the instructions above, inviting students to use continuous flow with pulsations to microbeats. Tell students that their engines are giving the engineers a very bumpy ride. Show the bumpy ride as pulsating movements. Be certain to put each microbeat pulsation in a different place in space, using various parts of the body. This models the use of space with flow. Again, observe students' movements. If students are successful coordinating pulsations with a variety of body parts, introduce the game.

Listening and Moving Game
Ask the students to label the two types of movement they have experienced (continuous flow and continuous flow with pulsations) in the Teaching Plan. Invite them to play a game. Tell them that, when they hear you chant "Engine, Engine," their engines will give the engineers a bumpy ride. (They should move using continuous

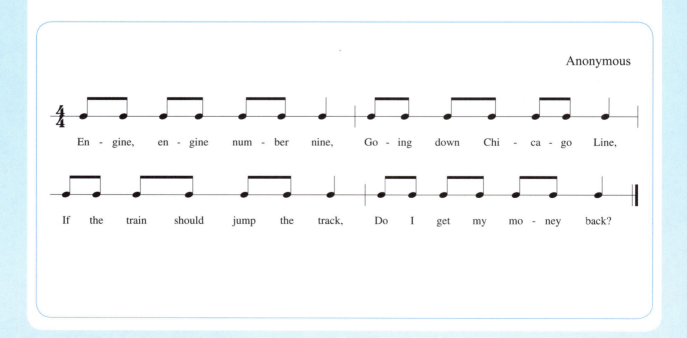

194

flow with pulsations.) When they hear you chant rhythm patterns, they should give the engineers a smooth ride. (They should move continuously without pulsations.) Tell them that you will model the appropriate movements as you chant.

After at least one repetition of the chant, improvise four, four-macrobeat rhythm patterns in Usual Duple meter. As students are able to change their movements with coordination, cease modeling for them. Also, sometimes perform "Engine, Engine" twice before performing patterns, or improvise only two four-macrobeat patterns.

Rhythm Imitation
After the students have had opportunities to hear the chant and many patterns, invite them to echo your patterns as they move with flow.

OLD MACDONALD HAD A FARM

Activity Type: Movement, Singing

Tonality: Major

Resting Tone:

Meter: Usual Duple

Macrobeats:

Microbeats:

Keyality: G

Disc Three
Track 24

Piano Bk
Page 98

Range: d–b

Materials Needed: Enough space for everyone to move comfortably.

Purpose:
1. To give students experience with movement using body awareness and continuous flow.
2. To help students remember sequences of movement.
3. To give students experience moving with bound and free flow.
4. To give students experience with a familiar song.

196

TEACHER'S EDITION • KINDERGARTEN

TEACHING PLAN
Everyone should be standing in stationary self space.

Audiate and Move
Invite the students to audiate this familiar song. Ask them not to sing out loud yet, even if they recognize the song. Later, you will invite them to sing the song for you. Tell them that they should imitate your movements now.

Move using continuous flow with your whole body each time you sing the phrase "Old MacDonald had a farm, E–I–E–I–O!" When you sing the animal name and sound for a given verse, isolate one part of the body, and move it in circular pathways as you sing. For example, rotate your hips in circles and figure eights while you sing the verse about chicks. During the verse about ducks, move your hands continuously. Accumulate verses of the songs so that after you sing about ducks and move your hands, you return to the verse about chicks and move your hips. Continue this until you also have moved your back, shoulders, head, knees, and wrists. Remember to move your whole body with continuous flow for the opening and closing repeating phrase.

Observe and notice whether students are able to move as you are moving while remaining coordinated and balanced. When they are ready, invite them to sing as they move.

Students Lead the Movements
On a different day, invite students to suggest and lead movements during the verses.

Recreate the Sequence
After students are familiar with the activities suggested, invite them to incorporate another activity.

After they have made five movements, invite them to perform those movements one after the other in silence at the end of the singing. First, invite them to close their eyes and recall the movements they performed on that day. If five movements are too many for them to recall, try fewer. Then give them a signal to begin, and observe their movements. Encourage students to flow from one movement to the next rather than perform one movement, stop, perform the next, stop, and so on. Model with them, and compliment their use of space and coordination as you observe success.

Bound and Free Flow
Invite the students to move a part of the body as though they were moving in the thickest, muddiest parts of the farm. Tell them that this mud is not runny and slippery because there hasn't been enough rain recently. Everyone's movements should be bound so they can stop easily in the thick mud. Then have them move in a rain shower that washes the mud away. Finally, have them move after the sun has dried them. Movements should be freer in the sun than in the mud. They are less easy to stop. Tell them that, "When moving in the mud, your movements will be more bound than when you are moving in the sun."

COORDINATION WITH INSTRUMENTAL MUSIC
Play the solo trombone recording of "Old MacDonald Had a Farm" from *Jump Right In: The Instrumental Series* (J229CD, track 94). Show the students a picture of the trombone using Instrument Card 23. Ask the students to imitate your movements at you play the recording again. Perform macrobeat movements using several parts of the body, changing parts of the body at phrase points in the song to facilitate the audiation of phrases.

JUMP RIGHT IN: THE MUSIC CURRICULUM

THE OLD GRAY CAT

Activity Type: Movement

Tonality: Major

Resting Tone:

Do

Meter: Usual Triple

Macrobeats:

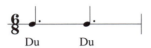
Du Du

Microbeats:

Du Da Di Du Da Di

Keyality: G

Range: d–b

 Disc Three Track 25   Piano Bk Page 96

Materials Needed: Recording. Enough space for everyone to move comfortably.

Purpose:
1. To help students imitate and learn to audiate macrobeats in Usual Triple meter.
2. To give students experience with strong and gentle movement in association with music.

TEACHING PLAN
Everyone should be seated in self space.

Identify Macrobeats
Ask the students to listen to the song and watch you move. Sing the song for the students while patting your lap in parallel motion to macrobeats. Tell the students that you are patting to the macrobeats of the song. Invite the students to join you in patting macrobeats as you sing the song again. Ask one student where you should pat macrobeats. Sing the song several more times

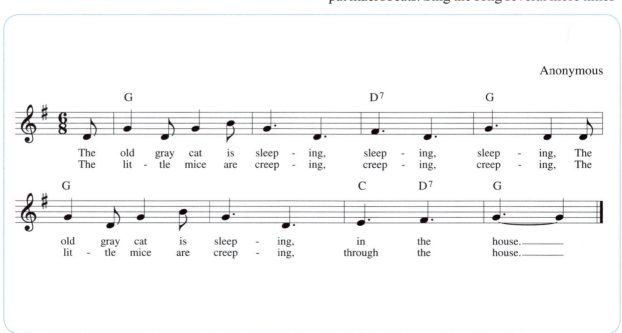

Anonymous

The old gray cat is sleep-ing, sleep-ing, sleep-ing, The old gray cat is sleep-ing, in the house.
The lit-tle mice are creep-ing, creep-ing, creep-ing, The lit-tle mice are creep-ing, through the house.

198

while incorporating different student suggestions. Then place your hands in front of you, and pat in an alternating motion as if your hands were walking in place. Ask the students to join you in that movement as you sing the song again.

Move to Macrobeats

Ask the students to stand in self space and move their feet to macrobeats by tiptoeing in place. Remind them that "in place" means that they do not move around the room, but stay in one spot. Sing the song again as you and the students tiptoe. After the students are able to do this successfully, play the recording, and ask them to tiptoe around the room to macrobeats. Then ask them to tell you about the text of the song. They should be able to identify that there is a cat sleeping and that mice are tiptoeing around, trying not to wake the cat.

Play the Game

Choose one student to be the sleeping cat. Ask that student to curl up on the floor in the middle of the room and pretend to be sleeping. Tell the rest of the students that they are the mice. During the song, they should tiptoe gently around the room, trying not to wake the cat. At the end of the song, the mice should stamp their feet in place as loudly as they can to wake up the cat. The cat should catch a mouse, who will become the cat in the next repetition of the game.

TEACHING TIP
Many of the students may not be able to walk to macrobeats. If this is the case, you can gently play a hand drum to macrobeats to accompany their movement. Even if the students mostly are unable to walk to macrobeats, they will learn from the activity. All students will experience strong and gentle movement, and they will hear macrobeats reinforced.

FOR THE MUSIC TEACHER
If your students are not able to move to macrobeats, they may need to develop more readiness. By engaging them in many activities that focus on flow with and without pulsations in a variety of meters, you will provide them with the readiness that they need to audiate and eventually move to macrobeats.

LITTLE WIND

Activity Type: Solo Singing, Movement

Tonality: Dorian

Resting Tone:

Meter: Usual Duple

Macrobeats:

Microbeats:

Keyality: E

Range: d–c-sharp'

Disc Three
Track 26

Piano Bk
Page 82

Materials Needed:
Hoberman sphere. Enough space for everyone to move comfortably.

Purpose:
1. To help students audiate resting tone in Dorian tonality.
2. To give students an opportunity to perform a pattern in solo.
3. To give students experience with continuous, fluid movement with pulsations.

TEACHING PLAN
Everyone should be seated in self space.

Flow with Pulsations
Sing the song for the students, and ask them to tell you about the text of the song. They should tell you that it is about the wind. Ask the students to watch your movement and to be prepared to

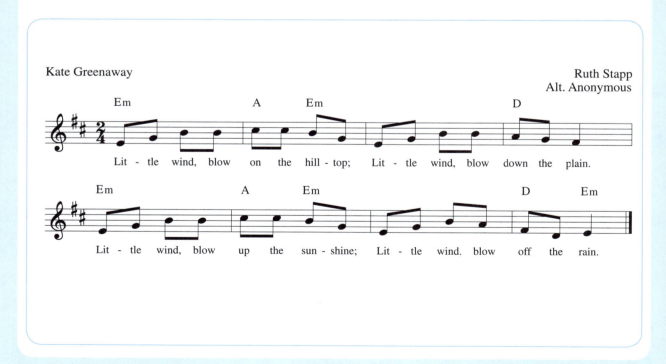

TEACHER'S EDITION • KINDERGARTEN

describe it for you when you are finished. Stand and sing the song again, pretending to be a tree whose branches are swaying in the wind. Your movement should be flowing but have pulsations on macrobeats. Ask the students to describe your movement. They should comment both on the flowing nature of the movement as well as on the pulsations. Perform the song again, and ask the students to move with you.

Sing the Resting Tone

Get out the Hoberman sphere. Open it, and sing the fifth scale degree. Then close it, and sing the resting tone. Open it, and place it on the ground. Spin it, singing the fifth scale degree, and when it closes naturally, sing the resting tone.

Then tell the students that you want them to sing what you sang when the ball is open and closed. Practice once with them singing when you open and close the ball. Do not sing with them. Then sing the song. When you open the ball at the end of the song, the students should sing the fifth scale degree. When you close the ball, they should sing the resting tone. Repeat this process several times. As you sing the song, walk around the classroom, weaving among the students and moving with the ball in a fluid manner.

Sing in Solo

Tell the students that they are going to have an opportunity to open and close the ball and that they should sing the pattern while they do it. Ask the students to move like the trees in the wind again as you sing the song. At the end of the song, stop in front of a student, and place the ball on the ground. That student should open and close the ball while singing the pattern that goes with it (fifth scale degree when the ball is open and resting tone when it closes). Sing the song again, and at the end, place the ball in front of a different student, who will open it and sing. You can choose several students to open and close the ball before you sing the song again so that more students get an opportunity to sing in solo.

FOR THE MUSIC TEACHER

Games that include opportunities for students to sing in solo provide an opportunity for you to document students' music achievement. Carry a class list or a seating chart and pencil with you as you teach this activity. After the student sings and as you begin to sing the song again, record his or her singing achievement on the class list or seating chart using the following rating scale.

5. The student takes an audiation breath before performing and sings the pattern with tonal accuracy.
4. The student performs the pattern with tonal accuracy but no audiation breath.
3. The student performs the pattern in singing voice with some accuracy.
2. The student maintains the melodic contour of the pattern but not the exact pitches.
1. The student is working toward use of singing voice.

If you do this several times during the school year, you will have a record of the student's singing development.

TEACHING TIP

Students will be excited about opening and closing the ball, which will make them less self-conscious about singing. However, they may also forget to sing. Remind them that they should sing at the same time. If a student gives you an inaccurate response, sing the correct pattern immediately afterward so that the student can compare the two performances.

WHO HAS SEEN THE WIND?

Activity Type: Singing, Solo Singing, Melodic Creativity, Vocal Exploration, Movement

Tonality: Phrygian

Resting Tone:

Meter: Usual Duple

Macrobeats:

Microbeats:

 Disc Three Track 27

 Piano Bk Page 150

Keyality: C

Range: c–e-flat'

Materials Needed: Enough space for everyone to move comfortably.

Purpose:
1. To give students an opportunity to experience Phyrgian tonality.
2. To give students an opportunity to create and perform a melodic pattern in solo.
3. To give students an opportunity to explore their voices.

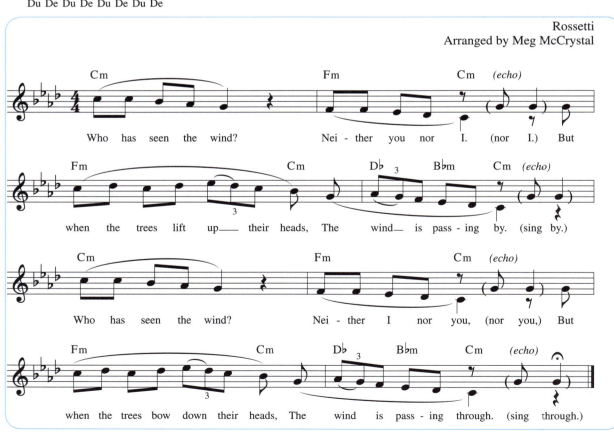

202

TEACHING PLAN
Everyone should be seated in self space.

Vocal Exploration
Sing the song for the student using the text. After you have finished, tell the students that you are going to make wind sounds with your voice. Then perform gentle vocal slides through all registers of your voice using the syllable OO. Ask the students to make similar wind sounds with their voices. Give them a breath cue, and gesture to perform. After about ten seconds, make a cut-off conducting gesture to quiet them down. Tell the students that their job is to make wind sounds when you gesture. Sing the first two phrases of the song (the A section), and then breathe and gesture for the students to make their wind sounds. After about five to ten seconds, cut them off and perform the last two phrases of the song (the B section). Again cue the students to make wind sounds.

Creativity
Ask the students what question is asked at the beginning of the song. (Answer: "Who has seen the wind?") Then ask them the answer to that question. (Answer: "Neither you nor I.") Tell them that you are going to ask individual students the question by singing and that they should make up their own answers using the words of the song. Demonstrate how this might sound. For example:

I would sing

Who has seen the wind?

and you might sing

Nei-ther you nor I.

Or, I would sing

Who has seen the wind?

and you might sing

Nei-ther you nor I.

Help the students to notice that the responses above are musically different from those in the original song.

Give several students a chance to create a melodic pattern to "Neither you nor I" outside of the context of the entire song. Sing the question and ask a volunteer to make up an answer. Do this several times. Then tell the students that you will sing the song and gesture to a student to make up and answer. Go on singing the song. When the question comes again, gesture to a different student. Continue this process several times, gesturing to different students each time.

OPHELIA' LETTER BLOW 'WAY

Activity Type: Singing, Solo Singing, Movement

Tonality: Major

Resting Tone:

Do

Meter: Usual Duple

Macrobeats:

Du Du Du Du

Microbeats:

Du De Du De Du De Du De

 Disc Three Track 28   Piano Bk Page 103

Keyality: F

Range: c–f'

Materials Needed: Recording. Small plush bean bag. Enough space for everyone to move comfortably.

Purpose: To help students audiate and sing the resting tone in Major tonality.

TEACHING PLAN
Everyone should be seated in a circle.

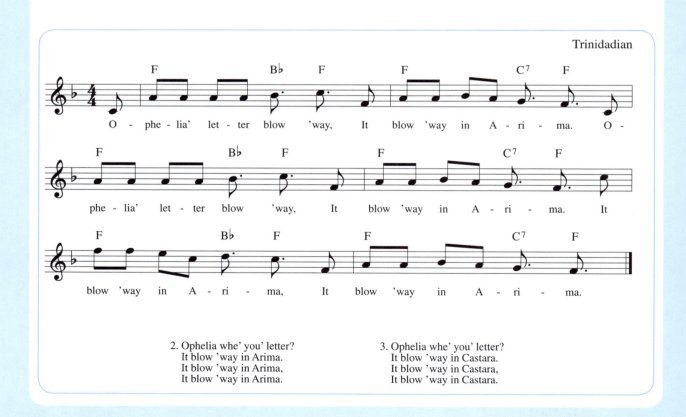

Trinidadian

O-phe-lia' let-ter blow 'way, It blow 'way in A-ri-ma. O-phe-lia' let-ter blow 'way, It blow 'way in A-ri-ma. It blow 'way in A-ri-ma, It blow 'way in A-ri-ma.

2. Ophelia whe' you' letter?
   It blow 'way in Arima.
   It blow 'way in Arima,
   It blow 'way in Arima.

3. Ophelia whe' you' letter?
   It blow 'way in Castara.
   It blow 'way in Castara,
   It blow 'way in Castara.

Sing

Play the recording to introduce the song. Teach the resting tone of the song using BUM, and ask the students to sing it every time you pause. Pause at the end of each phrase; then breathe, and gesture for the students to sing BUM on the resting tone.

Use the Toy

Sit in the center of the circle with a plush bean bag. Sing the song, and toss the bean bag to a student when you pause. Have that student sing the resting tone using BUM. Repeat this several times until all of the students have had an opportunity to sing alone or until the students lose interest.

TEACHING TIP

At first you may need to sing the resting tone in duet with the students until they have developed the confidence to sing it alone. However, most kindergarten students will be delighted to have an opportunity to have their turn. Also, many will focus on the toy and the playful nature of the activity rather than their concerns about singing in solo.

JUMP RIGHT IN: THE MUSIC CURRICULUM

FIREMAN, FIREMAN

Activity Type: Singing, Movement

Tonality: Harmonic Minor

Resting Tone:

Meter: Usual Duple

Macrobeats:

Microbeats:

Keyality: D

Range: d–b-flat

 Disc Three Track 29

 Piano Bk Page 50

Materials Needed: Enough space for everyone to move comfortably.

Purpose:
1. To give students an opportunity to create action movements to the lyrics of a song.
2. To give students an opportunity to echo tonic and dominant Harmonic Minor tonal patterns.
3. To give students an opportunity to create different tonal patterns.

TEACHING PLAN

Everyone should be standing in stationary self space.

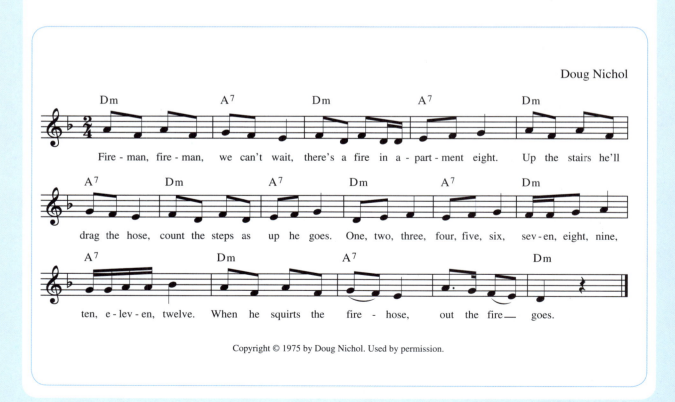

Doug Nichol

Fire-man, fire-man, we can't wait, there's a fire in a-part-ment eight. Up the stairs he'll drag the hose, count the steps as up he goes. One, two, three, four, five, six, sev-en, eight, nine, ten, e-lev-en, twelve. When he squirts the fire-hose, out the fire goes.

Copyright © 1975 by Doug Nichol. Used by permission.

206

TEACHER'S EDITION • KINDERGARTEN

Introduce the Song
Invite students to audiate silently while you play the recording or sing "Fireman, Fireman." Ask them to listen to the words and copy your movement. Move using continuous flow as you sing.

Create Pantomimed Movements
Invite the students to help you create movements to pantomime the action of the words to the song. Repeat the song, and perform their created movements several times through.

Sing Tonal Patterns
Pantomime squirting the firehose at the end of the song. While you are pretending to squirt, take a breath and establish tonality by singing the sequence of tones notated below using a neutral syllable.

Invite the students to breathe and be your echo as you sing tonal patterns suggested below.

Sing a Different Pattern: Creativity
Invite the students to help you put out the fire by breathing and singing a different tonal pattern from yours. Sing the whole song for students again. At the end, breathe and pantomime squirting the firehose. While you squirt, sing a tonic pattern. Assist children in knowing when it is their turn by breathing and lifting your imaginary hose in their direction.

Any pattern students sing is acceptable. If students sing functions other than tonic, their responses might confuse them and others. Help them enjoy the differences. Repeat this activity several times, asking different groups and individual students to sing patterns that are different from yours. For example, you could invite all of the boys, all of the girls, anyone who brushed their teeth this morning, or everyone in the first row. Gradually invite fewer students to be different until students are comfortable being different in solo. Student leaders can take turns singing tonal patterns for their classmates to respond to with a different pattern.

Intersperse repetitions of "Fireman, Fireman" and the pantomimed movements to reestablish tonality after you have sung several sets of patterns.

Sing the Song
After students have silently audiated the song several times, invite them to sing it. Do not sing with them. Instead, listen. If they struggle, return to singing the song or playing the recording for them, asking them to listen while they move.

LULLABY FROM CYPRUS

Activity Type: Listening, Movement

Tonality: Aeolian

Resting Tone:

Meter: Unusual Paired

Macrobeats:

Microbeats:

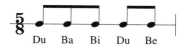

 Disc Three Track 30

 Piano Bk Page 84

Keyality: D

Range: c–g

Materials Needed: Enough space for everyone to move comfortably.

Purpose:
1. To give students an opportunity to listen and move to Unusual meter.
2. To give students experience moving continuously with pulsations.
3. To introduce students to music of another culture.

TEACHING PLAN

Everyone should be seated in self space.

TEACHER'S EDITION • KINDERGARTEN

Listen and Move While Seated

Tell the students that they will be listeners and movers. Remind them that listening is the most important job of a musician.

Have the students sit with crossed legs and copy your movements as you perform the song with bilateral microbeat pulsations in your hands. Never perform the microbeat pulsations in the same place twice in a row. Keep moving them around on the floor, on your legs, and in the air. Use your spine to assist your use of continuous, fluid movement.

Sing the song again, this time pulsating macrobeats. Have the students copy your bilateral macrobeat pulsations.

Then sing the song a third time, pulsating microbeats again. Now have the students copy your bilateral microbeat pulsations while they chant TUH to help coordinate their tongues with their body movements.

Sing the song again, pulsating macrobeats. Now have the students copy your bilateral macrobeat pulsations while they chant BAH to aid in awareness of the difference between microbeats and macrobeats and to facilitate the audiation of meter.

Stand and Rock

Use this song as an opportunity to assist students in feeling the differences between microbeats and macrobeats in Unusual Paired meter. When students become comfortable with each type of movement, have them stand and rock from side to side and simultaneously chant BAH on the macrobeats. Remind the students to use their weight on the balls of their feet and to raise their heels alternately as they rock.

Stand and Pulsate

Next, have the students copy your bilateral microbeat pulsations while they chant TUH to help coordinate their tongues with their body movements. Again, never perform the microbeat pulsations in the same place twice in a row. Keep moving them around on your legs and in the air. Use your spine to assist your use of continuous, fluid movement.

209

THE NOTHING SONG

Activity Type: Movement

Tonality: Major

Resting Tone:

Meter: Usual Duple

Macrobeats:

Microbeats:

Keyality: F

Range: d–d'

Materials Needed: Enough space for everyone to move comfortably.

Disc Three Track 31

Piano Bk Page 90

Purpose:
1. To give students experience moving in locomotor pathways.
2. To give students experience with strong and gentle movement.

TEACHING PLAN

Everyone should be standing in self space.

Move and Freeze in Locomotor Pathways

Tell the students that they will be traveling to empty spaces when they hear you sing and that they will freeze when you are not singing. Tell them that empty spaces are spaces with nothing and no one in them. If someone beats them to their chosen spots, they must choose another space.

TEACHER'S EDITION • KINDERGARTEN

Begin singing the song. Pause after each phrase to make sure that the students are listening to the musical cues to move and the cues to freeze.

Add the Effort of Weight
When the students have demonstrated success with simple locomotor pathways, add the effort of weight to their movements. When becoming aware of weight in movement, students need to practice being heavy and being light. Ask the students to talk about things that are heavy. Discuss how it feels to be heavy.

Tell the students to move like a heavy dinosaur or a large freight train (or something else that is heavy of their choosing) as they move and freeze when you sing and pause the song again. Change the word "nothing" to "heavy" during this repetition.

Discuss how it feels to be light. Tell the students to move lightly like a butterfly or a feather floating in the wind (or something else that is light of their choosing) as they move and freeze when you repeat the activity. Change the word "nothing" to "light" during this repetition.

Sing the song and play the move-and-freeze game again, allowing students to choose to be heavy or light.

THE BELL PETER

Activity Type: Movement

Tonality: Aeolian

Resting Tone:

La

Meter: Usual Triple

Macrobeats:

Du   Du

Microbeats:

Du Da Di Du Da Di

Keyality: A

Range: e–e'

Disc Three Track 32

Piano Bk Page 19

Materials Needed: Recording. Enough space for everyone to move comfortably.

Purpose:
1. To give students experience with macrobeat movement in Usual Triple meter.
2. To give students an opportunity to move in shared space.

TEACHING PLAN

Listen and Move

Everyone should be standing in self space. Play the recording of "The Bell Peter." As students listen, model rocking back and forth to macrobeats. Ask the students to move with you. Play the song again, this time swaying from side to side to macrobeats. Ask the students to move with you again.

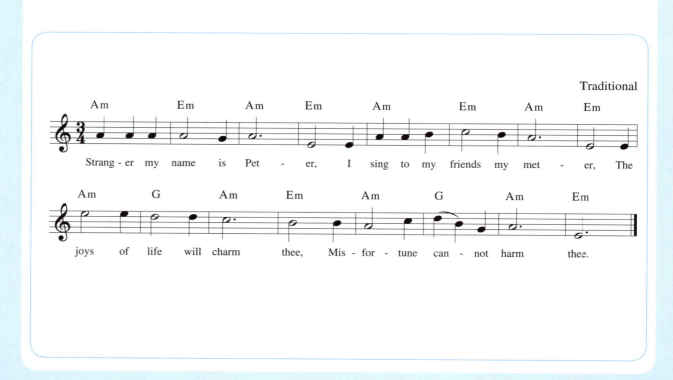

Move with a Partner

Tell the students you would like them to move to macrobeats, but instead of moving alone, they will move with a partner. Model rocking back and forth or swaying side to side with a partner for the students. Be sure to model the displacement of weight from one foot to the other. Pair your students with a partner, and sing the song again. Allow students time to practice moving their body in sync with each other. Invite the students to create other macrobeat movements in shared space (e.g., seated). Sing the song again, observing pairs moving to macrobeats. Invite a group to perform their macrobeat movement for the class, and ask class members to explain how the pair is moving. Invite the class to move in the same way.

COORDINATION WITH INSTRUMENTAL MUSIC

Play the flugelhorn recording of "The Bell Peter" from *Jump Right In: The Instrumental Series* (J199CD, track 60). Show the students a picture of the flugelhorn using Instrument Card 20. Ask the students if it reminds them of any other instrument. Tell them that it is similar to a trumpet, only larger. Because the instrument is larger, it sounds lower.

Give each student a bean bag. Sing the resting tone of the song in the key of the flugelhorn recording, and give the students a breath cue to sing the resting tone. Tell them that, when the recording is playing, they should balance their bean bags on a part of the body of their choosing and move that part of the body with continuous flow.

When you pause the recording, they should dump their bean bags on the floor, wait for your breath gesture, and then sing the resting tone. Then they should pick up their bean bags and place them on a different part of the body. Continue stopping and starting the recording to give them multiple opportunities to move and sing the resting tone.

GIPSY IPSY

Activity Type: Singing

Tonality: Pentatonic

Resting Tone:

Do

Meter: Usual Triple

Macrobeats:

Microbeats:

Keyality: C

Range: e–g

Disc Three Track 33   Piano Bk Page 58

TEACHING PLAN ONE

Materials Needed: Enough space for everyone to move comfortably.

Purpose:
1. To give students experience with continuous, fluid movement.
2. To imitate tonal patterns.
3. To identify tonal patterns as same or different.

Everyone should be seated in self space in a circle.

Listen, Move, and Sing

Sing the song a few times without the words, and have the students copy your movements.

Continuously roll your fists and forearms as you sing. Then invite the students to sing the song with you as they continuously roll their fists and forearms. Repeat the song several times.

Imitate and Identify Same and Different Tonal Patterns

Sing the following tonal patterns using the neutral syllable BUM. Give the students a breath gesture, and have them repeat each pattern after you sing it. It may help the students to breathe before they sing if they continue to roll their fists and forearms when they repeat after you.

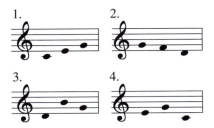

Tell the students to listen as you sing the first two patterns again. Explain to the students that the two patterns are different. Have the students hold up two different-looking hands (one open and the other closed) and repeat the word "different."

Next, sing the second two patterns. Again, tell the students that the two patterns are different. Have the students hold their different-looking hands and repeat the word "different."

Sing the first pattern, and then sing it again. Tell the students that the two patterns are the same. Have the students hold up two hands that look the same and repeat the word "same." (Both hands should be closed or open.)

Play the Game

Play a game using the four patterns. Sing pairs of patterns for the students. Have them show you with their hands if the two patterns you perform are the same or different.

GIPSY IPSY (continued)

TEACHING PLAN TWO

Activity Type: Singing, Tonal Creativity

Materials Needed: Enough space for everyone to move freely.

Purpose:
1. To give students experience moving continuously while pulsating macrobeats.
2. To give students an opportunity to imitate tonal patterns.
3. To give students an opportunity to create tonal patterns.

Everyone should be seated in self space in a circle. Students should be familiar with the activities in Teaching Plan One. Invite the students to sing the song with you as they continuously roll their fists and forearms. Repeat the song several times.

Tonal Pattern Imitation
Sing the tonal patterns from Teaching Plan One using BUM. Give the students a breath gesture, and have them repeat each pattern.

Then tell the students that when they repeat after you they are imitating you; they are performing the same pattern. Tell them that sometimes musicians perform differently from each other so that they can have musical conversations.

Tonal Pattern Creation
Tell the students that you are going to sing a tonal pattern, and they will get to sing a tonal pattern that is different from yours. Ask for a volunteer to demonstrate. Perform one of the four tonal patterns from Teaching Plan One. Gesture for the student to perform his or her pattern. Have the class repeat the student's pattern and determine if it the pattern is different from yours. They can show you their decisions by using their "same" or "different" hands.

TEACHER'S EDITION • KINDERGARTEN

If the student's tonal pattern is different from yours, say, "Yes, that was different." Accept all student attempts at being different from you in this lesson. Be sure to have the class repeat each student's tonal pattern for reinforcement, even if the student performs a pattern without using his or her singing voice. The point of the lesson is to make it safe to be different. In their first attempts to be different, students may not be accurate. With practice, accuracy will increase.

If the student's tonal pattern is the same as yours, say, "Thank you. That was the same pattern as mine. Here is a pattern that is different." Then demonstrate a different tonal pattern, and have the students imitate the different tonal pattern.

Give each student the opportunity to create a tonal pattern. If a student does not want to be different from you, allow the student to be the same as you.

THE SKY HAS CLOUDED

Activity Type: Movement, Chanting

Tonality: Harmonic Minor

Resting Tone:

Meter: Usual Duple

Macrobeats:

Microbeats:

Keyality: E

Range: e–b

Disc Three
Track 34

Piano Bk
Page 122

Materials Needed: Enough space for everyone to move comfortably.

Purpose:
1. To give students experience moving in a continuous, fluid style with pulsations.
2. To help students discriminate whether rhythm patterns are the same or different in Usual Duple meter.

TEACHING PLAN

Everyone should be standing in stationary self space.

Move, Establish Tonality, and Sing the Melody

Invite the students to audiate silently and imitate your movement. Model continuous, fluid movement with your whole body. As you move,

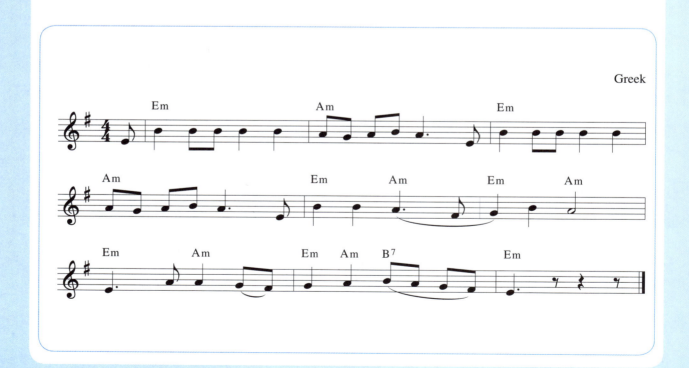

establish tonality by singing the sequence of tones notated below, followed by the resting tone using BUM. Continue moving as you sing the song.

Freeze when you finish singing the song. Resume moving to sing the resting tone using BUM, and invite the students to sing it after you by giving a breath gesture. Encourage them to imitate your movement as well as your singing.

Move Using Continuous Flow with Pulsations

Again, invite the students to imitate your movement. This time move using continuous flow with pulsations to macrobeats as you sing the melody or play the recording. Be certain to put each pulsation in a different place in space, using a variety of body parts as you move. Observe the students who are able to coordinate themselves while using continuous flow with pulsations. If students have difficulty, return to modeling continuous flow while they audiate the melody.

Rhythm Imitation in Usual Duple Meter

Establish Usual Duple meter. Then invite the students to be your echo by giving them a breath gesture on the fourth macrobeat of your pattern. They should begin to echo you on the first macrobeat following your pattern. Improvise four-macrobeat patterns in Usual Duple meter. During your improvisation, be certain to include the first one suggested below.

Suggested Usual Duple Patterns

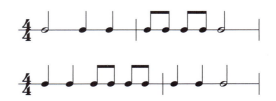

Same and Different

Repeat one of the patterns above, and invite the students to echo you. Ask them to audiate that pattern silently. Then invite them to play a game. Tell them that when you chant that pattern they will breathe and chant the same pattern. If your pattern is different from that pattern, they should breathe and audiate silently. Always provide the breath gesture as a cue for them to sing. Intersperse their patterns among different patterns. An alternate way to play is for the students to silently audiate your pattern when it is the same and echo the patterns that are different.

CLAPPING LAND

Tonality: Major

Resting Tone:

Meter: Usual Duple

Macrobeats:

Microbeats:

Keyality: D

Range: d–d'

 Disc Three
Track 35

 Piano Bk
Page 30

TEACHING PLAN ONE

Activity Type: Movement, Singing

Materials Needed: Enough space for everyone to move comfortably.

Purpose:
1. To move continuously with pulsations.
2. To imitate a tonal pattern.

Everyone should be seated in self space.

Listen and Move

Have the students sit with crossed legs and copy your movements as you perform the song with bilateral microbeat pulsations in your hands. Never perform the microbeat pulsations in the same place twice in a row. Keep moving them

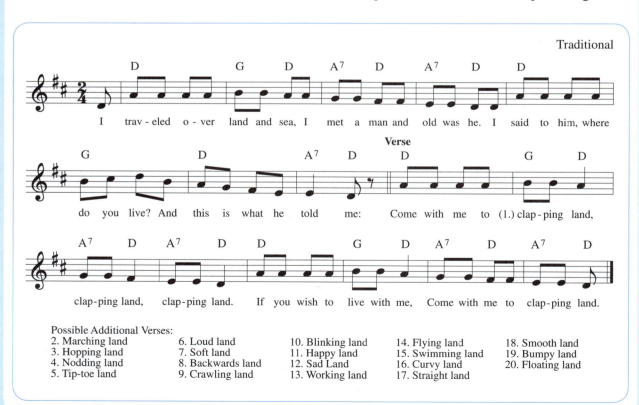

Possible Additional Verses:
2. Marching land
3. Hopping land
4. Nodding land
5. Tip-toe land
6. Loud land
7. Soft land
8. Backwards land
9. Crawling land
10. Blinking land
11. Happy land
12. Sad Land
13. Working land
14. Flying land
15. Swimming land
16. Curvy land
17. Straight land
18. Smooth land
19. Bumpy land
20. Floating land

all around on the floor, on your legs, and in the air. Use your spine to assist your use of continuous flow, being certain to keep the movements relaxed and fluid.

Sing the song again. This time, pulsate macrobeats, and have the students copy your bilateral macrobeat pulsations.

Move and Chant
Sing the song a third time, and move with microbeat pulsations again. Have the students copy your microbeat pulsations while they chant TUH to microbeats to coordinate their tongues with their body movements.

Sing the song again, moving with macrobeat pulsations. Now have the students copy your bilateral macrobeat pulsations while they chant BAH to help develop awareness of the differences between microbeats and macrobeats and to facilitate the audiation of meter.

When students become comfortable with the movements, encourage them to sing the song with text as they move.

Tonal Pattern Imitation
Sing the following tonal pattern using the syllable BUM. Use a clear preparatory breath gesture to cue the students to repeat the pattern.

Tell the students that this is the first tonal pattern of the song and the first tonal pattern of the second phrase. Sing the beginning of the song and the second phrase to demonstrate the tonal pattern.

Using a neutral syllable, sing the song for the students. Have them insert the tonal pattern at the beginning of phrase one and phrase two. Be sure to use a clear preparatory breath gesture before you have the students sing the tonal pattern.

TEACHING PLAN TWO
Activity Type: Movement

Materials Needed: Enough space for everyone to move comfortably.

Purpose:
1. To develop body awareness.
2. To give students experience with strong and gentle movement.

Everyone should be standing in self space.

Move and Freeze in Locomotor Pathways
Tell the students that they will be traveling to empty spaces when you sing and that they should freeze when you do not sing. Explain that empty spaces are spaces with nothing and no one in them. Tell the students that someone else may move to spaces that they were planning on using. If that is the case, they must simply choose another space.

Begin singing the song. Pause after each phrase to make sure the students listen to the music cues to move and the silence cues to freeze.

Adding the Effort of Weight
Once students have demonstrated success at simple locomotor pathways, add the effort of weight to their movements. When becoming aware of weight in movement, students should practice being strong and being gentle.

Tell the students to be very strong in their arms, backs, and legs as they move and freeze when you sing the song again. Change the word "clapping" to "strong" during this repetition of the song.

Next, tell the students to be very gentle in their arms, backs, and legs as they move and to freeze when you sing the song again. Change the word "clapping" to "gentle" during this repetition of the song.

CLAPPING LAND (continued)

Ask the students to talk about times when you have to be strong or gentle. Discuss how it feels to be strong. Discuss how it feels to be gentle.

Sing the song, and play the move-and-freeze game again. Allow the students to choose to move being strong or to move being gentle. Use the original text of the song.

Repeat the weight activity in stationary movement without using locomotor space. Discuss how it feels to be strong and to be gentle without traveling.

TEACHING PLAN THREE

Activity Type: Movement, Chanting, Rhythm Creativity

Materials Needed: Enough space for everyone to move comfortably.

Purpose:
1. To move continuously with pulsations.
2. To create rhythm patterns.

Everyone should be seated in self space.

Listen and Move
Have the students sit with crossed legs and copy your movements as you review the differences between microbeats and macrobeats. Perform the song, moving with bilateral microbeat pulsations as you did in Teaching Plan One. Ask the students to copy your bilateral microbeat pulsations while they chant TUH to help coordinate their tongues with their body movements. Then sing the song again and have the students copy your bilateral macrobeat pulsations while they chant BAH.

Imitate and Identify Same and Different Rhythm Patterns
Now tell the students you are going to perform two rhythm patterns that are different from one another. Perform each of the following rhythm

Possible Additional Verses:
2. Marching land
3. Hopping land
4. Nodding land
5. Tip-toe land
6. Loud land
7. Soft land
8. Backwards land
9. Crawling land
10. Blinking land
11. Happy land
12. Sad Land
13. Working land
14. Flying land
15. Swimming land
16. Curvy land
17. Straight land
18. Smooth land
19. Bumpy land
20. Floating land

patterns using the neutral syllable BAH. Pause between the patterns, and hold up one finger for the first pattern and two fingers for the second pattern to allow the students to identify each.

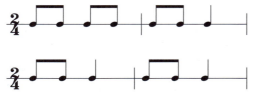

Next, have the students imitate each of the two rhythm patterns. Tell them that those two rhythm patterns are the only rhythm patterns in the second half of the song. Perform the second half of the song to demonstrate the patterns.

Rhythm Pattern Creation

Tell the students that you are going to chant a rhythm pattern and that they will get to chant a rhythm pattern that is different from yours. Ask for a volunteer to demonstrate. Perform one of the rhythm patterns notated above. Gesture for the student to perform his or her pattern. Have the class repeat the student's pattern and determine if the pattern was different from yours. They can show you their decisions by using their same (two fists) or different (one fist and one open) hands.

Accept all student attempts at being different from you in this lesson. If the student's rhythm pattern is different from yours, say, "Yes, that was different." Be sure to have the class repeat each student's rhythm pattern for reinforcement. The point of the lesson is to make it safe to be different. In their first conscious attempts to be different, students may not maintain beat or tempo. Given opportunity and practice, this will improve.

If the student's rhythm pattern is the same as yours, say, "Thank you. That was the same pattern as mine. Here is a pattern that is different." Then demonstrate a different rhythm pattern, and have everyone demonstrate the different rhythm pattern.

JUMP RIGHT IN: THE MUSIC CURRICULUM

ONLY MY OPINION

Activity Type: Singing, Movement

Tonality: Mixolydian

Resting Tone:

So

Meter: Usual Duple

Macrobeats:

Du Du

Microbeats:

Du De Du De

Keyality: E

Range: d–c-sharp'

Materials Needed: Enough space for everyone to move comfortably.

 Disc Three Track 36

 Piano Bk Page 101

Purpose:
1. To give students an opportunity to experience and audiate the resting tone Mixolydian tonality.
2. Help students develop body awareness through locomotor movement.

TEACHING PLAN
Everyone should be seated in self space.

Focus on Resting Tone
Sing the song for the students using text. Then sing the resting tone and label it as such for the students. Sing the resting tone again, and give a preparatory breath and gesture for them to echo you. After you have finished, ask the students to tell you what the song is about. You may need to sing the song again to help them understand the text.

Debbie Artz

Is a cat-er-pil-lar tick-lish? Well, it's al-ways my be-lief that he gig-gles as he wig-gles a-cross a hair-y leaf.

Movement

Hold your hand out with the palm pointed down, as though you are balancing something on the back of your hand. Tell the students that you have an imaginary caterpillar on the back of your hand. Ask them to show you the caterpillars on the backs of their hands. Then carefully stand, being sure not to let your imaginary caterpillar fall; ask the students to do the same. Remind them that they must be very careful not to let their caterpillars fall.

Then ask the students to walk around the room, balancing their caterpillars while you sing the song. At the end of the song, sing on the resting tone, "Now we are going to gently move our caterpillars." Sing the fifth scale degree as you gently pick up your imaginary caterpillar, and sing the resting tone as you gently place it on your head. Ask the students to do the same. Then sing the song as everyone moves around the room again, this time balancing the caterpillars on their heads.

Ask the students where else you could balance your caterpillars. Each time you move the imaginary caterpillars, sing the fifth scale degree as you lift it; sing the resting tone as you place it on the new part of the body.

FOR THE MUSIC TEACHER

After students are comfortable with this activity and have developed some body awareness, you can extend the activity by playing a game. Ask a student to balance his or her caterpillar without telling you where. Then sing the song as the student moves across the room. Ask the class to guess where the student is balancing his or her caterpillar. The student who guesses correctly is the next student who moves and balances the imaginary caterpillar.

TEACHING TIP

If the students do not demonstrate the desired level of body awareness as they carry their imaginary caterpillars, they may need more concrete experience to prepare them for the imaginary. Cut rectangles of construction paper so that they are approximately two inches long and a half-inch wide. Have the students balance these "real" caterpillars as they move around the room, rather than imagining caterpillars. Balancing a real object gives students feedback about how successful they are. If the caterpillar falls off, they know that they need to work on keeping that part of the body more level as they move.

JUMP RIGHT IN: THE MUSIC CURRICULUM

RAIN ON THE GREEN GRASS

Activity Type: Listening, Movement

Meter: Unusual Paired

Macrobeats:

Microbeats:

Materials Needed: Enough space for everyone to move comfortably.

Purpose:
1. To help students audiate Unusual Paired meter.
2. To give students experience using stationary and locomotor space.
3. To help students develop body awareness.

Disc Three Track 37

Piano Bk Page 111

TEACHING PLAN
Everyone should be seated in self space, prepared to move using stationary and locomotor self space.

Learn or Review Types of Movement
Ask the students to observe your movement. Tell them that when you have finished moving you will ask them to describe what you did when you began your movements and what you did when you stopped moving.

First, move with continuous flow and travel to a new spot. Stay in self space. Chant "Rain on the Green Grass" as you flow and travel. When you finish the chant, stop moving.

Anonymous

Rain on the green grass, Rain on the tree, Rain on the roof top, But not on me.

226

Ask the students to describe your movement. Invite discussion when accurate and inaccurate descriptions are given. Model the same movements again, this time emphasizing three labels: continuous flow, locomotor space, and self space. Be certain the students realize that your movement began and ended while you were in self space. If necessary, model what beginning or ending in shared space looks like so that they are able to make a comparison.

Repeat this process, this time moving with continuous flow in one place as you perform the chant and move in stationary self space. Again, ask the students to describe your movement, guiding them to three labels: continuous flow, stationary space, and self space. Remind them that you began and ended your movement in self space.

Move to Standing Self Space

Invite a few students to stand and model stationary self space using continuous flow as you perform the chant. Challenge all students to imagine what everyone will look like when they are all standing in the room demonstrating stationary self space and continuous flow. Perform the chant as they imagine the movements. Then invite rows or groups of students to join the students already standing when you begin your chant. Once all students are standing, repeat the sequence using locomotor self space with continuous flow. When all students are successful with both types of movements, introduce the next part of the Teaching Plan.

Is It Raining?

On a different day, chant several repetitions of "Rain on the Green Grass." Tell the students that the chant you have been performing for them is called "Rain on the Green Grass." If they hear you chant "Rain on the Green Grass," they should move in locomotor self space using continuous flow. If they hear a different chant (one that is not "Rain on the Green Grass"), they should move using continuous flow in stationary self space. Chant "Rain on the Green Grass" and other chants in unpredictable sequences. Do not move with the students; rather, observe their movements to learn who can aurally identify the chant.

THIS OLD MAN

Activity Type: Movement, Singing, Tonal Creativity

Tonality: Major

Resting Tone:

Do

Meter: Usual Duple

Macrobeats:

Du Du

Microbeats:

Du De Du De

Keyality: F

Range: f–d'

Materials Needed: Enough space for everyone to move comfortably.

 Disc Three Track 38

 Piano Bk Page 138

Purpose:
1. To help students develop body awareness and give them experience with continuous, fluid movement.
2. To help students learn to discriminate whether tonal patterns in Major tonality are the same or different.
3. To give students the opportunity to create tonal patterns.

TEACHING PLAN

Everyone should be standing in stationary self space.

Dance for Most Important Part of the Body

Tell the students to audiate the melody you are about to sing and to imitate your movement. Sing the song, doing a continuous, flowing dance for the part of the body each verse suggests.

Traditional

This old man, he played one, He played knick knack on his thumb. With a knick knack, pad-dy whack, give your dog a bone, This old man came rol-ling home.

2. This old man, he played two,
   He played knick knack on his shoe.
   With a knick knack, paddy whack,
   Give your dog a bone,
   This old man came rolling home.

3. This old man, he played three,
   He played knick knack on his knee…

4. This old man, he played four,
   He played knick knack on the floor…

5. This old man, he played five,
   He played knick knack on his hives…

6. This old man, he played six,
   He played knick knack on his sticks…

TEACHER'S EDITION • KINDERGARTEN

If the words do not specify, improvise movement using a part of the body you have not emphasized (hips, shoulders, head, legs). Remember to move your whole body even as you emphasize one part of the body in your movement.

Observe the students as they move. Notice students who coordinate continuous flow while emphasizing one body part.

Sing the Resting Tone

On a different day, after you have sung the melody several times, sing the resting tone, and invite the students to be your echo, using a breath gesture as a cue to sing. Then invite them to move when they hear you sing the melody. Tell them that when you stop singing they are to freeze and watch you. You will give them a breath gesture and invite them to sing the resting tone while they are frozen; they should watch you and be prepared to sing, either as individuals or as a class.

Same and Different Endings

Tell the students that you will sing only the first verse of the song. When the verse is complete, you will sing the last pattern by itself. Ask them to listen for the pattern because you will ask them to sing it after you.

Sing the first verse, and pause. Then sing the last measure with words. Give the breath gesture to invite students to echo that pattern. Tell the students to audiate that pattern silently and then gesture for them to sing it again. Ask the students to audiate and remember that pattern because they will need it during this next activity.

Tell the students that you will sing the verse again and that you will either finish the verse with the same pattern or a different pattern. Then tell them that the rhythm of the pattern will stay the same, but that you might sing something different from Mi–Re–Do. (Model that pattern using BUM.) Each time you finish singing the verse, you will ask them to indicate whether the

pattern you sang at the end sounded the same or different. At the end of the song, you will give them the breathe-and-sing gesture. This time, they will not sing. Instead, they will breathe and signal whether they hear the same or a different pattern (two hands closed or two hands open = same; one hand open and one closed = different). Be prepared to improvise different endings using the same rhythm pattern but different tonic patterns. Observe their answers.

Invite Other Endings

Ask for volunteers to audiate an ending different from the original. Tell the volunteers you will sing the song and give a breath gesture when it is time to sing. Because this is a tonal creativity activity, embrace all responses. Remember, the student might be able to audiate patterns without being ready to perform them.

COORDINATION WITH INSTRUMENTAL MUSIC

Play the solo flute recording of "This Old Man" from *Jump Right In: The Instrumental Series* (J229CD, track 25). Ask the students if, without looking at the picture of the instrument, they can identify the instrument that they heard. If a student is able, ask how he or she knew. If they are unable to identify the instrument, show them a picture of the flute using Instrument Card 8. Tell the students that the flute is called a wind instrument because it makes a sound when you blow into it. Ask them to name other wind instruments with which they are familiar.

Ask the students how they could keep macrobeats in their bodies. Take a student movement suggestion, and ask everyone to perform that movement to macrobeats as you play the flute recording again. Play the recording several more times, using different student movement suggestions for each repetition of the song.

229

JUMP RIGHT IN: THE MUSIC CURRICULUM

JOHNNY WORKS WITH ONE HAMMER

Activity Type: Movement, Chanting, Rhythm Creativity

Tonality: Major

Resting Tone:

Meter: Usual Duple

Macrobeats:

Microbeats:

Keyality: F

Range: f–c'

Disc Three Track 39

Piano Bk Page 74

Materials Needed: Enough space for everyone to move comfortably.

Purpose:
1. To give students experience with moving their whole bodies using continuous, fluid movement.
2. To give students an opportunity to improvise rhythm patterns in Usual Duple meter.

TEACHING PLAN

Everyone should be standing in self space.

Sing and Move

Ask students to audiate silently while you sing the song. Tell them you will be moving using continuous, fluid movement and that they should imitate your movement as they audiate.

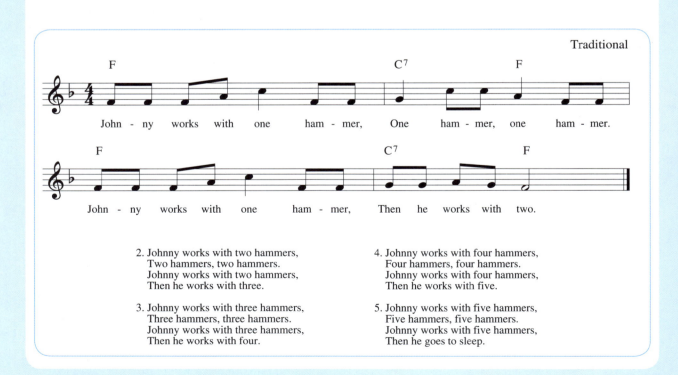

230

Move only one part of the body using continuous flow while you sing the first verse. Add another part of the body each time Johnny adds a hammer in the song. Continue adding verses until you are modeling continuous, fluid movement with your whole body. Hips, shoulders, back, elbows, knees, and the head are parts of the body that are most useful in assisting continuous flow. Repeat this activity several times. Change the order of the movements each time. Observe the students, and notice those who are able to coordinate their movement using lots of space and flexibility as they move additional body parts.

Invite Students to Sing and Move
On a different day, sing the melody while you perform the macrobeat movements traditionally associated with this song. Invite students to move as you do. For one hammer, make a fist with one hand and "hammer" the ground, desk, or the air.

Add the other fist for two hammers, a foot for three hammers, the other foot for four hammers, and the head for five hammers. Then pantomime exhaustion, and rest your head in your hands. Again, observe students who can coordinate movement and singing.

Establish Duple Meter
Signal the students to audiate while you establish meter. Invite the students to be your echo. Perform a four-macrobeat pattern in Usual Duple meter. To indicate when it is the students' turn to chant, give a breath gesture on the fourth macrobeat of each pattern you want them to echo. Indicate for them to begin chanting on the first macrobeat following each of your patterns. There should be no break in tempo, meter, or chanting between your pattern and the students' echo.

Same and Different
Invite students to perform a pattern that is different from yours. When you provide the breath gesture, do not chant. Listen only. If necessary, invite a student or two to perform their different patterns for the students in class. Extend this activity by asking them to chant two different patterns (from each other and from your first), three different, and, finally, four different patterns. When most students are chanting four patterns in a row that are different from each other and yours, move on to the next section of the Teaching Plan.

Improvise Rhythm Patterns for a B Section
Use their four four-macrobeat improvised patterns as a B section between each verse of the song. Students should move to the song, wait for your gesture to breathe, and improvise four patterns, either as a group or as individuals. They can continue their one-hammer movement during the first B section, their two-hammer movement during the second B section, and so on.

THE CHICKENS THEY ARE CROWIN'

Activity Type: Movement

Tonality: Aeolian

Resting Tone:

La

Meter: Multimetric (Usual Duple, Usual Triple)

Macrobeats:

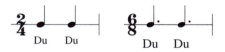

Microbeats:

 Disc Three Track 40   Piano Bk Page 28

Keyality: F

Range: d–d-flat'

Materials Needed: Enough space for everyone to move comfortably.

Purpose:
1. To help students audiate a multimetric song.
2. To give students experience making straight or curvy shapes that are open or closed.
3. To give students experience making shapes that are the same or different from the model.

TEACHING PLAN
Everyone should be standing in stationary self space in scattered formation.

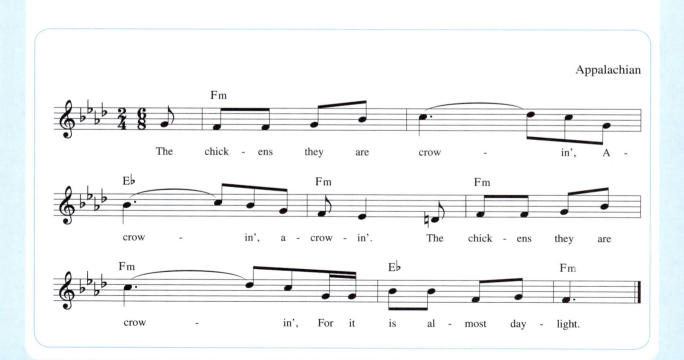

232

TEACHER'S EDITION • KINDERGARTEN

Introduce Straight Shapes: Same and Different

Using your body, make a variety of straight shapes at high, medium, and low levels. After you make each shape, invite the students to make their bodies look like yours. Remind them that straight shapes are angular, not flexible. After they are successful making straight shapes, make a straight shape, and ask them to make a straight shape that is different from yours.

Model Open and Closed Straight Shapes

Perhaps on a different day, ask students to audiate silently and imitate your movement while you sing the song or play the recording. Without interrupting the music, pause at the end of the first phrase (beginning of measure 4) in a straight, open shape. Open shapes use a lot of space. Begin flowing again as the second phrase begins. By the time you reach the end of the second phrase (last measure), make a straight, closed shape. Closed shapes use very little space.

Ask students to describe what they observed and experienced. Guide the discussion as needed so that they realize they made an open shape first and a closed shape second. Repeat the activity if needed.

Introduce Curvy Shapes: Same and Different

Repeat the sequence for introducing same and different straight shapes, only this time with curvy shapes. Curvy shapes are not as angular; they are flexible and rounded. Repeat the activity for modeling open and closed straight shapes, replacing straight shapes with curvy shapes. As before, ask students to describe what they observe and experience.

Student Leaders Model Movement

On a different day, after students have successfully coordinated moving into straight or curvy and open or closed shapes, review the previous activities as a warm-up. Notice students who move in a coordinated way with the melody. Invite one of them to lead their classmates in movement. The student leader should say, "Audiate silently, and move like I do." At the end of the turn, the leader can say, "Raise your hand if you can name the shapes we made."

On yet a different day, student leaders can invite their classmates to make a shape that is either straight, curvy, open, or closed, but different from the leader's. If necessary, play this game first without any melody. Have the leader move with flow and freeze in a shape. Once children are successful being different from the leader, play the recording or sing the melody, and repeat the activity of moving to the phrases of the song.

LAZY BONES

Activity Type: Movement

Tonality: Major

Resting Tone:

Do

Meter: Multimetric (Usual Duple, Usual Triple)

Macrobeats:

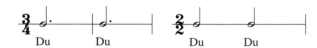

Microbeats:

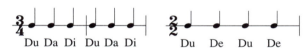

Keyality: E-flat

Range: d–c'

Disc Three Track 41 Piano Bk Page 78

Materials Needed: Recording. Enough space for everyone to move comfortably.

Purpose:
1. To give students experience with multiple meters in the context of a single song.
2. To give students an opportunity to perform microbeat movement in duple meter.
3. To give students experience with quick movements.

TEACHING PLAN

Everyone should be standing in a circle.

Listen and Move

Sing the song or play the recording, and pantomime the text of the song in the Usual Triple meter portion of the song (looking for lost cows or sheep and then laying down and pretending to go to sleep).

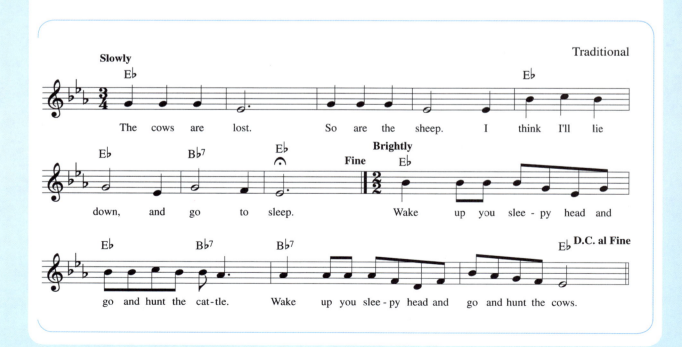

TEACHER'S EDITION • KINDERGARTEN

When the Usual Duple meter section begins, stand up quickly, and pat microbeats in bilateral motion on your legs. Choose one student to wake up the class on the Usual Duple meter section by standing up and patting microbeats on his or her legs. Then perform the song again so that the student can model for the class when to stand and pat. Tell the other students that they should wait until the leader stands, even if they think the leader should already be standing.

TEACHING TIP
By giving students opportunities to perform or move in solo, we can gather meaningful records of students' musical development over time. This activity can be used to evaluate students' audiation of microbeats as demonstrated through movement. Observe the student who is in charge of waking up the class, and evaluate that student's microbeat accuracy. Keep a written record of the quality of his or her performance using a rating scale as a guide.

CONNECTION TO LITERATURE
Read the classic children's book *Big Red Barn* by Margaret Wise Brown (Harper Collins 1956). Name and discuss the animals that live on a farm. As a means of developing reading readiness, you could list the animals on the board.

FOR THE MUSIC TEACHER
Since students learn from watching each other, choose students who are rhythmically strong to wake up the class before giving the rhythmically weak students a turn. This will allow all students to see the movement modeled correctly and facilitate learning.

JUMP RIGHT IN: THE MUSIC CURRICULUM

NANNY GOAT

Activity Type: Movement, Tonal Creativity

Tonality: Aeolian

Resting Tone:

La

Meter: Usual Duple

Macrobeats:

Du   Du

Microbeats:

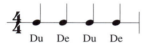
Du De Du De

Keyality: D

Range: d–a

Disc Three
Track 42

Piano Bk
Page 89

Materials Needed: Enough space for everyone to move comfortably.

Purpose:
1. To help students audiate the resting tone in Aeolian tonality.
2. To help students discriminate whether tonal patterns are the same or different in Aeolian tonality.

TEACHING PLAN

Everyone should be standing in self space in a scattered formation.

Audiate and Move

Invite the students to audiate the song. After you sing the song twice, ask the students whether they heard the directions being given in the song ("hop on one foot"). Then ask them to audiate

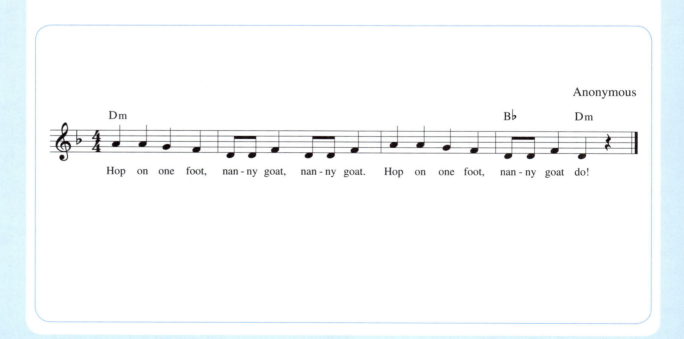

236

and observe. Repeat the song several times using the pattern below. For each movement direction ("hop on one foot"), repeat the song twice.

The first time through the song, model continuous, fluid movement. During the repetition of the song, model the movement described in the song. After you have demonstrated a few repetitions, invite students to join you if they have figured out the movement pattern. You might also try to incorporate "Rock like this," "Push and pull," and "Twist like this" in the song lyrics.

Establish Tonality

Establish tonality by singing the sequence of tones notated below using a neutral syllable. Sing the resting tone using BUM, and give a breath gesture for students to echo you.

Sustain the Resting Tone

Return to the movement pattern established in the first activity. Invite students to sustain the resting tone while they move with continuous flow and listen to hear which part of the body they will move in the next repetition. During the second repetition, the students should stop singing the resting tone and perform the movement identified in the lyrics of the song.

Invite small groups of students to take turns sustaining the resting tone during the first repetitions. When students are familiar with the activity, invite all students to move, but only one to sing the resting tone to accompany you.

Compare Endings

Ask the students to audiate as you sing the last measure of the song with the words. Then gesture for students to breathe and sing it after you. Tell the students to listen carefully to "Nanny goat do" when they hear you sing the whole song. Explain that, when you sing the end of the song, you will sing either the same pattern (model without words in rhythm) or a different pattern (do not model) to finish the song. At the end of the song, you will give them the breathe-and-sing gesture. This time, they will not sing. Instead, they will breathe and signal whether they hear the same pattern or a different pattern (two hands closed or two hands open = same; one hand open and one closed = different). Be prepared to improvise different endings using the same rhythm pattern but different tonic patterns. Observe their answers.

Invite Other Endings

Ask for volunteers to audiate an ending that is different from the original. Tell the volunteers you will sing the song and give a breath gesture when it is time to sing. Because this is a tonal creativity activity, embrace all responses; any music response is acceptable. Remember that the student might be audiating patterns, but might not be ready to perform them yet.

JUMBO ELEPHANT

Activity Type: Singing, Movement

Tonality: Harmonic Minor

Resting Tone:

La

Meter: Usual Duple

Macrobeats:

Du Du

Microbeats:

Du De Du De

Keyality: D

Range: d–d'

Disc Three
Track 43

Piano Bk
Page 76

Materials Needed: Enough space for everyone to move comfortably.

Purpose:
1. To help students audiate resting tone in Harmonic Minor tonality.
2. To give students an opportunity to move with weight.

TEACHING PLAN
Everyone should be seated in self space.

Identify Macrobeats
Ask the students to listen to the song and watch you move. Sing the song for the students while patting your lap in bilateral motion to macrobeats. Tell the students that you are patting to the macrobeats of the song. Invite the students

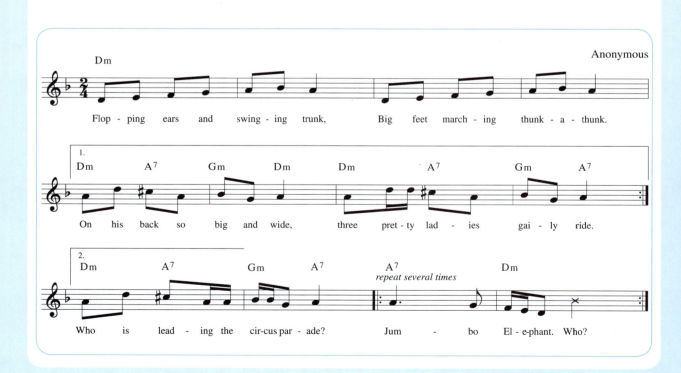

TEACHER'S EDITION • KINDERGARTEN

to join you in patting macrobeats as you sing the song again. Ask the students to put their hands on the floor in front of them and walk their hands in place to macrobeats. Remind the students that when they walk they do not move both feet at once, so their hands should also alternate. Sing the song again as the students move.

Moving with Weight

Ask the students whether elephants would move with heavy steps or light steps. (They should answer "heavy.") Ask them to walk their hands with heavy steps as you sing the song. Then ask the students to stand. Have several students demonstrate what a heavy elephant would look like as it walked around the room. Ask all of the students to walk around the room like very heavy elephants to macrobeats as you sing the song. Remind them that every one of their steps should shake the entire school building.

Then ask the students to move around the room like baby elephants. Tell them that when baby elephants walk you cannot hear their steps. This time, as you sing the song, the students should walk gently around the room.

Tell the students that they can choose to be a big elephant or a little elephant. Sing the song, and have the students move either like a baby elephant or a large, adult elephant. As the students move, sing the song. After the song is complete, identify which size elephant several of the students tried to emulate. Repeat, identifying the movement qualities of different students.

TEACHING TIP

Not all students will walk to macrobeats during this activity. This may be because they are focusing on the quality of weight in their movements rather than on coordinating to beat. It may also be because they are not audiating macrobeats, which is especially difficult to demonstrate with locomotor movement. You can provide macrobeat reinforcement by performing them on a hand drum as the students move and you sing. When performing them, play strongly when you want them to move with heavy movement and gently when you want them to move gently.

EXTENDING THE ACTIVITY

After the students are comfortable moving with weight, you can extend this activity by incorporating pathways. Remind the students that in the circus elephants walk in a line. Ask the students to stand in an elephant line with you as the leader. Have them walk with strong steps as you sing the song and move in a curvy pathway. The students should follow you. When you have completed the song, ask the students whether you moved in a straight or a curvy pathway. Repeat, this time moving in a straight pathway. Let students take turns leading the elephant line. Whisper in the leader's ear whether you want him or her to move in a straight or a curvy pathway, and have the rest of the students identify the type of pathway following the movement.

239

SCARBOROUGH FAIR

Activity Type: Movement

Tonality: Dorian

Resting Tone:

Re

Meter: Usual Triple

Macrobeats:

 Disc Three Track 44

 Piano Bk Page 116

Microbeats:

Keyality: D

Range: c–d'

Materials Needed: Recording. Enough space for everyone to move comfortably.

2. Bid her make me a cambric shirt,
   Parsley, sage, rosemary and thyme,
   Sewn without seams or fine needlework,
   If she would be a true love of mine.

3. Have her wash it in yonder dry well,
   Parsley, sage, rosemary and thyme,
   Where spring ne'er flowed, nor rain water fell,
   Or never be a true love of mine.

4. Bid her dry it on yonder thorn,
   Parsley, sage, rosemary and thyme,
   Which blossomed not since Adam was born,
   Then she will be a true love of mine.

5. Have him find me an acre of land,
   Parsley, sage, rosemary and thyme,
   Lying between sea foam and sea sand,
   Or he'll not be a true love of mine.

6. Tell him to plough it with a lamb's horn,
   Parsley, sage, rosemary and thyme,
   And sow it well with one peppercorn,
   Ere he can be a true love of mine.

7. When at last he has finished his work,
   Parsley, sage, rosemary and thyme,
   He'll come to claim his cambric shirt,
   And ever be a true love of mine.

Purpose: To give students experience moving gently in shared space to macrobeats and microbeats in Usual Triple meter.

TEACHING PLAN

Everyone should be seated in self space.

Introduce the Music

Play the recording of the song, and invite the students to audiate and imitate your movement. Model macrobeat movements such as rocking, swaying, pushing and pulling, twisting, or stretching using alternating movements with gentle, relaxed expression. Observe the students, and notice which ones are coordinating their movements.

Model Shared Space Movement

Invite one student who moved nicely to be your partner. Model the same movements as before, this time as you share space holding your partner's hands. Invite another student to take your place, and ask the rest of the class to move in the same way in self space (still without a partner). Tell them to notice how gentle and relaxed the movements are. Play the recording, and watch everyone as they move.

Assign partners, and give them a moment to practice moving in shared space. Call out each of the movements they experienced in self space. After they have moved without the music, play the recording. Again, call out movements for them to perform as they move to the recording.

Move Using Continuous Flow with Pulsations

Ask the students to return to standing self space. Invite them to audiate the song again and imitate your movements. Sing the song, or play the recording; move using continuous flow, pulsating microbeats. Place each pulsation in a different place in space and in various parts of the body, using sustained flow from one place to another. Observe the students, and notice who coordinates microbeat pulsations with continuous flow.

Move to Macrobeats and Microbeats

On a different day, once most students have accomplished the previous portion of the Teaching Plan, ask the students to move in two different ways. Again, invite them to audiate and imitate your movement. Play the recording, or sing the melody and put macrobeats in your heels and microbeats in your fingertips as you pat your thighs. Observe the students, and notice which ones coordinate simultaneous macrobeat and microbeat movement.

COORDINATION WITH INSTRUMENTAL MUSIC

Play the alto saxophone recording of "Scarborough Fair" from *Jump Right In: The Instrumental Series* (J229CD, track 16). Ask the students if any of them can identify the instrument in the recording. Show the students a picture of the alto saxophone using Instrument Card 16, and ask them if they know anyone who plays saxophone. Listen to their answers.

Play a move-and-freeze game using the saxophone recording. Tell the students that when they hear the music they should move throughout the room using continuous flow, but when the music stops, they should freeze. Play the recording, pausing it at phrase points to give the students an opportunity to freeze.

JUMP RIGHT IN: THE MUSIC CURRICULUM

PUNCHINELLA

Activity Type: Movement, Singing Game

Tonality: Pentatonic

Resting Tone:

Meter: Usual Duple

Macrobeats:

Microbeats:

Keyality: G

Range: d–g

Disc Three
Track 45

Piano Bk
Page 110

Materials Needed: Enough space for everyone to move comfortably.

Purpose: To give students an opportunity to play variations of a traditional circle game that allows them to create movement, tonal patterns, or rhythm patterns.

TEACHING PLAN
Everyone should be standing in a circle.

Introduce the Song and Movement
Enter the center of the circle. Tell the students that the music you will sing includes directions to a game. To play the game, they will use the movements that you will be modeling. Ask students to audiate silently as they imitate your movements, and ask them to remember the ways they moved.

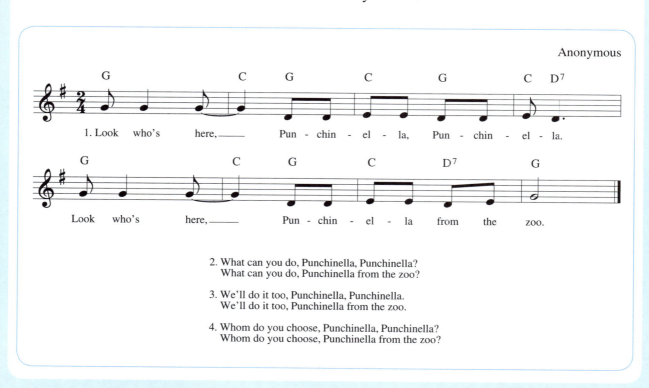

2. What can you do, Punchinella, Punchinella?
   What can you do, Punchinella from the zoo?

3. We'll do it too, Punchinella, Punchinella.
   We'll do it too, Punchinella from the zoo.

4. Whom do you choose, Punchinella, Punchinella?
   Whom do you choose, Punchinella from the zoo?

TEACHER'S EDITION • KINDERGARTEN

From the center of the circle, sing the melody. As you sing, model different macrobeat movements. Movements might include twisting, rocking side to side, stretching, bending, hopping on both feet, jumping (where there is a preparation to jump with both feet to another location), nodding, stomping, and marching. To help students successfully coordinate their macrobeat movements, follow the sequence of movements for "Humpty Dumpty" on page 252.

After you have finished singing and moving, invite the students to label the movements they remember using during that activity. Ask them to help you spell the words as you write them on the board.

Teach the Game

On a different day, make a circle, and stand in it with the students. Tell them you will sing the song with all of the words and that they should listen for four directions. Be the first leader to show how the game works. Tell the students that you will sing and that they are to join in when they know what to sing. When students are singing the song, stop singing with them. Try the following movements:

Verse One: When verse one begins, all students in the circle should clap macrobeats. When you model clapping, hold the palm of one hand facing up. That hand will remain stationary, and the fingertips of the other hand will clap the palm. The leader moves to the center of the circle, also clapping. (Alternatively, the leader can improvise any movement.)

Verse Two: The leader should perform a movement of his or her choice to macrobeats during this whole verse. Students in the circle should continue to clap to macrobeats. (For this activity, you are observing whether the student can lead a movement you modeled previously. In the traditional game, the leader can move however he or she chooses.)

Verse Three: Students in the circle should imitate the leader's movement as the leader continues the same movement.

Verse Four: Students in the circle walk clockwise, clapping macrobeats. The leader turns in a counterclockwise circle with an outstretched arm. On the word "zoo," the leader will point to a new leader, with whom he will exchange places when verse one begins again. Repeat.

Switch It Up!

On a different day, change the lyrics "What can you do?" to "What can you sing?" or "What can you chant?" All students should move with continuous flow during verse two. Between verses two and three, everyone should pause for the leader to either sing or chant a pattern for the class to echo. Then the game should continue as usual.

243

TO MARKET, TO MARKET

Activity Type: Singing, Chanting, Movement

Tonality: Major

Resting Tone:

Do

Meter: Usual Triple

Macrobeats:

Du Du

Microbeats:

Du Da Di Du Da Di

Keyality: D

Range: d–d'

 Disc Three Track 46

 Piano Bk Page 140

Materials Needed: Tambourine. Enough space for locomotor movement.

Purpose:
1. To give students an opportunity to perform rhythm patterns in solo.
2. To give students an opportunity to audiate and move to macrobeats in Usual Triple meter.

TEACHING PLAN
Everyone should be standing in self space.

Locomotor Movement
Tell the students that as you sing the song they should gallop to macrobeats. Demonstrate by galloping and playing macrobeats in the tempo of the song on a tambourine. Then sing the song and have the students move while you accompany your singing and their movement by playing macrobeats on the tambourine.

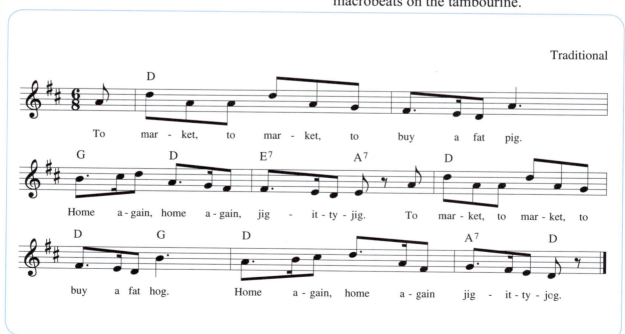

Echo Rhythm Patterns

Tell the students that you want them to freeze their movements at the end of each performance of the song. Then you will perform a pattern, and the student whose shoulder you tap should echo that pattern. Sing the song with macrobeat tambourine accompaniment as the students gallop. On the last beat of the song, tap a student on the shoulder. Between repetitions of the song, create a four-macrobeat rhythm pattern using BAH, and gesture for the student whose shoulder you tapped to echo your pattern. Without breaking tempo or meter, start singing the song again. The students should begin galloping again when you begin singing. Repeat this process several times so that several students have an opportunity to echo a pattern.

TEACHING TIP

Activities that include solo performances enable the teacher to adapt instruction to individual differences. If you choose a student who is strong rhythmically, give that student a difficult pattern to echo so that you stretch his or her rhythm audiation. If you choose a student who is less rhythmically strong, create an easier pattern. In this way, you challenge the stronger students without frustrating those who are still learning to audiate.

FOR THE MUSIC TEACHER

In this activity, students gallop freely around the room rather than in a circle. This helps them develop awareness of their bodies and how their bodies move through space. To be successful, they need to maneuver around the classroom without touching their peers.

HOT DOG

Activity Type: Movement

Tonality: Major

Resting Tone:

Meter: Unusual Paired

Macrobeats:

Microbeats:

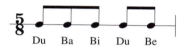

Keyality: G

Range: d–b

Disc Three Track 47 Piano Bk Page 67

Materials Needed: Tambourine. Enough space for everyone to move comfortably.

Purpose:
1. To give students experience with locomotor movement in Unusual Paired meter.
2. To give students experience with continuous, fluid movement.
3. To help students experience AB form through movement.

TEACHING PLAN

Everyone should be standing in self space.

Move

Sing the song without text, and walk to macrobeats while tapping the tambourine as an aural cue. Ask the students to stand. Then sing the song again, and have students walk to macrobeats. Do not expect accuracy in the macrobeat movement.

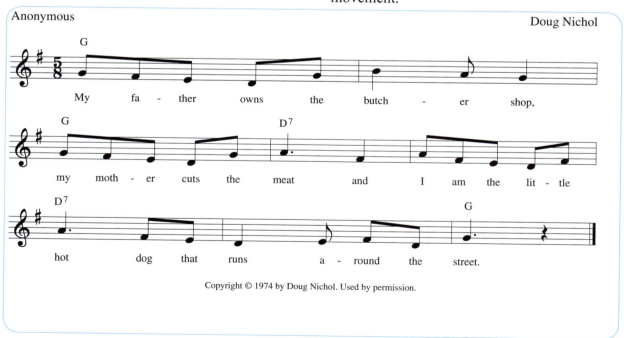

Copyright © 1974 by Doug Nichol. Used by permission.

Move and Listen

Explain to the students that you are going to sing the song twice and that you want them to walk to macrobeats as before. Then, after the second repetition of the song, you want them to stop their feet and freeze in place.

Tell the students that, while their feet are not moving, you are going to perform a chant (improvise a chant on BAH), and as you chant you want them to move their arms and upper bodies using continuous, fluid movement. Their feet should remain in place.

Repeat the activity several times, alternating between the song with locomotor movement to the beat and the improvised chant with flowing movement in place.

TEACHING TIP

Sing the song without text first so that the students focus on Unusual Paired meter and Major tonality rather than on the words. Once students are familiar with the song, add the text.

Teacher's Edition • Kindergarten

TOODALA

Activity Type: Singing, Movement, Melodic Creativity

Tonality: Major

Resting Tone:

Do

Meter: Usual Duple

Macrobeats:

Du Du

Microbeats:

Du De Du De

Keyality: G

Range: d–d'

Disc Three
Track 48

Piano Bk
Page 141

Materials Needed: Enough space for everyone to move comfortably.

Purpose:
1. To give students experience moving in self and shared space.
2. To give students an opportunity to sing a familiar song and create a different ending.

TEACHING PLAN

Everyone should be standing in self space.

Introduce the Song

Invite the students to audiate the song silently and imitate your movement as you sing. Sing "Toodala" with these suggested movements:

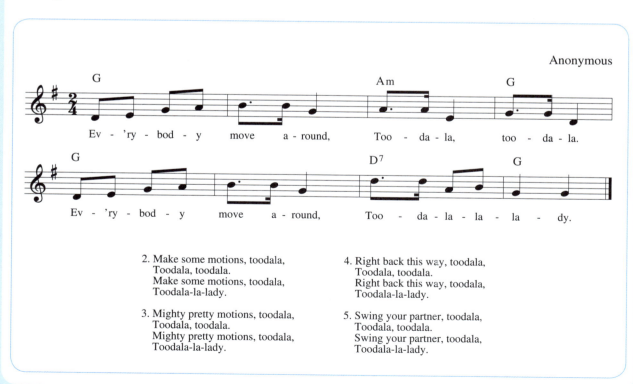

2. Make some motions, toodala,
   Toodala, toodala.
   Make some motions, toodala,
   Toodala-la-lady.

3. Mighty pretty motions, toodala,
   Toodala, toodala.
   Mighty pretty motions, toodala,
   Toodala-la-lady.

4. Right back this way, toodala,
   Toodala, toodala.
   Right back this way, toodala,
   Toodala-la-lady.

5. Swing your partner, toodala,
   Toodala, toodala.
   Swing your partner, toodala,
   Toodala-la-lady.

Verse One: Move in stationary space using continuous flow. Explore high, medium, and low levels and the space all around you as you move.

Verse Two: Move using continuous flow with pulsations to macrobeats. Be certain to put each pulsation in a different place in space and in various parts of the body as you move.

Verse Three: Invite the students to move using either continuous flow or continuous flow with pulsations.

Verse Four: Model moving forward four steps and back four steps; repeat.

Verse Five: Hold your right elbow out, and walk clockwise in a small circle back to your place for eight macrobeats. Repeat, holding your left elbow out (to model swinging *without* a partner).

Model swinging to the verse with a student partner. Assign student partners, and assist them with coordinating a swing in shared space. Allow them to practice coordinating their swings while you sing the song or play the recording.

Students Sing

After the students have had an opportunity to move while listening to the song, invite them to sing it. Sing the preparatory sequence below to assist them in singing together. Do not sing the song with them.

Create a New Ending

After the students are able to sing the melody without your assistance, ask them to audiate and sing only the last two measures of the song. You will need to demonstrate these measures. Then give the students a breath cue to imitate you.

Ask the students to raise their hands when they hear the demonstrated pattern as you sing the whole song and watch. Once students can identify the pattern correctly, ask them to listen again. Tell them you will not sing the end and that you would like them to audiate a different ending. Explain that their new part should have the same rhythm and words ("Toodalalalady"). Model this in your instructions by chanting the rhythm and words in tempo and meter. Their song should be different from So–Re–Mi–Do. (Model using BUM for aural/oral instruction.)

Demonstrate several possible endings. Then sing the song; gesture for the group and then individuals to sing their new endings. Return to this activity on different days. Try the same approach with other songs that students have learned. After the students offer new endings, guide them to audiate an ending on the resting tone.

JUMP RIGHT IN: THE MUSIC CURRICULUM

THESSALY *SYRTOS* DANCE

Activity Type: Movement

Tonality: Aeolian

Resting Tone:

Meter: Unusual Unpaired

Macrobeats:

Microbeats:

Keyality: E

Range: d–c'

 Disc Three Track 49

 Piano Bk Page 136

Materials Needed: Tambourine. Enough space for everyone to move comfortably.

Purpose:
1. To give students experience with Unusual Unpaired meter.
2. To give students experience with heavy and light movements.

TEACHING PLAN

Everyone should be standing in self space.

Sing

Sing the song, and walk using heavy movements to macrobeats. Ask students to imitate your movements.

Sing the song again, and pretend to fly while walking lightly to macrobeats. Ask the students to imitate your movements.

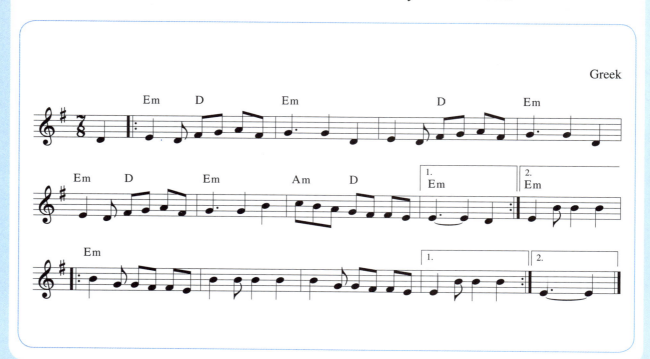

TEACHER'S EDITION • KINDERGARTEN

Stomping and Flying Game

Tell students that when they hear you tap the tambourine they are to walk using heavy movements and that when you shake the tambourine they are to fly.

Sing the song again. Tap the tambourine during the phrases or sections of the song when you want them to stomp, and shake the tambourine when you want them to fly. At first, change only at phrase points. As the students become more comfortable alternating between these two movements, you can change at other points in the song.

Continue singing and alternating between stomping and flying.

CONNECTION TO SCIENCE

Bring in objects such as plastic golf balls, rocks, and pencils, and have students sort them into heavy and light categories. Then bring out a bucket of water, and ask students which objects will float and which will sink. Have students make predictions. Place each object into the bucket of water, and evaluate if it sinks or floats.

JUMP RIGHT IN: THE MUSIC CURRICULUM

HUMPTY DUMPTY

Activity Type: Movement, Chanting

Meter: Usual Triple

Macrobeats:

Du Du

Microbeats:

Du Da Di Du Da Di

 Disc Three
Track 50

 Piano Bk
Page 68

Materials Needed: Enough space for everyone to move comfortably.

Purpose: To help students learn to audiate, move, and chant Usual Triple meter.

Introduce the Rhyme
Ask the students to audiate silently and move with you while you chant. Tell them that they might know the rhyme that you chant. If they know the rhyme, they should think it silently in their heads rather than chant it with you.

Chant "Humpty Dumpty" in a comfortable tempo for moving to macrobeats and microbeats simultaneously, which you will do eventually. You should model continuous, fluid movement as you chant. Make a note of the tempo you choose so you can return to the same one on a different day.

TEACHING PLAN
Everyone should be seated in self space.

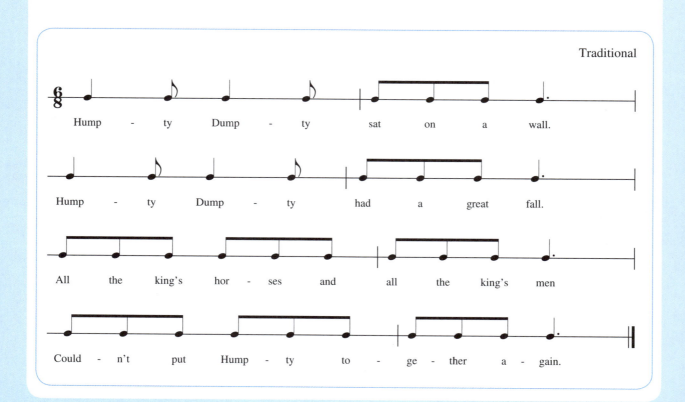

252

Once students have had an opportunity to audiate silently and move with continuous flow the way you do many times and when they can coordinate themselves with the movements suggested, introduce the following activity.

Suggested Movements for Subsequent Repetitions of the Chant
The following movements can be performed for subsequent repetitions of the chant during the same class period or for subsequent class periods.

- Continuous flow
- Continuous flow with pulsations to microbeats
- Continuous flow with pulsations to macrobeats
- Strong and/or gentle flow
- Flow using a lot and/or a little space
- Quick and/or slow flow
- Macrobeat movement or microbeat movement
- Macrobeats and microbeats together

Refer to the Scope and Sequence or Index sections in this Teacher's Edition for more activities supporting the movements suggested above.

Rhythm Pattern Imitation
Ask the students to imitate you and silently audiate. Sit on the floor with your feet under your legs in self space. Chant the rhyme in the same tempo as before. As you chant, sway from side to side to macrobeats, gently bouncing your hips and tapping your thighs to microbeats. Observe which students are able to perform this movement. In between performances of the chant, invite students to echo your four-macrobeat patterns in Usual Triple meter while you move.

Chant the Macrobeats
Model large macrobeat movements, and chant BAH on each macrobeat in the same tempo as before. Invite the students to stand and imitate your movement and chanting. Once they are able to chant macrobeats and move in a steady tempo without your support, continue to move and chant the rhyme as they chant macrobeats. Tell students that if you chant patterns they should continue moving and echo your patterns.

Chant the Microbeats
Continue to model large macrobeat movements. However, this time chant TUH on each microbeat. Invite the students to imitate your movements and chanting. Once they are able to chant and move in a steady tempo without your support, continue to move and chant the rhyme as they chant microbeats.

When the students are able, invite half of them to chant BAH and the other half to chant TUH. You chant the rhyme with them. Switch parts. Invite a soloist to chant the rhyme.

LITTLE RONDO

Activity Type: Singing, Movement

Tonality: Pentatonic

Resting Tone:

Meter: Usual Duple

Macrobeats:

Microbeats:

Keyality: D

Range: d–d'

Disc Three Track 51

Piano Bk Page 80

TEACHING PLAN ONE

Materials Needed: Enough space for everyone to move comfortably.

Purpose:
1. To give students experience with continuous, fluid movement.
2. To give students an opportunity to imitate tonal patterns.
3. To help students discriminate whether tonal patterns are the same or different.

Everyone should be seated in self space in a circle.

Listen, Move, and Sing

Sing the song a few times without the words. As you sing, continuously roll your fists and

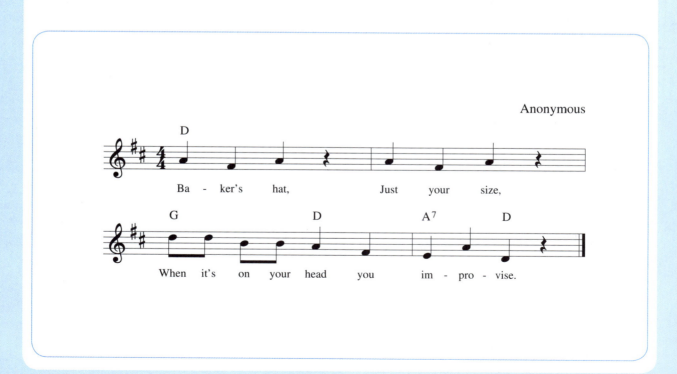

forearms. Then invite the students to sing the song with you as they copy your movements.

Imitate and Identify Tonal Patterns as Same or Different

Sing the following tonal patterns using the neutral syllable BUM. Give the students a breath gesture, and have them repeat each pattern after you sing. This may help the students breathe before they sing if they continue to roll their fists and forearms when they repeat after you.

Tell the students to listen as you sing the first two patterns. Again, tell the students that the two patterns are different. Have the students hold up two hands that are different (one in a fist and the other open) and repeat the word "different."

Next, sing the second two patterns. Tell the students that the two patterns are different. Have the students hold up their "different" hands and repeat the word "different."

Sing the first patterns, and repeat. Tell the students that the two patterns are the same. Have the students hold up two hands that are same (either both in a fist or both open) and repeat the word "same."

Play the Game

Play a game using the four patterns. Sing pairs of patterns for the students. Have them show you with their hands if the two patterns you perform are the same or different.

TEACHING PLAN TWO
Activity Type: Singing, Tonal Creativity

Materials Needed: Enough space for everyone to move comfortably.

Purpose:
1. To give students experience moving continuously to macrobeats.
2. To give students an opportunity to imitate tonal patterns.
3. To give students an opportunity to create tonal patterns.

Everyone should be seated in self space in a circle. Students should be familiar with the activities in Teaching Plan One. Invite the students to sing the song with you as they continuously roll their fists and forearms. Repeat the song several times.

Tonal Pattern Imitation

Sing the tonal patterns from Teaching Plan One using the neutral syllable BUM. Give the students a breath gesture, and have them repeat each pattern after you sing.

Tell the students that, when they repeat after you, they are imitating you; they are the same as you. Explain that sometimes musicians are different from each other so that they can have musical conversations.

Tonal Pattern Creation

Tell the students that you are going to sing a tonal pattern, and they will sing a tonal pattern different from yours. Ask for a volunteer to demonstrate. Perform one of the four tonal patterns from Teaching Plan One. Gesture for the student to perform his or her pattern. Have the class repeat the student's pattern and determine if the pattern was different from yours. They can show you their decisions by using their "same" or "different" hands.

LITTLE RONDO (continued)

If the student's tonal pattern was different from yours, say, "Yes, that was different." Accept all student attempts at being different from you in this lesson. Be sure to have the class repeat each student's tonal pattern for reinforcement, even if the student performs a pattern without using her singing voice. The point of the lesson is to make it safe to be different. In their first conscious attempts to be different, students may not be accurate. With practice, accuracy will increase.

If the student's tonal pattern was the same as yours, say, "Thank you. That was the same pattern as mine. Here is a pattern that is different." Then demonstrate a different tonal pattern, and have everyone imitate the different tonal pattern.

Give each student the opportunity to create a tonal pattern. If a student does not want to be different from you, allow the student to be the same as you.

TEACHING PLAN THREE

Activity Type: Singing, Chanting

Materials Needed: Enough space for everyone to move comfortably.

Purpose:
1. To give students experience with continuous, fluid movement.
2. To give student an opportunity to imitate rhythm patterns.
3. To help students learn to discriminate whether rhythm patterns are the same or different.

Everyone should be seated in self space in a circle.

Listen, Move, and Sing
Sing the song a few times without the words, as you continuously roll your fists and forearms as you sing. Then invite the students to sing the song with you and copy your movements.

Imitate and Identify Rhythm Patterns as Same or Different
Perform the following rhythm patterns using the neutral syllable BAH. Give the students a breath gesture, and have them repeat the patterns after you perform them. It may help the students to breathe before they perform if they continue to roll their fists and forearms when they repeat after you.

Tell the students to listen as you perform the first two patterns again. Explain that the two patterns are different. Have the students hold up two hands that are different and repeat the word "different."

Next, perform the second two patterns. Tell the students that those two patterns are different. Have the students hold up two hands that are different and repeat the word "different."

Now, perform the first pattern and then perform it again. Tell the students that the two patterns are the same. Have the students hold up two hands that are same and repeat the word "same."

TEACHER'S EDITION • KINDERGARTEN

Play the Game
Play a game using the four patterns. Perform pairs of patterns for the students. Have them show you with their hands if the two patterns you perform are the same or different.

TEACHING PLAN FOUR

Activity Type: Chanting, Rhythm Creativity

Materials Needed: Enough space for everyone to move comfortably.

Purpose:
1. To give students experience moving in a continuous, fluid style with pulsations to macrobeats.
2. To give students and opportunity to imitate rhythm patterns.
3. To give students an opportunity to create rhythm patterns.

Everyone should be seated in self space in a circle.

Listen, Move, and Sing
Students should be familiar with the activities in Teaching Plan Three. Invite the students to sing the song with you as they continuously roll their fists and forearms. Repeat the song several times.

Imitate and Identify Rhythm Patterns as Same or Different
Perform the rhythm patterns from Teaching Plan Three using the neutral syllable BAH. Give the students a breath gesture, and have them repeat each pattern after you. It may help the students to breathe before they perform if they continue to roll their fists and forearms when they repeat after you.

Tell the students that, when they repeat after you, they are imitating you and being the same as you. Explain that sometimes musicians are different from each other so that they can have musical conversations.

Rhythm Pattern Creation
Tell the students that you are going to perform a rhythm pattern and that they will get to perform a rhythm pattern that is different from yours. Ask for a volunteer to demonstrate. Perform one of the previous rhythm patterns. Gesture for the student to perform his or her pattern. Have the class repeat the student's pattern and determine if it the pattern was different. They can show you their decisions by using their "same" or "different" hands.

Accept all student attempts at being different from you in this lesson. If the student's rhythm pattern is different from yours, say, "Yes, that was different." Be sure to have the class repeat each student's rhythm pattern for reinforcement. The point of the lesson is to make it safe to be different.

If the student's rhythm pattern is the same as yours, say, "Thank you. That was the same pattern as mine. Here is a pattern that is different." Then demonstrate a different rhythm pattern and have everyone imitate the different rhythm pattern.

Give each student the opportunity to create a rhythm pattern. If a student does not want to be different from you, allow the student to be the same as you.

257

JUMP RIGHT IN: THE MUSIC CURRICULUM

DRAW A BUCKET OF WATER

Activity Type: Movement

Tonality: Major

Resting Tone:

Do

Disc Three
Track 52

Piano Bk
Page 39

Meter: Usual Duple

Macrobeats:

Du   Du

Microbeats:

Du De Du De

Keyality: G

Range: d–b

Materials Needed: Enough space for everyone to move comfortably.

Purpose:
1. To give students experience with moving in shared space.
2. To give students an opportunity to explore strong and gentle movement.

TEACHING PLAN

Everyone should be seated in self space.

Move in Self Space with Weight

Ask the students if they have ever seen a water well. Draw or show a picture of a well with a rope and a bucket. Demonstrate how to use your arms to bring up a bucket from the bottom of the well by pulling a rope, hand over hand. Have the students copy your movement.

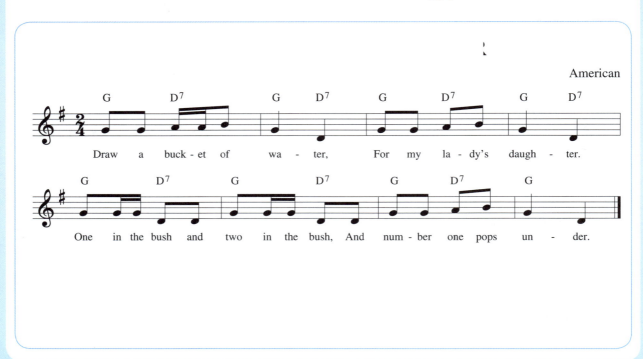

American

Draw a buck-et of wa-ter, For my la-dy's daugh-ter.
One in the bush and two in the bush, And num-ber one pops un-der.

Sing the song as the students copy your hand-over-hand movements on macrobeats. Repeat, and tell the students to be very strong because the bucket is full of water and heavy.

Then tell the students that the bucket is empty, so they should be very gentle because the bucket is light. Sing the song again, and have the students make the hand-over-hand movement to macrobeats with a gentle style.

Move in Shared Space with Weight
Tell the students to stay seated and face a partner without using language. (Practice choosing partners without using language to facilitate future activities that require shared space.)

Find a partner for yourself. Hold your partner's hands, and demonstrate bilateral alternating rowing movement on macrobeats. Ask the students to tell you if you were using self space or shared space. (The correct answer is shared space.)

Ask the students to hold their partner's hands. Have them practice the bilateral, alternating rowing movement on macrobeats while you sing the song. They will row forward to one macrobeat and back to the next.

Tell the students that this time you want them to be very strong because the bucket is full of water and heavy. Remind the students that being strong does not mean being rough. Sing the song again as they move.

Explain to the students that this time you want them to be very gentle because the bucket is empty and light. Sing the song again as they move.

Try this activity in standing shared space as a readiness for the play party game to the same song in the Grade Four book.

FAIR ROSIE

Tonality: Major

Resting Tone:

Meter: Usual Duple

Macrobeats:

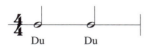

Microbeats:

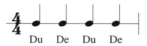

Keyality: D

Range: d–b

 Disc Three Track 53

 Piano Bk Page 48

TEACHING PLAN ONE

Activity Type: Movement, Singing

Materials Needed: Enough space for everyone to move comfortably.

Purpose:
1. To give students experience with continuous, fluid movement with pulsations to microbeats.
2. To help students discriminate whether tonal patterns are the same or different.

Everyone should be seated in self space.

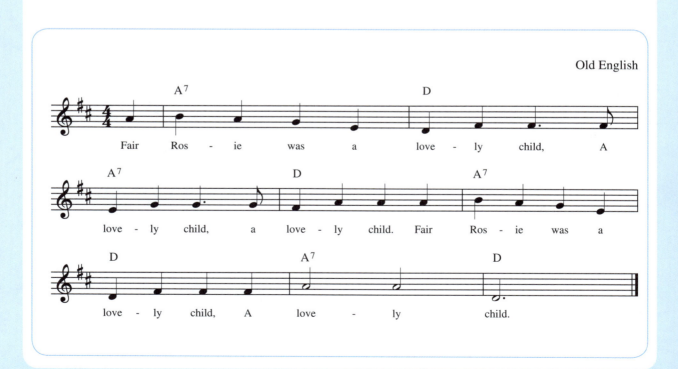

260

Listen and Move

Sing the song a few times, and have the students copy your movements. As you sing, use your hands to pulse or tap microbeats. Never perform the microbeats in the same place twice in a row. Keep moving them all around on the floor, on your legs, and in the air. Use your spine to assist your use of continuous flow, being certain to keep the movement relaxed and fluid.

Imitate and Identify Same and Different Tonal Patterns

Sing the following tonal pattern using the neutral syllable BUM. Give the students a breath gesture, and have them repeat the pattern.

Tell the students that although this pattern is not in the song it helps us to audiate the song. Sing the pattern again. Give the students a breath gesture, and have them repeat the tonal pattern again.

Sing the following tonal pattern using BUM. Give the students a breath gesture, and have them repeat the pattern.

Explain to the students that this pattern is in the song. Sing the second tonal pattern again using BUM. Give the students a breath gesture, and have them repeat the second tonal pattern. Demonstrate where this pattern occurs in the song.

Tell the students to listen as you sing the two patterns. Explain that the two patterns are different. Have the students hold up two hands that are different (one open and one closed) and repeat the word "different."

Next, sing the first pattern; repeat. Tell the students that this time the two patterns were the same. Have the students hold up two hands that are same (both open or both closed) and repeat the word "same."

FAIR ROSIE (continued)

TEACHING PLAN TWO

Activity Type: Movement, Singing, Tonal Creativity

Materials Needed: Enough space for everyone to move comfortably.

Purpose:
1. To give students experience with continuous, fluid movement with pulsations to microbeats.
2. To give students an opportunity imitate tonal patterns.
3. To give students an opportunity to create tonal patterns.

Everyone should be seated in self space.

Listen and Move
Sing the song a few times, and have the students copy your movements. As you sing, use your hands to pulse or tap microbeats. Never perform the microbeats in the same place twice in a row. Keep moving them all around on the floor, on your legs, and in the air. Use your spine to assist your use of continuous flow, being certain to keep the movement relaxed and fluid.

Find a Tonal Pattern in the Song
Sing the following tonal pattern using the neutral syllable BUM. Give the students a breath gesture, and have them repeat the pattern.

Tell the students that the tonal pattern is the last one of the song. Explain that you will sing the song again, but not that tonal pattern. That is their job. Sing the song again, this time without words. Omit the last tonal pattern, and give a breath gesture for the students to sing the tonal pattern.

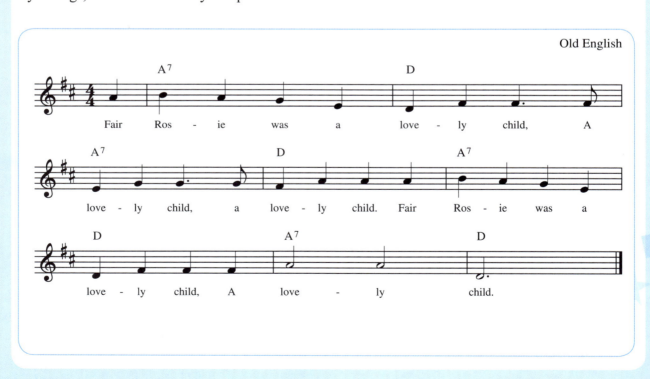

Create a New Ending

Tell the students that there are other ways that the song might end. Substitute the following tonal patterns as examples. Sing each using BUM.

Tell the students that each of the tonal patterns is different. Sing the two patterns above, and give a breath gesture for the students to imitate each pattern. Then ask them as a class to choose one of the patterns as the new ending for the song. Have them repeat that pattern several times. Use clear breathe-and-sing gestures.

Tell the students that you will sing the song again and that they will be responsible for singing the new ending. Sing the song again, this time without words. Omit the last tonal pattern, and give a breath gesture for the students to sing the new ending.

Ask individual students to create new endings for the song. Have the class sing those endings. In tonal creation, all endings are acceptable.

MARY WORE A RED DRESS

Activity Type: Movement, Tonal Imitation

Tonality: Major

Resting Tone:

Do

Meter: Usual Duple

Macrobeats:

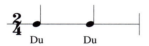
Du Du

Microbeats:

Du De Du De

Keyality: G

Range: d–d'

Disc Three Track 54

Piano Bk Page 85

TEACHING PLAN ONE

Materials Needed: Enough space for everyone to move comfortably.

Purpose:
1. To give students experience moving continuously to macrobeats.
2. To help students learn to discriminate whether tonal patterns are the same or different.

Everyone should be seated in self space.

Listen and Move
Sing the song a few times, and have the students copy your movements. Use your hands to pulsate or pat macrobeats as you continuously sway with your spine. Never pulsate or pat in the same place twice.

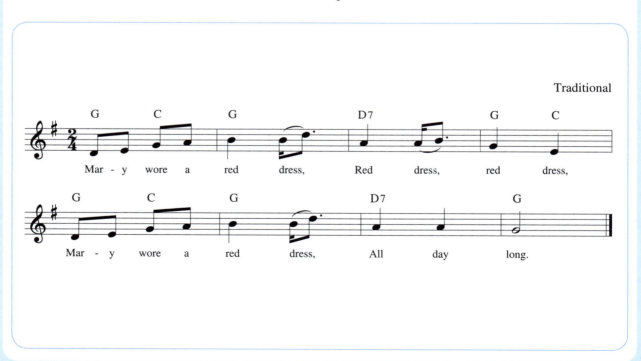

TEACHER'S EDITION • KINDERGARTEN

Imitate and Identify Same and Different Tonal Patterns

Sing the following tonal pattern using the neutral syllable BUM. Give the students a breath gesture, and have them repeat the pattern.

Tell the students, "Although this pattern is not in the song, it helps us to audiate the song." Sing the tonal pattern again using BUM. Give the students a breath gesture, and have them repeat the pattern.

Sing the following tonal pattern using BUM. Give the students a breath gesture, and have them repeat the pattern.

Explain to the students, "Although this pattern is not in the song, it also helps us to audiate the song." Sing the tonal pattern again using BUM. Give the students a breath gesture, and have them repeat the tonal pattern.

Tell the students to listen as you sing the two tonal patterns again. Explain to the students that the two patterns are different. Have the students hold up two hands that are different (one a fist and the other open) and repeat the word "different."

Next, sing the first pattern, and then sing it again. Tell the students that the two patterns are the same. Have the students hold up two hands that are the same (both open or both closed) and repeat the word "same."

TEACHING PLAN TWO

Activity Type: Movement, Singing, Tonal Creativity

Materials Needed: Enough space for everyone to move comfortably.

Purpose:
1. To give students experience moving in a continuous, fluid style while pulsating macrobeats.
2. To give students the opportunity to imitate tonal patterns.
3. To help students learn to create tonal patterns.

Everyone should be seated in self space.

Listen and Move
Sing the song a few times, and have the students copy your movements. Use your hands to pulsate or pat to microbeats as you continuously sway your spine. Never pulsate or pat in the same place twice.

Identify the Pattern
Sing the following tonal pattern using the neutral syllable BUM. Give the students a breath gesture, and have them repeat the pattern.

Explain to the students that the tonal pattern is the last one of the song. Tell them that you will sing the song again, but you will not sing that tonal pattern at the end of the song. That will be their job. Sing the song again, this time without words. Omit the last tonal pattern, and give a breathe-and-sing gesture for the students to sing the pattern.

MARY WORE A RED DRESS (continued)

Create a New Ending
Tell the students that there are other ways that song might end. Sing one of the following tonal patterns using BUM, give a breath gesture, and have the student imitate you. Then end the song with that tonal pattern. Repeat that process with the other tonal pattern.

Tell the students that those two tonal patterns are different. Ask them to choose one of the patterns as the new ending for the song. Using clear breathe-and-sing gestures, have them repeat that pattern several times.

Tell the students that you will sing the song again and that they will be responsible for singing the new ending. Sing the song again, this time without words. Omit the last tonal pattern and give a breathe-and-sing gesture for the students to sing the new ending.

Ask individual students to create new endings for the song. Have the class sing those endings. In tonal creation, all endings are acceptable.

TEACHING PLAN THREE

Materials Needed: Enough space for everyone to move comfortably.

Purpose: To help students discriminate whether rhythm patterns are the same or different in Usual Duple meter.

Everyone should be seated in self space.

Greet the Children and Introduce the Song
Ask the students to audiate silently and imitate your movements while you sing the melody. Sing the song using the words as written. Model macrobeat movements in seated self space while you sing. If there is anyone named Mary in your class, sing words that describe what she is wearing. Otherwise, sing the song using a student's name and a description of what he or she is wearing. Invite each child to pick the clothing you should sing about in describing him or her. Invite students to listen as you sing.

Invite Students to Sing the Song
On a different day, review the song for students. Invite them to sing the song. Sing the preparatory sequence notated below, and give them the breath gesture to indicate when they are to begin singing.

Introduce the Chord Root Melody
Tell the students that you have a new song to teach them and that this new song goes with "Mary Wore a Red Dress." Invite students to take a walking trip on the macrobeats. Ask them to audiate silently as they move. Encourage students to walk in pathways different from yours and to stay in self space.

Sing the preparatory sequence notated on this page with the words "Walk with me" instead of "Ready, sing." Walk while you sing the song, the chord root melody, and then the song again (without stopping, if possible).

Teach the Chord Root Melody

Ask the students to stand in one place, audiate silently, and imitate your movement. For steps one through four, sing the chord root melody.

1. Model macrobeat movement in your heels.
2. Model microbeat movement in your fingertips.
3. Model macrobeats in heels and microbeats in fingertips simultaneously.
4. Establish tonality; sing Do. Invite students to breathe and sing Do when you stop singing, and offer the breath gesture.
5. Invite students to audiate the chord root melody silently, and to raise their hands when they have finished.
6. Use the preparatory sequence with the instructions "Ready, sing" to invite students to sing the chord root melody.

FOR THE MUSIC TEACHER

Once the students can sing the chord root melody with confidence, you can sing the melody of the song as they sing the chord root melody. Your students may or may not be ready to take this step in kindergarten. Simply introducing the chord root melody, even if they never hear it directly with the song, will develop their harmonic audiation.

Chord Root Melody

Mary Wore a Red Dress

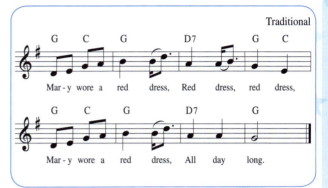

JUMP RIGHT IN: THE MUSIC CURRICULUM

ROW, ROW, ROW YOUR BOAT

Activity Type: Movement, Singing

Tonality: Major

Resting Tone:

Meter: Usual Triple

Macrobeats:

Microbeats:

Keyality: D

Range: d–d'

Disc Three
Track 55

Piano Bk
Page 112

Materials Needed: Enough space for everyone to move comfortably.

Purpose:
1. To help students audiate the resting tone in Major tonality.
2. To give students an opportunity to sing tonal patterns in Major tonality.
3. To give students experience with continuous, fluid movement.

TEACHING PLAN

Everyone should be standing in stationary self space in scattered formation.

Tell the students that each person in the room is in a boat flowing on the river. In a flowing boat, one can either ride the river's current (flowing using minimal stationary space), or make the boats move more swiftly down the river (flowing using maximum stationary space). These special

268

flowing boats do not travel from their spots; they also need singing to move. Ask the students to audiate silently and imitate your movement. Explain that, although they might recognize the song, you want them to listen and move rather than sing. Also tell them that if you stop singing, they should freeze.

Sing the song while you move with maximum continuous flow in stationary space. After a few repetitions of the song, pause at the end of a phrase. Everyone should stop moving in the silence. Sing the sequence of tones notated below. Pause, and then continue with the next phrase of the song. Randomly intersperse the sequence of tones in between silent, frozen, pauses.

Sing Patterns
On a different day, after the students have had several opportunities to complete the previous activity, invite the students to be your echo. Sing tonic, dominant, and subdominant Major tonal patterns. Include the patterns notated below. After each pattern, give a breath gesture as a cue for students to echo that pattern. Move continuously as you sing the patterns, and invite the students to imitate your movement as well as your singing.

Sing a Resting Tone Accompaniment
On another day, invite the students to sing the melody. As soon as the students are able to sing the melody without your assistance, accompany them by singing the resting tone on every other macrobeat.

Play a Game
Invite the students to sing the melody. Tell them that if you do not sing, they should move using continuous flow in stationary space. However, if you accompany their singing with the resting tone accompaniment, they should add pulsations to macrobeats to their continuous, fluid movement.

Invite Students to Sing the Resting Tone Accompaniment
After the students have heard the resting tone accompaniment several times on different days, invite them to sing it while you sing the melody. Do not expect correctness. Instead, compliment their efforts, and return to their singing the melody while you sing the resting tone accompaniment.

COORDINATION WITH INSTRUMENTAL MUSIC
Play the clarinet recording of "Row, Row, Row Your Boat" from *Jump Right In: The Instrumental Series* (J229CD, track 15). Show your students a picture of the clarinet using Instrument Card 12. Explain that it is a wind instrument, which means that it makes a sound when you blow into it. Ask the students if they know anyone who plays clarinet, and listen to their answers.

Assign each student a partner, and ask them to sit, face their partners, and hold hands. Tell them that they are going to row to the clarinet recording, but first you want them to practice, using your tambourine beat as a cue. Strike the tambourine at the tempo of alternating macrobeats in the recording, and chant "row" each time you strike the tambourine. Watch to see if the students are able to coordinate their rowing movement. If they are, play the recording, and gently strike the tambourine and chant "row" on alternating macrobeats to help guide their partner movement.

TEACHER'S EDITION • KINDERGARTEN

Index A
Alphabetical Listing of Songs and CD Tracks

CD	Track	Title	Page	CD	Track	Title	Page
1	5	All Pretty Little Horses	10	1	14	Floppy Scarecrow	28
2	8	America	88	1	19	Full Moonlight Dance	38
1	16	America the Beautiful	32	3	14	Funny Puppy	174
1	27	The Ardelean Woman	54				
1	6	*Arirang*	12	1	15	The Ghost of John	30
2	11	As Joseph Was A-Walking	94	3	33	Gipsy Ipsy	214
2	14	Away in a Manger	100	1	21	Go to Sleep	42
				1	18	Graceful Simo (*Simo Ligeri*)	36
3	19	Baa, Baa, Black Sheep	184	3	11	The Greenland Whale Fishery	168
2	9	Baloo, Lammy	90				
3	7	Barnacle Bill	160	3	2	*Hani Kouni*	150
3	32	The Bell Peter	212	1	25	*Hato Popo* (Little Pigeons)	50
2	22	*Bi, Bi, Og Blaka* (Flip, Flap, and Flutt'ring)	116	1	1	Hello, Everybody	2
1	30	*Bim Bam*	60	3	6	High Bird	158
1	12	Blow the Balloon	22	2	28	Horses	128
2	34	Blow the Man Down	138	3	47	Hot Dog	246
3	35	Blow the Winds Southerly	140	3	50	Humpty Dumpty	252
1	2	The Braes O'Yarrow	4				
3	17	Bre'r Rabbit, Shake It	180	2	12	I Wonder as I Wander	96
				2	18	I'm a Little Snowflake	108
3	40	The Chickens They Are Crowin'	232	2	5	In the Window	82
2	16	Children's Lullaby	104				
3	4	City Line Avenue	154	1	4	Jeremiah, Blow the Fire	8
3	35	Clapping Land	220	3	16	Jim Along Josie	178
2	10	Coventry Carol	92	3	39	Johnny Works with One Hammer	230
				3	43	Jumbo Elephant	238
2	23	Dance from Zalongou	118				
2	31	Dancing Bear	134	3	41	Lazy Bones	234
2	20	Darling, Goodnight	112	3	51	Little Rondo	254
1	24	Do You See That Bird There?	48	3	22	Little Train	190
1	10	Down in Village of Valtou	18	3	26	Little Wind 2	00
3	52	Draw a Bucket of Water	258	2	25	London Bridge	122
				3	30	Lullaby from Cyprus	208
1	31	Early to Bed	62				
1	9	The Elephant	16	3	54	Mary Wore a Red Dress	264
2	2	The Elephant Song	76	1	35	*Mos Mos* (Cat Song)	70
3	5	Elephants and Kitty Cats	156	2	3	My Little Ducklings	78
3	23	Engine, Engine	192	3	21	My Name Is Little Yellow Bird	188
2	29	Everybody Do This!	130				
				3	42	Nanny Goat	236
3	53	Fair Rosie	260	3	31	The Nothing Song	210
3	12	Fire House	170				
3	29	Fireman, Fireman	206	2	13	O Little Town of Bethlehem	98
1	34	Five Little Muffins	68	2	17	Oh, I'll Build a Snowman	106
1	13	Five Little Pumpkins	24	3	25	The Old Gray Cat	198
2	27	Five Little Speckled Frogs	126	3	24	Old MacDonald Had a Farm	196

271

JUMP RIGHT IN: THE MUSIC CURRICULUM

CD	Track	Title	Page
1	23	One Summer Day	46
3	36	Only My Opinion	224
1	17	Open-Close	34
3	28	Ophelia' Letter Blow 'Way	204
1	32	Over the River and through the Wood	64
1	8	Peas	14
2	7	*Personent Hodie* (Celebrate Joyously)	86
2	6	Popcorn	84
3	45	Punchinella	242
3	37	Rain on the Green Grass	226
3	1	Roll That Big Ball Down to Town	146
3	55	Row, Row, Row Your Boat	268
3	20	*Sakura*	186
3	3	Scandinavian Folk Song	152
3	44	Scarborough Fair	240
3	9	See How I'm Jumping	162
1	28	Shake, Shake, Shake	56
3	10	*Shalom Chaverim*	166
3	15	Sidewalk Talk	176
3	34	The Sky Has Clouded	218
2	1	Sleep, My Babe (*Dors, Dors, 'Tit Bébé*)	74
1	11	Sleep, My Darling (*Sofda Unga Astin Min*)	20
2	15	Softly	102
1	22	Sometimes I Feel Like a Motherless Child	44

CD	Track	Title	Page
1	26	The Squirrel	52
2	24	The Star-Spangled Banner	120
1	20	The Sure Hope	40
2	30	Swing a Lady	132
3	49	Thessaly *Syrtos* Dance	250
1	3	This Lady She Wears a Dark Green Dress	6
3	38	This Old Man	228
3	18	Tisket, A-Tasket	182
3	46	To Market, To Market	244
3	48	Toodala	248
2	26	Toss and Catch	124
2	36	*Tsamico* Dance	142
1	33	Turkey Song	66
1	36	Two Little Sausages	72
1	29	The Volga Boat Song	58
2	19	Walking with My Mom	110
3	27	Who Has Seen Wind?	202
3	13	Wild Dog on Our Farm	172
2	37	Will Winter End?	144
2	33	Yangtze Boatmen's Chantey	136
2	21	You'll Sound as Weird as Me	114
2	4	Zion's Children	80

Index B
Songs by Arranger, Composer, or Transcriber

Artz, Debbie

Only My Opinion 224

Bailey, Charity

Hello, Everybody 2

Bailey, Jennifer

City Line Avenue 154

Beth, Karen

Full Moonlight Dance 38

Child, Lydia Maria

Over the River and through the Wood 64

Gade, Jacob

One Summer Day 46

Gordon, Edwin E.

High Bird 158

Walking with My Mom 110

Holsaert, Eunice

Hello, Everybody 2

Johnson, Dinah

Sidewalk Talk   176

Jordon, Grace Olin

Elephants and Kitty Cats. 156

Jung, Kyungsil

The Squirrel 52

Key, Francis Scott

The Star-Spangled Banner 120

McChrystal, Meg

Who Has Seen Wind? 202

Meade, Cheryl

Will Winter End?. 144

Müller, Carl

Away in a Manger 100

Nash, Grace C.

Little Train   190

Nelson, Esther L.

My Name Is Little Yellow Bird 188

Nichol, Doug

Dancing Bear   134

Fireman, Fireman 206

Hot Dog   246

Oh, I'll Build a Snowman 106

Peas   14

Popcorn 84

You'll Sound as Weird as Me 114

Post, Isabel D.

The Sure Hope 40

Redner, Lewis H.

O Little Town of Bethlehem 98

Ricky, Alice

Elephants and Kitty Cats. 156

Rossetti

Who Has Seen Wind? 202

Stapp, Ruth

Little Wind   200

Valerio, Wendy H.

Sidewalk Talk   176

Ward, Samuel A.

America the Beautiful 32

Index C
Songs by Chanting

Chant: Listening and Performing

The Elephant 16
Five Little Muffins 68
Floppy Scarecrow 28
Humpty Dumpty 252
I'm a Little Snowflake 108
Little Rondo 254
Rain on the Green Grass 226
Shake, Shake, Shake 56
Sidewalk Talk 176
The Squirrel 52
To Market, To Market 244
Two Little Sausages 72
Walking with My Mom 110

Rhythm Pattern Creativity

Clapping Land 220
Coventry Carol 92
Early to Bed 62
I'm a Little Snowflake 108
Jim Along Josie 178
Johnny Works with One Hammer 230
Little Rondo 254
See How I'm Jumping 162
Tsamico Dance 142
Turkey Song 66
Two Little Sausages 72

Rhythm Pattern Imitation

Clapping Land 220
The Elephant Song 76
Engine, Engine 192
Humpty Dumpty 252
Open-Close 34
Over the River and through the Wood 64
Peas 14
See How I'm Jumping 162
The Sky Has Clouded 218
Tsamico Dance 142

Index D
Songs by Connections:
Art, Literature, Social Studies, and Science

Art

Old MacDonald Had a Farm 196
One Summer Day 46

Literature

The Elephant 16
Engine, Engine 192
Five Little Muffins 68
Lazy Bones 234
Little Train 190
My Little Ducklings 78
Over the River and through the Wood 64
The Sure Hope 40

Science

Sometimes I Feel Like a Motherless Child 44
Thessaly *Syrtos* Dance 250

Social Studies

Jim Along Josie 178

Index E
Songs by Coordination with Instrumental Music

Alto Saxophone

Scarborough Fair 240
Sometimes I Feel Like a Motherless Child 44

Band

***An American Festival Overture* by Jenkins**
    Barnacle Bill 160
***Dance of Jesters* by TchaikovThe Sky**
    Dancing Bear 134
"Pere Lachaise" from *Paris Sketches* by Marin Ellerby
    Arirang 12

Bass

The Volga Boat Song 58

Bassoon

Coventry Carol 92

Cello

America the Beautiful 32

Euphonium

Down in Village of Valtou 18

Flugelhorn

The Bell Peter 212

Flute

All Pretty Little Horses 10

Away in a Manger .100

This Old Man 228

Oboe

America 88

Ophelia' Letter Blow 'Way 204

Recorder

As Joseph Was A-Walking 94

Tenor Saxophone

Shalom Chaverim 166

Trombone

Blow the Man Down 138

Old MacDonald Had a Farm 196

Trumpet

The Star-Spangled Banner 120

Index F
Songs by Form

AB

Barnacle Bill 160

Hot Dog 246

ABA

Dancing Bear 134

Call-and-Response

Bre'r Rabbit Shake It 180

Index G
Songs by Games and Dances

Action Songs

Everybody Do This! 130

Fire House 170

Fireman, Fireman .206

Five Little Muffins .68

Five Little Pumpkins 24

Jumbo Elephant 238

Lazy Bones 234

London Bridge 122

The Old Gray Cat .198

Only My Opinion .224

Turkey Song 66

Circle Games

Punchinella 242

Swing a Lady 132

Tisket, A-Tasket 182

Finger Play

Five Little Muffins .68

Open-Close 34

Greeting Song

Jim Along Josie 178

Same and Different

The Elephant 16

The Elephant Song .76

Fair Rosie 260

Funny Puppy 174

Gipsy Ipsy 214

Go to Sleep 42

The Sky Has Clouded 218

This Old Man 228

Toss and Catch 124

Two Little Sausages 72

Zion's Children 80

Index H
Songs by Listening

All Pretty Little Horses	10
America	88
As Joseph Was A-Walking	94
Baa, Baa, Black Sheep	184
Bim Bam	60
Bre'r Rabbit Shake It	180
Dancing Bear	134
Engine, Engine	192
Five Little Pumpkins	24
Hato Popo (Little Pigeons)	50
Lullaby from Cyprus	208
Personet Hodie (Celebrate Joyously)	86
Popcorn	84
Sidewalk Talk	176
Softly	102
The Star-Spangled Banner	120
This Lady Wears a Dark Green Dress	6
Walking with My Mom	110
You'll Sound as Weird as Me	114

Index I
Songs by Listening Lesson

***An American Festival Overture* by Jenkins**

Barnacle Bill	160

***Dance of Jesters* by TchaikovThe Sky**

Dancing Bear	134

"Pere Lachaise" from *Paris Sketches* by Marin Ellerby

Arirang	12

Index J
Songs by Manipulative

Bean Bags

Bí, Bí, Og Blaka	116
Go to Sleep	42
Ophelia' Letter Blow 'Way	204
Sleep My Darling (*Sofda Unda Astin Min*)	20
Sometimes I Feel Like a Motherless Child	44

Co-op Band

Blow the Winds Southerly	140

Hoberman Sphere

Little Wind	200

Parachute

America the Beautiful	32
Tisket, A-Tasket	182

Pom Poms

Graceful Simo (*Simo Ligeri*)	36
Zion's Children	80

Puppets

Early to Bed	62
The Elephant	16
Five Little Speckled Frogs	126
Funny Puppy	174

Rhythm Sticks

Little Train	190
The Sure Hope	40
Wild Dog on Our Farm	172

Ropes

The Volga Boat Song	58
Yangtze Boatman's Chantey	136

Scarves

Arirang	12
Darling, Goodnight	112
Jeremiah, Blow the Fire	8
Will Winter End?	144

Streamers

Fire House	170
Will Winter End?	144

Toy Microphone

My Name Is Little Yellow Bird	188

Index K
Songs by Meter

Multimetric

The Chickens They Are Crowin'	232
Children's Lullaby	104
Do You See That Bird There?	48
Horses	128
Lazy Bones	234

TEACHER'S EDITION • KINDERGARTEN

Unusual Paired

Full Moonlight Dance 38
Hot Dog 246
Lullaby from Cyprus. 208
The Squirrel 52

Unusual Unpaired

Dance from Zalongou 118
Rain on the Green Grass 226
Thessaly Syrtos Dance. 250

Usual Duple

All Pretty Little Horses 10
America the Beautiful 32
The Ardelean Woman 54

Baa, Baa, Black Sheep. 184
Bí, Bí, Og Blaka .116
Bim Bam 60
Blow the Balloon 22
Bre'r Rabbit Shake It 180

City Line Avenue 154
Clapping Land 220

Dancing Bear 134
Darling, Goodnight 112
Draw a Bucket of Water 258

The Elephant Song. 76
Elephants and Kitty Cats. 156
Engine, Engine. .192
Everybody Do This! 130

Fair Rosie 260
Fire House 170
Fireman, Fireman 206
Five Little Muffins 68
Five Little Pumpkins. 24
Five Little Speckled Frogs. 126
Floppy Scarecrow 28
Funny Puppy. 174

The Ghost of John 30
Go to Sleep. 42
Graceful Simo (*Simo Ligeri*). 36
The Greenland Whale Fishery 168

Hani Kouni. 150
Hato Popo (Little Pigeons) 50

Hello, Everybody 2
High Bird 158

I'm a Little Snowflake 108

Jeremiah, Blow the Fire 8
Jim Along Josie .178
Johnny Works with One Hammer 230
Jumbo Elephant .238

Little Rondo 254
Little Train 190
Little Wind 200
London Bridge 122

Mary Wore a Red Dress 264
Mos Mos (Cat Song). 70
My Little Ducklings 78
My Name is Little Yellow Bird 188

Nanny Goat 236
The Nothing Song 210

O Little Town of Bethlehem 98
Old MacDonald Had a Farm. 196
Only My Opinion 224
Open-Close 34
Ophelia' Letter Blow 'Way 204

Peas 14
Personent Hodie (Celebrate Joyously) 86
Popcorn 84
Punchinella. 242

Roll That Big Ball Down to Town 146
Sakura 186
See How I'm Jumping 162
Shake, Shake, Shake 56
Shalom Chaverim 166
Sidewalk Talk 176
The Sky Has Clouded 218
Sleep My Babe (*Dors, Dors, 'Tit Bébé*) 74
Sleep My Darling (*Sofda Unda Astin Min*) 20
Sometimes I Feel Like a Motherless Child 44
Swing a Lady 132

This Lady Wears a Dark Green Dress 6
This Old Man 228
Tisket, A-Tasket .182
Toodala. 248

277

JUMP RIGHT IN: THE MUSIC CURRICULUM

Toss and Catch 124

Turkey Song 66

Two Little Sausages 72

The Volga Boat Song 58

Walking with My Mom 110

Who Has Seen Wind? 202

Wild Dog on Our Farm 172

Will Winter End? 144

Yangtze Boatman's Chantey 136

Zion's Children 80

Usual Triple

America 88

Arirang 12

As Joseph Was A-Walking 94

Away in a Manger .100

Baloo, Lammy 90

Barnacle Bill 160

The Bell Peter 212

Blow the Man Down 138

Blow the Winds Southerly 140

The Braes O'Yarrow 4

Coventry Carol 92

Down in Village of Valtou 18

Early to Bed 62

The Elephant 16

Gipsy Ipsy 214

Humpty Dumpty .252

I Wonder as I Wander 96

In the Window 82

Oh, I'll Build a Snowman 106

The Old Gray Cat .198

One Summer Day 46

Over the River and through the Woods 64

Peas 14

Popcorn 84

Row, Row, Row Your Boat 268

Scandinavian Folk Song 152

Scarborough Fair .240

Softly 102

The Star-Spangled Banner 120

The Sure Hope 40

To Market, To Market 244

Tsamico Dance 142

You'll Sound as Weird as Me 114

Index L
Songs by Movement

Beat
Alternate

Little Train 190

Bilateral

Barnacle Bill 160

Clapping Land 220

Fire House 170

Funny Puppy 174

Little Train 190

My Name Is Little Yellow Bird 188

The Old Gray Cat .198

Tisket, A-Tasket 182

Wild Dog on Our Farm 172

Body Parts

Baloo, Lammy 90

Bre'r Rabbit Shake It 180

Full Moonlight Dance 38

I Wonder as I Wander 96

Johnny Works with One Hammer 230

Only My Opinion .224

Sometimes I Feel Like a Motherless Child 44

This Old Man 228

Macrobeat/Microbeat

America 88

Away in a Manger .100

City Line Avenue .154

Coventry Carol 92

Dancing Bear 134

Engine, Engine 192

Funny Puppy 174

TEACHER'S EDITION • KINDERGARTEN

The Greenland Whale Fishery 168
Hani Kouni. 150
Humpty Dumpty 252
Lullaby from Cyprus. 208
Oh, I'll Build a Snowman 106
Scandinavian Folk Song 152
Scarborough Fair. 240
See How I'm Jumping 162
Softly. 102
The Star-Spangled Banner 120
You'll Sound as Weird as Me 114

Macrobeats

Barnacle Bill. 160
The Bell Peter 212
Blow the Man Down. 138
Blow the Winds Southerly 140
Early to Bed 62
Jumbo Elephant 238
London Bridge. 122
Oh, I'll Build a Snowman 106
The Old Gray Cat 198
This Lady She Wears a Dark Green Dress. 6
Tisket, A-Tasket 182
To Market, To Market 244
Wild Dog on Our Farm 172
Yangtze Boatmen's Chantey. 136

Microbeat

City Line Avenue 154
Fair Rosie .260
Fire House .170
Toss and Catch. 124

Pulsate

America 88
Clapping Land 220
Coventry Carol. 92
Dance from Zalongou 118
Engine, Engine. 192
Everybody Do This! 130
Fair Rosie .260
Floppy Scarecrow 28
Hato Popo (Little Pigeons) 50
In the Window 82
Little Wind 200
Lullaby from Cyprus. 208
Mary Wore a Red Dress 264
Oh, I'll Build a Snowman 106
One Summer Day 46

Peas 14
Popcorn 84
Scarborough Fair. 240
Shake, Shake, Shake 56
Sidewalk Talk 176
The Sky Has Clouded 218
Softly. 102
The Star-Spangled Banner 120
Toodala. .248
Toss and Catch. 124
Turkey Song 66
Two Little Sausages 72
The Volga Boat Song 58
You'll Sound as Weird as Me 114
Zion's Children 80

Rock

Popcorn 84
You'll Sound as Weird as Me 114

Sway

Away in a Manger 100
The Bell Peter 212
Early to Bed 62
Five Little Muffins. 68
Sakura 186
Scandinavian Folk Song 152

Locomotor
Crawl

Mos Mos (Cat Song) 70

Gallop

Horses 128
Over the River and through the Woods 64
To Market, To Market 244

Jump

Five Little Speckled Frogs. 126
Jim Along Josie 178
See How I'm Jumping 162

Tiptoe

The Old Gray Cat 198
Softly. 102

Walk

As Joseph Was A-Walking. 94
City Line Avenue 154
Clapping Land 220

279

JUMP RIGHT IN: THE MUSIC CURRICULUM

The Elephant Song. 76
Elephants and Kitty Cats. 156
Engine, Engine. 192
High Bird .158
Horses 128
Hot Dog 246
Jumbo Elephant 238
London Bridge. 122
My Little Ducklings 78
Nanny Goat 236
The Nothing Song 210
One Summer Day 46
Rain on the Green Grass. 226
Scandinavian Folk Song 152
Sidewalk Talk 176
Tisket, A-Tasket 182

Partner

Mirrors

Do You See That Bird There? 48

Rock

The Bell Peter 212
Draw a Bucket of Water 258
Row, Row, Row Your Boat 268

Stylistic

Body Awareness

The Ardelean Woman 54
As Joseph Was A-Walking. 94
Baloo, Lammy 90
Bí, Bí, Og Blaka 116
Bre'r Rabbit, Shake It 180
Children's Lullaby. 104
Down in Village of Valtou 18
Full Moonlight Dance 38
Hello, Everybody 2
I Wonder as I Wander 96
Mos Mos (Cat Song) 70
Old MacDonald Had a Farm. 196
Personent Hodie (Celebrate Joyously) 86
Punchinella. 242
Rain on the Green Grass. 226
Sidewalk Talk 176
Sleep My Darling (Sofda Unda Astin Min) 20
This Old Man 228

Flow

All Pretty Little Horses 10
America the Beautiful 32
The Ardelean Woman 54
Arirang. 12
As Joseph Was A-Walking. 94

Baa, Baa, Black Sheep. 184
Bim Bam. 60
Blow the Balloon 22
The Braes O'Yarrow 4
Bre'r Rabbit Shake It 180

Children's Lullaby 104

Dance from Zalongou 118
Darling, Goodnight 112
Do You See That Bird There? 48
Down in Village of Valtou 18

Engine, Engine. 192
Everybody Do This! 130

The Ghost of John 30
Gipsy Ipsy 214
Go to Sleep. 42
Graceful Simo (Simo Ligeri). 36
The Greenland Whale Fishery. 168

Hani Kouni. 150
Hato Popo (Little Pigeons) 50
Hot Dog 246
Humpty Dumpty. 252

I Wonder as I Wander 96
I'm a Little Snowflake. 108
In the Window 82

Jeremiah, Blow the Fire 8

Little Rondo 254
Lullaby from Cyprus. 208

The Old Grey Cat 198
Old MacDonald Had a Farm. 196
One Summer Day 46

Personet Hodie (Celebrate Joyously) 86

Rain on the Green Grass. 226

Row, Row, Row Your Boat 268

Sakura 186
Scandinavian Folk Song 152
Shalom Chaverim 166
Sidewalk Talk 176
The Sky Has Clouded 218
Sleep My Darling (*Sofda Unda Astin Min*) 20
Sleep, My Babe (*Dors, Dors, 'Tit Bébé*) 74
Softly 102
Sometimes I Feel Like a Motherless Child 44
The Sure Hope 40

This Lady She Wears a Dark Green Dress 6
This Old Man 228
Toodala 248

The Volga Boat Song 58

Shared Space

The Bell Peter .212
Blow the Man Down 138
Draw a Bucket of Water 258
Peas 14
Scarborough Fair 240
Shalom Chaverim 166
Walking with My Mom 110

Space

Arirang 12
Blow the Balloon 22
Blow the Man Down 138
The Chickens They Are Crowin' 232
Dancing Bear 134
Down in Village of Valtou 18
Floppy Scarecrow 28
Full Moonlight Dance 38
Hello, Everybody 2
High Bird 158
I Wonder as I Wander 96
I'm a Little Snowflake 108
In the Window 82
Johnny Works with One Hammer 230
My Little Ducklings 78
The Nothing Song 210
O Little Town of Bethlehem 98
Only My Opinion 224
Roll That Big Ball Down to Town 146
The Squirrel 52
Will Winter End? 144

Time

Baloo, Lammy 90
Blow the Balloon 22
Lazy Bones 234
Sakura 186
Shake, Shake, Shake 56

Weight

The Ardelean Woman 54
Clapping Land .220
Dance from Zalongou 118
Draw a Bucket of Water 258
The Elephant Song 76
Elephants and Kitty Cats 156
Engine, Engine .192
I'm a Little Snowflake 108
Jumbo Elephant 238
The Nothing Song 210
Oh, I'll Build a Snowman 106
The Old Gray Cat 198
Rain on the Green Grass 226
Roll That Big Ball Down to Town 146
Thessaly *Syrtos* Dance 250
Will Winter End? 144

Index M
Songs by Music Concept

Breath

Barnacle Bill 160
Bí, Bí, Og Blaka 116
Bim Bam 60
Blow the Balloon 22
Five Little Pumpkins 24
Five Little Speckled Frogs 126
Jeremiah, Blow the Fire 8
See How I'm Jumping 162
This Lady Wears a Dark Green Dress 6

Chord Roots

In the Window 82
Mary Wore a Red Dress 264

Conducting Readiness

Bim Bam 60
Five Little Pumpkins 24
This Lady Wears a Dark Green Dress 6

JUMP RIGHT IN: THE MUSIC CURRICULUM

Flow

All Pretty Little Horses	10
America the Beautiful	32
The Ardelean Woman	54
Arirang	12
As Joseph Was A-Walking	94
Baa, Baa, Black Sheep	184
Bim Bam	60
Blow the Balloon	22
The Braes O'Yarrow	4
Bre'r Rabbit Shake It	180
Children's Lullaby	104
Dance from Zalongou	118
Darling, Goodnight	112
Do You See That Bird There?	48
Down in Village of Valtou	18
Engine, Engine	192
Everybody Do This!	130
The Ghost of John	30
Gipsy Ipsy	214
Go to Sleep	42
Graceful Simo (Simo Ligeri)	36
The Greenland Whale Fishery	168
Hani Kouni	150
Hato Popo (Little Pigeons)	50
Hot Dog	246
Humpty Dumpty	252
I Wonder as I Wander	96
I'm a Little Snowflake	108
In the Window	82
Jeremiah, Blow the Fire	8
Jim Along Josie	178
Little Rondo	254
London Bridge	122
Lullaby from Cyprus	208
The Old Gray Cat	198
Old MacDonald Had a Farm	196
One Summer Day	46
Personet Hodie (Celebrate Joyously)	86

Punchinella	242
Rain on the Green Grass	226
Row, Row, Row Your Boat	268
Sakura	186
Scandinavian Folk Song	152
Shake, Shake, Shake	56
Shalom Chaverim	166
Sidewalk Talk	176
The Sky Has Clouded	218
Sleep My Darling (*Sofda Unda Astin Min*)	20
Sleep, My Babe (*Dors, Dors, 'Tit Bébé*)	74
Softly	102
Sometimes I Feel Like a Motherless Child	44
The Squirrel	52
The Star-Spangled Banner	120
The Sure Hope	40
This Lady She Wears a Dark Green Dress	6
This Old Man	228
Toodala	248
Toss and Catch	124
Turkey Song	66
Two Little Sausages	72
The Volga Boat Song	58

Form

Barnacle Bill	160
Bre'r Rabbit, Shake It	180
Dancing Bear	134
Hot Dog	246

Macrobeat/Microbeat

America	88
Away in a Manger	100
City Line Avenue	154
Coventry Carol	92
Dancing Bear	134
Engine, Engine	192
Funny Puppy	174
The Greenland Whale Fishery	168
Hani Kouni	150
Humpty Dumpty	252
Lullaby from Cyprus	208
Oh, I'll Build a Snowman	106
Scandinavian Folk Song	152
Scarborough Fair	240
See How I'm Jumping	162

Softly. 102
The Star-Spangled Banner. 120
You'll Sound as Weird as Me 114

Macrobeats

Barnacle Bill. 160
The Bell Peter 212
Blow the Man Down. 138
Blow the Winds Southerly. 140
Early to Bed 62
Jumbo Elephant .238
London Bridge. .122
Oh, I'll Build a Snowman 106
The Old Gray Cat 198
This Lady She Wears a Dark Green Dress. 6
Tisket, A-Tasket .182
To Market, To Market 244
Wild Dog on Our Farm 172
Yangtze Boatmen's Chantey 136

Microbeat

City Line Avenue 154
Fair Rosie 260
Fire House 170
Toss and Catch .124

Ostinato

Coventry Carol. 92

Phrases

America the Beautiful 32
As Joseph Was A-Walking. 94
Hani Kouni. 150

Resting Tone

All Pretty Little Horses 10
America 88
Arirang. 12

Baa, Baa, Black Sheep. 184
Barnacle Bill. 160
Bí, Bí, Og Blaka 116
Bim Bam 60
Blow the Winds Southerly. 140
The Braes O'Yarrow. 4

Children's Lullaby. 104
City Line Avenue 154

Darling, Goodnight 112
Five Little Pumpkins. 24
Five Little Speckled Frogs. 126
Go to Sleep. 42
Hani Kouni. 150
Hato Popo (Little Pigeons) 50
I Wonder as I Wander 96
In the Window 82
Jeremiah, Blow the Fire 8
Jim Along Josie .178
Johnny Works with One Hammer 230
Jumbo Elephant .238
Little Wind. 200
My Name Is Little Yellow Bird 188
Nanny Goat 236
One Summer Day 46
Open-Close 34
Ophelia' Letter Blow 'Way 204
Peas 14
Personent Hodie (Celebrate Joyously) 86
Roll that Big Ball Down to Town 146
Row, Row, Row Your Boat 268
Sleep, My Darling (*Sofda Unda Astin Min*) 20
Sometimes I Feel Like a Motherless Child 44
The Star-Spangled Banner. 120
This Lady Wears a Dark Green Dress 6
This Old Man 228
Tisket, A-Tasket .182
Will Winter End?. 144
Yangtze Boatman's Chantey 136

Rhythm Patterns

Clapping Land 220
Coventry Carol. 92
Early to Bed 62

JUMP RIGHT IN: THE MUSIC CURRICULUM

Engine, Engine 192

Hot Dog 246

Humpty Dumpty 252

I Wonder as I Wander 96

I'm a Little Snowflake 108

Johnny Works with One Hammer 230

Little Rondo 254

Over the River and through the Woods 64

See How I'm Jumping 162

The Sky Has Clouded 218

To Market, To Market 244

Tsamico Dance 142

Turkey Song 66

Two Little Sausages 72

Walking with My Mom 110

Zion's Children 80

Same and Different

Clapping Land 220

Coventry Carol 92

The Elephant 16

The Elephant Song 76

Fair Rosie .260

Five Little Pumpkins 24

Five Little Speckled Frogs 126

Funny Puppy 174

The Ghost of John 30

Gipsy Ipsy .214

Go to Sleep 42

I Wonder as I Wander 96

I'm a Little Snowflake 108

Johnny Works with One Hammer 230

Little Rondo 254

Mary Wore a Red Dress 264

Nanny Goat 236

Sakura 186

See How I'm Jumping 162

The Sky Has Clouded 218

This Old Man 228

Toss and Catch 124

Two Little Sausages 72

Walking with My Mom 110

Zion's Children 80

Sound and Silence

As Joseph Was A-Walking 94

Peas 14

Personent Hodie (Celebrate Joyously) 86

Tonal Patterns

Baa, Baa, Black Sheep 184

Blow the Winds Southerly 140

Bre'r Rabbit Shake It 180

Clapping Land 220

Darling, Goodnight 112

The Elephant Song 76

Fair Rosie .260

Fireman, Fireman 206

Five Little Speckled Frogs 126

Funny Puppy 174

Gipsy Ipsy .214

Go to Sleep 42

The Greenland Whale Fishery 168

Little Rondo 254

London Bridge 122

Mary Wore a Red Dress 264

Personent Hodie (Celebrate Joyously) 86

Roll that Big Ball Down to Town 146

Row, Row, Row Your Boat 268

Sakura 186

See How I'm Jumping 162

Shalom Chaverim 166

Sleep My Babe (*Dors, Dors, 'Tit Bébé*) 74

This Old Man 228

Toss and Catch 124

Will Winter End? 144

Voice Exploration

Engine, Engine 192

Fire House .170

Who Has Seen Wind? 202

Index N
Songs by National, State, or Ethnic Origin

African-American

All Pretty Little Horses 10

Sometimes I Feel Like a Motherless Child 44

Tisket, A-Tasket 182

Zion's Children 80

American

Blow the Man Down 138

Bre'r Rabbit Shake It 180

Draw a Bucket of Water 258

The Ghost of John 30

TEACHER'S EDITION • KINDERGARTEN

Appalachian
As Joseph Was A-Walking 94
The Chickens They Are Crowin' 232

Armenian
The Sure Hope 40

Austrian
My Little Ducklings 78

British
Baa, Baa, Black Sheep. 184
Blow the Winds Southerly 140
The Braes O'Yarrow .4
Fair Rosie 260
Scarborough Fair. 240

Cajun . . . .
Sleep My Babe (*Dors, Dors, 'Tit Bébé*) 74

Chinese
Yangtze Boatman's Chantey. 136

Danish
One Summer Day 46

Flemish
See How I'm Jumping 162

Greek
Dance from Zalongou 118
Down in Village of Valtou 18
Lullaby from Cyprus. 208
The Sky Has Clouded 218
Thessaly *Syrtos* Dance. 250
Tsamico Dance 142

Hopi
Mos Mos (Cat Song) 70

Icelandic
Bí, Bí, Og Blaka 116
Sleep My Darling (*Sofda Unda Astin Min*) 20

Irish
Jeremiah, Blow the Fire 8

Japanese
Hato Popo (Little Pigeons) 50
Sakura 186

Jewish
In the Window 82
Shalom Chaverim 166

Kentucky
Swing a Lady 132

Korean
Arirang. 12

Macedonian
Graceful Simo (*Simo Ligeri*). 36

Native American
Hani Kouni. 150
Toss and Catch 124

Newfoundland
The Greenland Whale Fishery 168

North Carolina
I Wonder as I Wander 96

Nova Scotian
Do You See That Bird There? 48

Romanian
The Ardelean Woman 54

Russian
The Volga Boat Song 58

Scandinavian
Scandinavian Folk Song 152

Scottish
Baloo, Lammy 90

Slovakian
Darling, Goodnight 112

Swedish
Go to Sleep. 42

Trinidadian
Ophelia' Letter Blow 'Way 204

Virginia
Wild Dog on Our Farm 172

285

JUMP RIGHT IN: THE MUSIC CURRICULUM

Wisconsin

Turkey Song 66

Yiddish

Bim Bam 60

Index O
Songs by Performance Instrument

Hand Drum

The Ardelean Woman 54

London Bridge. 122

The Volga Boat Song 58

Recorder

As Joseph Was A-Walking 94

Rhythm Sticks

Little Train 190

The Sure Hope 40

Wild Dog on Our Farm 172

Tambourine

The Ardelean Woman 54

Hot Dog 246

Thessaly *Syrtos* Dance 250

To Market, To Market 244

Temple Blocks

Over the River and through the Wood 64

Tone-bar Instruments

In the Window 82

Train Whistle

Engine, Engine. .192

Index P
Songs by Singing

Chord Root

Mary Wore a Red Dress 264

Melodic Creativity

Fair Rosie 260

Mary Wore a Red Dress 264

My Name Is Little Yellow Bird 188

Nanny Goat 236

This Old Man 228

Toodala. 248

Who Has Seen Wind? 202

Readiness: Vocal Exploration

Engine, Engine. 192

Fire House 170

Who Has Seen Wind? 202

Resting Tone

All Pretty Little Horses 10

America 88

Arirang 12

Baa, Baa, Black Sheep. 184

Barnacle Bill 160

Bim Bam 60

Blow the Winds Southerly 140

Children's Lullaby 104

City Line Avenue 154

Five Little Pumpkins. 24

Five Little Speckled Frogs. 126

The Ghost of John 30

Go to Sleep. 42

Hato Popo (Little Pigeons) 50

I Wonder as I Wander 96

In the Window 82

Jim Along Josie 178

Little Wind 200

Nanny Goat 236

Ophelia' Letter Blow 'Way 204

Peas 14

Personent Hodie (Celebrate Joyously) 86

Row, Row, Row Your Boat 268

The Sky Has Clouded 218

Sleep, My Darling (*Sofda Unga Astin Min*) 20

Sometimes I Feel Like a Motherless Child 44

The Star-Spangled Banner. 120

286

This Lady She Wears a Dark Green Dress 6
This Old Man 228
Tisket, A-Tasket 182

Will Winter End?. 144

Yangtze Boatmen's Chantey 136

Solo

Bí, Bí, Og Blaka (Flip, Flap, and Flutt'ring) 116
Blow the Winds Southerly 140
Children's Lullaby 104
Darling, Goodnight 112
Fair Rosie 260
Fireman, Fireman 206
Funny Puppy 174
Gipsy Ipsy 214
I Wonder as I Wander 96
Jim Along Josie 178
Little Rondo 254
Little Wind 200
London Bridge 122
Mary Wore a Red Dress 264
My Name Is Little Yellow Bird 188
Nanny Goat 236
Only My Opinion 224
Ophelia' Letter Blow 'Way 204
Shalom Chaverim 166
Sleep, My Babe (*Dors, Dors, 'Tit Bébé*). 74
This Old Man 228
Who Has Seen Wind? 202
Will Winter End?. 144
Yangtze Boatmen's Chantey 136

Tonal Patterns

Creativity

Fair Rosie 260
Fireman, Fireman 206
Five Little Speckled Frogs 126
Funny Puppy 174
Gipsy Ipsy 214
Little Rondo 254

Imitation

Baa, Baa, Black Sheep 184
Bre'r Rabbit, Shake It 180
Clapping Land 220

Darling, Goodnight 112
Fair Rosie 260
Fireman, Fireman 206
Five Little Pumpkins. 24
Funny Puppy. 174
Gipsy Ipsy 214
The Greenland Whale Fishery 168
Little Rondo 254
London Bridge. 122
Mary Wore a Red Dress 264
Personent Hodie (Celebrate Joyously) 86
Roll That Big Ball Down to Town. 146
Row, Row, Row Your Boat 268
See How I'm Jumping 162
Shalom Chaverim 166
Sleep, My Babe (*Dors, Dors, 'Tit Bébé*). 74
Toss and Catch 124

Unison

Everybody Do This! 130
Fireman, Fireman 206
The Ghost of John 30
Gipsy Ipsy 214
Hani Kouni. 150
Jeremiah, Blow the Fire 8
Jim Along Josie 178
Old MacDonald Had a Farm. 196
Open-Close 34
Row, Row, Row Your Boat 268
Toodala. 248

Index Q
Songs by Subject Matter

Animals and Birds

All Pretty Little Horses 10
Baa, Baa, Black Sheep. 184
Bre'r Rabbit Shake It 180
The Chickens They Are Crowin' 232
Dancing Bear 134
Do You See That Bird There? 48
The Elephant. 16
The Elephant Song. 76
Elephants and Kitty Cats. 156
Five Little Speckled Frogs. 126
Funny Puppy. 174
Hato Popo (Little Pigeons) 50
High Bird 158
Horses .128

Jumbo Elephant 238

Mos Mos (Cat Song) 70

My Little Ducklings 78

My Name is Little Yellow Bird 188

Nanny Goat 236

The Old Gray Cat 198

Only My Opinion 224

The Squirrel 52

Turkey Song 66

Wild Dog on Our Farm 172

Clothing

Mary Wore a Red Dress 264

This Lady Wears a Dark Green Dress 6

Counting

Barnacle Bill 160

Five Little Muffins 68

Five Little Pumpkins 24

Five Little Speckled Frogs 126

This Old Man 228

Farms

The Chickens They Are Crowin' 232

Lazy Bones 234

The Old Grey Cat 198

Old MacDonald Had a Farm 196

Wild Dog on Our Farm 172

Food

Five Little Muffins 68

Hot Dog 246

Over the River and through the Woods 64

Peas 14

Popcorn 84

Two Little Sausages 72

Holiday

Christmas

As Joseph Was A-Walking 94

Away in a Manger .100

Coventry Carol 92

O Little Town of Bethlehem 98

Halloween

Five Little Pumpkins 24

Floppy Scarecrow 28

The Ghost of John 30

Hanukkah

In the Window 82

Thanksgiving

Over the River and through the Wood 64

Turkey Song 66

Lullaby

Children's Lullaby 104

Coventry Carol 92

Darling, Goodnight .112

Go to Sleep 42

Lullaby from Cyprus 208

Sleep My Babe (*Dors, Dors, 'Tit Bébé*) 74

Sleep My Darling (*Sofda Unda Astin Min*) 20

Softly 102

Occupations

Blow the Man Down 138

Fire House 170

Fireman, Fireman 206

The Greenland Whale Fishery 168

Yangtze Boatman's Chantey 136

Patriotic

America 88

America the Beautiful 32

The Star-Spangled Banner 120

Playing

Clapping Land 220

Everybody Do This! .130

Gipsy Ipsy 21

Jim Along Josie 178

Oh, I'll Build a Snowman 106

Punchinella 242

Scarborough Fair 240

See How I'm Jumping 162

Sidewalk Talk 176

Toodala 248

Seasons and Weather

Blow the Winds Southerly 140

I'm a Little Snowflake 108

Little Wind 200

Oh, I'll Build a Snowman 106

Old MacDonald Had a Farm 196

One Summer Day 46

Ophelia' Letter Blow 'Way 204

Rain on the Green Grass 226

TEACHER'S EDITION • KINDERGARTEN

The Sky Has Clouded 218
The Sure Hope 40
Who Has Seen Wind? 202
Will Winter End?. 144

Travel

All Pretty Little Horses 10
Down in Village of Valtou 18
Engine, Engine. 192
Horses 128
Little Train 190
Ophelia' Letter Blow 'Way 204
Row, Row, Row Your Boat 268
Scarborough Fair. .240
To Market, To Market 244
The Volga Boat Song 58
Yangtze Boatman's Chantey. 136

Index R
Songs by Tonality

Aeolian

All Pretty Little Horses 10
The Bell Peter 212
The Braes O'Yarrow 4
The Chickens They Are Crowin' 232
Darling, Goodnight 112
Full Moonlight Dance 38
The Ghost of John .30
Hani Kouni. 150
I Wonder as I Wander 96
Lullaby from Cyprus. 208
Nanny Goat 236
See How I'm Jumping 162
Shalom Chaverim .166
Thessaly Syrtos Dance 250
Toss and Catch 124
Turkey Song 66
The Volga Boat Song 58
Yangtze Boatman's Chantey. 136

Dorian

Elephants and Kitty Cats. 156
Little Wind. 200
Personent Hodie (Celebrate Joyously) 86
Scarborough Fair. .240

Harmonic Minor

The Ardelean Woman 54

Bim Bam 60
Coventry Carol. 92
Down in Village of Valtou 18
Fire House 170
Fireman, Fireman .206
Funny Puppy. 174
Go to Sleep. 42
Graceful Simo (Simo Ligeri). 36
In the Window 82
Jumbo Elephant 238
Oh, I'll Build a Snowman 106
Old MacDonald Had a Farm. 196
Scandinavian Folk Song 152
The Sky Has Clouded 218
Sleep My Babe (Dors, Dors, 'Tit Bébé) 74
Sleep My Darling (Sofda Unda Astin Min) 20
Sometimes I Feel Like a Motherless Child 44
The Sure Hope. 40

Hungarian Minor

Tsamico Dance. 142

Lydian

Peas 14

Major

America 88
America the Beautiful 32
As Joseph Was A-Walking. 94
Away in a Manger .100

Baa, Baa, Black Sheep. 184
Baloo, Lammy 90
Barnacle Bill 160
Bí, Bí, Og Blaka 116
Blow the Balloon .22
Blow the Man Down. 138
Blow the Winds Southerly 140

Children's Lullaby. 104
Clapping Land 220

Dancing Bear 134
Draw a Bucket of Water 258

Early to Bed 62
The Elephant Song. 76
Everybody Do This! 130

Fair Rosie 260

289

JUMP RIGHT IN: THE MUSIC CURRICULUM

Five Little Pumpkins. 24
Five Little Speckled Frogs. 126

Hato Popo (Little Pigeons) 50
Hello, Everybody 2
Horses 128
Hot Dog 246

Johnny Works with One Hammer 230

Lazy Bones. 234
London Bridge. 122

Mary Wore a Red Dress 264
Mos Mos (Cat Song). 70
My Little Ducklings 78
My Name Is Little Yellow Bird 188

The Nothing Song 210

O Little Town of Bethlehem 98
The Old Grey Cat 198
Old MacDonald Had a Farm. 196
Open-Close 34
Ophelia' Letter Blow 'Way 204
Over the River and through the Wood 64

Popcorn 84

Rain on the Green Grass 226
Roll that Big Ball Down to Town 146

Softly. 102
The Star-Spangled Banner 120

This Lady Wears a Dark Green Dress 6
This Old Man 228
To Market, To Market 244
Toodala. 248

Zion's Children .80

Mixolydian

City Line Avenue 154
The Greenland Whale Fishery. 168
Only My Opinion 224
Swing a Lady 132
Wild Dog on Our Farm 172

Multitonal

Arirang. 12
Dance from Zalongou 118
Do You See That Bird There? 48
You'll Sound as Weird as Me 114

Pentatonic

Bre'r Rabbit, Shake It 180
Gipsy Ipsy 214
Jeremiah, Blow the Fire 8
Jim Along Josie 178
Little Rondo 254
Little Train 190
Punchinella. 242
Sakura 186
Tisket, A-Tasket 182

Phrygian

High Bird 158
Who Has Seen Wind? 202
Will Winter End?. 144

290